BN 8517957 4

BRIGHTON POLYTECHNIC
LEARNING RESOURCES

WITHDRAWN FROM
UNIVERSITY OF BRIGHTON
LIBRARIES

A SOCIALIST ANATOMY OF BRITAIN

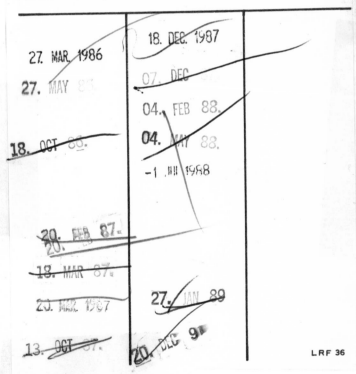

BRIGHTON POLYTECHNIC – FALMER LIBRARY

Please return by last date stamped below

27. MAR. 1986
27. MAY 86

18. OCT 86

18. DEC. 1987
07. DEC
04. FEB 88.
04. MAY 88.
-1 .III 1988

20. FEB 87.
18. MAR 87.
20. MAR 1987

13. OCT 87.

27. JAN 89
20. DEC 9

LRF 36

D1334064

A Socialist Anatomy of Britain

Edited by

DAVID COATES, GORDON JOHNSTON
AND RAY BUSH

Polity Press

320.53109 41
COA
851795 7

© David Coates, Gordon Johnston and Ray Bush, 1985

First published 1985 by
Polity Press, Cambridge, in association with Basil Blackwell, Oxford.

Editorial Office: Polity Press
Dales Brewery, Gwydir Street, Cambridge, CB1 2LJ.

Basil Blackwell Ltd
108, Cowley Road, Oxford, OX4 1JF, UK.

Basil Blackwell Inc.
432 Park Avenue South, Suite 1505, New York, NY 10016, USA.

All rights reserved. Except for the quotation of short passages for the purposes of criticism and review, no part of this publication may be reproduced, stored in a retrieval system, or transmitted, in any form or by any means, electronic, mechanical, photocopying, recording or otherwise, without the prior consent of the publisher.

Except in the United States of America this book is sold subject to the condition that it shall not by way of trade or otherwise be lent, hired out or otherwise circulated without the publisher's prior consent in any form of binding or cover other than that in which it is published and without a similar condition including this condition being imposed on the subsequent purchaser.

British Library Cataloguing in Publication Data

A Socialist Anatomy of Britain.
1. Socialism — Great Britain
I. Coates, David II. Johnston, Gordon, 1952- . III. Bush, Ray
335'.00941 HX244
ISBN 0-7456-0024-7
ISBN 0-7456-0025-5 Pbk

Library of Congress Cataloging in Publication Data

A Socialist anatomy of Britain.
Includes index.
1. Socialism — Great Britain — Addresses, essays, lectures.
I. Coates, David. II. Johnston, Gordon, 1952- . III. Bush, Ray.
HX244.S63 1985   335'.00941   84-26424
ISBN 0-7446-0024-7
ISBN 0-7446-0025-5 (pbk.)

Typeset by Banbury Typesetters Limited, Banbury

Printed in Great Britain by Bell and Bain Limited, Glasgow

*This book is dedicated to the memory of
Peter Sedgwick – a great socialist, colleague
and friend.*

Contents

Notes on Contributors

Anthony Arblaster is a lecturer in Politics, University of Sheffield and at one time was on the staff of *Tribune*. He is author of *Academic Freedom* (1974) and *The Rise and Decline of Western Liberalism* (1984). He is an active member of the Socialist Society.

Kum Kum Bhavnani is a psychologist who has been active in black, anti-racist, feminist and socialist politics for a number of years. She is currently researching youth unemployment in Britain.

Reena Bhavnani has been active in black women's groups, anti-racist groups and the broader feminist and socialist movements for many years. She is currently working in the area of anti-racism in education.

Ray Bush is a lecturer in Politics at the University of Leeds. He has researched and published in the areas of African politics, state formation and international resource allocation.

David Coates is Senior Lecturer, and currently Head of the Department of Politics at the University of Leeds. He has written extensively on the Labour Party and the question of socialism and has recently published a text to parallel this one: *The Context of British Politics* (1984).

Laurence Harris is Professor of Economics at the Open University and co-author (with Ben Fine) of *Re-reading Capital* and (with Jeremy Coakley) of *The City of Capital*.

Richard Hyman is Reader in Industrial Relations at Warwick University. He is the author of many books and articles on the history and current struggles of trade unions. He is now an independent socialist after 14 years membership of the International Socialists.

BRIGHTON POLYTECHNIC LEARNING RESOURCES

Gordon Johnston is a lecturer in Politics at Leeds Polytechnic. He is currently researching labourism, socialist thought and the British Labour Party.

Robert Looker is a lecturer in Politics at the University of York. His publications include *Rosa Luxemburg: selected writings* (1971). He is currently preparing (with David Coates) a book on the take-off of labour movements.

Doreen Massey is Professor of Geography at the Open University. She is the author of *Capital and Land* (with Alejandrina Catalano), *The Geography of Industrial Reorganisation* (with Richard Meegan), *The Anatomy of Job Loss,* and *Spatial Divisions of Labour: social structures and the geography of production.* She is a Board Member of The Greater London Enterprise Board.

Sarah Perrigo is a lecturer in the Department of Peace Studies at the University of Bradford. She has taught courses on women and society for several years. She is an active socialist feminist, a member of the Labour Party and is currently researching the history of women in the Labour Party.

John Scott is a lecturer in Sociology at the University of Leicester. He is the author of *Corporations, Classes and Capitalism, The Anatomy of Scottish Capital* (with M. Hughes), *The Upper Classes, Directors of Industry* (with C. Griff) and *Networks of Corporate Power* (joint editor and contributor).

Richard Taylor is Senior Lecturer in the Department of Adult and Continuing Education at the University of Leeds and is responsible for the 'Pioneer Work' programme of community based adult education. He is the co-author of three books, including *The Protest Makers* (1980), a study of CND.

John Urry is Professor of Sociology at the University of Lancaster. He is the author of *Social Theory as Science* (with R. Keat), *The Anatomy of Capitalist Societies, Capital Labour and the Middle Classes* (with N. Abercrombie) and joint editor of *Power in Britain* and *Social Relations and Spatial Structures.*

Acknowledgements

The editors, contributors and publisher are grateful to the following for permission to reprint previously published material in this book:

A. B. Atkinson and Oxford University Press for table 3.5, originally from Atkinson, A. B., *The Economics of Inequality*, Oxford, Oxford University Press, 1983.

A. B. Atkinson, A. J. Harrison and Cambridge University Press for tables 3.2 and 3.3, originally from Atkinson, A. B. and Harrison, A. J., *The Distribution of Personal Wealth in Britain*, Cambridge, Cambridge University Press, 1978.

George Bain, Robert Price and Basil Blackwell Ltd for tables 5.1–5.4, originally from Bain, G. S., *Industrial Relations in Britain*, Oxford, Basil Blackwell, 1983.

David P. Boyd for tables 2.6 and 2.7, originally from Boyd, D. P., *Elites and their Education*, London, NFER, 1973.

S. Fothergill, M. Kitson and Cambridge University Press for table 4.2, originally from *Regional Studies*, August 1983.

R. J. Johnston, J. C. Doornkamp and Methuen for figure 4.4, originally from Johnston, R. J. and Doornkamp, J. C., *The Changing Geography of the United Kingdom*, London, Methuen, 1982.

J. Ross and Pluto Press for table 2.8, originally from Ross, J., *Thatcher and Friends*, London, Pluto Press, 1983.

G. Routh and Macmillan London and Basingstoke for table 3.7, originally from Routh, G., *Occupation and Pay in Great Britain, 1906–1979*, London, Macmillan, 1980.

The Spare Rib collective for substantial sections of chapter 7, originally published in *Spare Rib* numbers 115–17, 1981.

Peter Townsend, University of California Press and Penguin Books Ltd for table 3.4, originally from Townsend, P., *Poverty in the United Kingdom* which was published in 1979 by Pelican Books in the United Kingdom and by the University of California Press in the United States.

Warrington and Runcorn Development Corporation and Royds Advertising Agency for figure 4.3, originally published in the *Financial Times*.

Editorial Introduction

A Socialist Anatomy of Britain is the third volume in a series aiming to gather together intellectual material which will place in the hands of left-wing activists the arguments, theories and information necessary to help them construct the case for socialism in their discussions with others: material that is both concise and compact in its presentation, and as rigorous and exhaustive in its quality and range as we can make it. The first volume, *Socialist Arguments*, attempted to bring together in one place the major socialist answers to the conventional wisdoms of the day: that there is no alternative to Thatcherism, that the unions have too much power, that society is too equal and overtaxed, that immigration is a problem and so on. The second volume, *Socialist Strategies*, offered Marxist explanations of the contemporary crisis, and brought together general discussions of possible left-wing strategies for its resolution. This third volume, while standing alone and complete in its own terms, sees itself as complementing those two, by offering *A Socialist Anatomy of Britain*. The purpose of this brief introduction is to explain what a socialist anatomy is all about.

Our title, and indeed our purpose, is partly modelled on the fascinating journalistic surveys of the contemporary power structure compiled by Anthony Sampson. Sampson has made a practice down the years of reporting regularly on the character and personnel of key elite groups in Britain; and his latest survey *The Changing Anatomy of Britain*[1] reports at length on political parties, Establishment figures, state personnel, and the leaders of business, finance and labour. His books are always fun to read, and are full of interesting anecdotes. But they are also, by their nature, brief and superficial, and reflective of the attitudes and assumptions of the Establishment on which they report. Sampson's own political preference for a party of the Centre colours his judgement of the people and institutions he discusses, and fixes the range of topics on which his anatomies concentrate. For what he does not choose to talk about tells us at least as much about the anatomy of Britain as do his books themselves. What is missing, in general, are the powerless and the dispossessed, the radicals and the rebels. So socialist anatomies have to be very different from his. They have to ask different questions. They have to have a different focus. They need a different set of preoccupations. They use a different mode of exposition; and they address a different audience. And they possess all these features because without them, and no matter how well researched and well written they may be, they are just not able to tell socialists the kinds of things they need to know.

Anatomies of Sampson's variety, fascinating though they are, cannot tell us, for example, about the underlying structures and processes of the society which place institutions and individuals in key positions of power. Nor do they explain (as distinct from report upon) the interests and preoccupations of office holders within the Establishment. Moreover, anatomies such as Sampson's, which attempt to catch a particular moment in time, can do that properly only if they are capable of situating that moment in the history which has produced it; and the strength of a good socialist history, when set against the histories of the Right and Centre, is that it does more than record the consolidation of the status quo. It actually draws attention to the contradictions within the dominant order, and to the social forces likely to be mobilized against it. That is vital. For a socialist anatomy must have the question of resistance as its central concern. Its job is not simply, or even primarily, to map the Establishment. Sampson does that well enough. Its prime job is rather to locate the progressive forces available for social change, and to specify the internal development, the organizations and the practices available within the potential constituency of the Left. *A Socialist Anatomy of Britain* has to probe beneath the surface, to locate the essential processes at work there. It has to go behind the present, to locate the contradictions of the past. It has to go beyond the powerful, to locate those who would sweep them away; and it has to provide a map of the society which is different from that provided by Anthony Sampson – one which uses different categories, different criteria of importance, and different specifications of the relevant.

A Socialist Anatomy of Britain has to begin with capitalism, and with a particular capitalism at that: a local capitalism in decline within a world system which is itself in a late state of its own development. Capitalism is in essence a system of generalized commodity production based on wage labour, and it has already moved from a phase of liberal capitalism (based on small production units and limited state activity) to a monopoly stage, in the reproduction of which the state is heavily involved. The British capitalist class and its state draw their strength from the health of the accumulation process at capitalism's core; and so *A Socialist Anatomy of Britain* has to capture the character of that accumulation process and its attendant social forces. This is attempted in part 1, where Laurence Harris analyses contemporary capitalism in Britain, and John Scott discusses the nature of the local ruling class. Ruling classes of course, exist only at the top of a pyramid of social inequality; and in contemporary capitalism that inequality derives from a complex interplay of class, race and gender. John Urry describes that interplay in chapter 3, and Doreen Massey examines its spatial dimensions in chapter 4. Part 2 then reports on the social forces generated on the Left by this experience of inequality within capitalism. Richard Hyman reports on working-class struggle and the trade unions, Sarah Perrigo looks at the women's movement, Kum Kum and Reena Bhavnani write about black oppression and resistance, Anthony Arblaster surveys the struggle for national liberation in Ireland, Richard Taylor reports on 'Green' politics, and David Coates surveys the parties of the Left. The tasks facing those parties are discussed by Robert Looker in the final chapter in the volume; and the detailed programmes of individual parties are listed in the appendix. The content of individual chapters remains, in the end, the personal responsibility of the author concerned; but the collection in total is offered as a comprehensive and coherent guide to British capitalism and its contradictory social forces.

We hope that this book will be of value and interest to socialists and radicals of all shades of opinion. We hope too that you will find within it concise and useful information about the capitalism we would transform and replace, and a detailed guide to the social forces, movements, organizations and programmes which are currently working on the Left to that end. At the very least, we hope that the volume will make clear how to contact any organization which looks potentially attractive to you, the better to enable you to decide for yourself where your energies might best be concentrated. We are aware that, even as a handbook, the need to be concise has meant that much has had to be left unsaid. Some of the general questions of socialist strategy are more fully discussed in volume II of the Socialist Primer series; and the issues raised in part 1 are also discussed in David Coates's *The Context of British Politics* (Hutchinson, 1984). In the end all we can hope is that there is sufficient here to whet the appetite for further reading and study, and that the information gathered in this volume will be of some assistance to those engaged in the vital task of rekindling left-wing forces in the United Kingdom in the 1980s.[2]

David Coates, Gordon Johnston and **Ray Bush**

Part 1
The Anatomy of British Capitalism

1

British Capital: Manufacturing, Finance and Multinational Corporations

LAURENCE HARRIS

I

The image of the British economy that people are given is both simple and static. In the ideas the media promulgate, a picture of a stultified economy, the sick patient paralysed by the British disease, has alternated with one where Tory medicine could liberate free enterprise and generate riches for all. In both, the Tory view that the economy consists of rational individual entrepreneurs on one hand – the embodiment of the spirit of progress – and powerful, obstructive trade unions on the other, summarizes the two unchanging forces at work. In fact, the British economy cannot be characterized in any such simple way. First, it is far from static. British capitalism is always changing; to understand what it is like at any one time it has to be seen as the product of its history. Second, it is highly complex and divided. As well as the conflict between workers and capitalists the competing interests of different sections of the capitalist class shape it. In this chapter I set out the main features of British capital bearing in mind these two aspects.[1]

In their editorial preface, David Coates, Ray Bush and Gordon Johnston referred to the general character of *capitalism* as a system that affects the whole of social life and whose impact is felt by both the working class and capitalists. Here we look at *capital* in the more limited economic sense; as the mass of resources, finance, property, machinery, raw materials and finished goods, largely owned and ultimately under the control of the capitalist class. It is not these things themselves, as lifeless assets, that are important as capital, but their operation: the industry that works with the machinery and materials for profit; the banks that manipulate and deal in financial assets; and the other trading, producing and money making activities of the economy. It is these activities that, in

Britain, comprise capital and have produced the changes that capitalism in Britain has undergone.

The modern British economy is a product of these changes but they have not been smooth and continuous. The greatest changes have occurred through the major crises that have disrupted the economy at times, for such crises overthrow the old economic order and lay the foundations for a new.[2] There have been two great turning points in this century. The inter-war decades of the 1920s and 1930s, marked by the crisis which produced peak unemployment in 1931 and 1932, not only changed the structure of industry, shrinking, for example, the old textile industries and generating new light engineering and consumer goods industries, but changed the ways in which capital worked, for these years laid the foundations for a wartime and post-war co-operation between trade unions, employers and state.[3] The second major upheaval of this century started in the early 1970s, was marked by the crisis of 1979 to 1982 which produced unemployment officially measured at over three million, and has produced large changes in capital's way of operating.[4]

II

Because the different sections of capital have different interests and roles, it is important to know how capital is divided between different types. But these divisions themselves have changed considerably. Since the Second World War, and especially since the start of the 1960s, manufacturing industry has accounted for a declining proportion of British capital and the position of manufacturing relative to services (and relative to extractive and other industries) has changed significantly. But there are other ways of slicing up British capital to examine its structure. For socialists it is important to identify sections which have distinct and conflicting *interests*. Financial capital is distinguishable from industrial capital with distinct and often conflicting interests in a way in which manufacturing and transport or retail services are not. Similarly, large firms with an international reach, the multinational corporations, have interests and modes of operating which differ from medium and small firms. Thus, there are three ways of examining the changing division of British capital: (a) between manufacturing, other industrial sectors, agriculture and services (or, in other words, according to the type of product); (b) between financial capital and capital employed in industry; and (c) between large firms and others ('monopoly capital' and 'non-monopoly capital'). If we examine each in turn we find that the relative size of manufacturing capital has decreased since the mid-1960s; that within it concentration has increased so that 'monopoly capital' has become more significant; and that the financial sector has grown in size and significance.

The decline in manufacturing industry hardly needs documenting for an unemployed trade unionist on Merseyside, Tyneside or even in Brent, Tower Hamlets and Newham in London. Factories which used to have large, well-organized workforces rationalized and closed in the 1970s and early 1980s, giving the word 'de-industrialization' a real meaning. Yet economists have had difficulty in pinning it down and measuring it, noting that the term 'gatecrashed the literature, thereby avoiding the entrance fee of a definition'. The relative decline of manufacturing is marked most clearly by the numbers employed. From 1956 onward the proportion of the labour force employed in manufacturing has fallen steadily (although the total numbers employed grew until 1966). Whereas it was 36 per cent in 1960, it had fallen to 30 per cent by 1976 and as low as 26 per cent by 1983. Until the late 1970s, however, the proportion of total *output* accounted for by manufacturing industry remained steady if measured at constant prices,[5] although the 1979–82 crisis dramatically worsened the relative share of manufacturing in the output of the whole economy. The greatest decline in the significance of manufacturing in Britain has been on an international scale. The simple image of Britain as 'the workshop of the world' was held unquestioningly in Britain long after it had lost its empirical basis, but the last two decades have completely undermined it. The OECD comprises the world's most advanced capitalist countries; between 1960 and 1975 the United Kingdom's manufacturing output fell from 9.6 per cent of the OECD total to 5.8 per cent and by 1982 it had fallen to 4.1 per cent. Another mark of the same decline in the international position of British manufacturing is the fact that whereas Britain has been a net exporter of manufactured goods since the Industrial Revolution, by 1984 the country was importing a greater value of manufactured goods than it exported.

The relative decline of manufacturing in Britain, that sector of industrial capital that profits directly from the factory and workshop, is thus most evident in the proportion of the labour force it absorbs and in its international weakness. Tories (and some left-wing commentators) argue that this is of little significance and hold out a vision of the future in which jobs lost in manufacturing will be compensated for by increased employment in the service sector. As long as we are referring to the proportions of the labour force employed in each sector this is almost a truism, for manufacturing and services are defined so that the only other sectors are agriculture, construction, and extractive industries which are small and not easily expanded. Thus, a decline in the proportion of the labour force employed in manufacturing has been accompanied by a rise in the proportion employed in services (the latter rising from 47 per cent to 62 per cent of the labour force between 1960 and 1982). This information, however, does not support the view that the number of service jobs has expanded, or will do so, to absorb those lost from manufacturing. The increase in the proportion of employees in the service sector would arise even if all who lost their jobs when a factory closed (or all school leavers who would have got a factory job when apprenticeships were more plentiful) stayed unemployed; as manufacturing jobs are lost the total number in work in the economy as a whole would fall. In fact, this is what has happened; the number of jobs in services has not increased to absorb those lost from manufacturing. The future is even more problematic. Even if new service sector jobs are created by the growth of computer applications, old types of office work will decline as computers have their effect.

The exercise of comparing the loss of jobs in manufacturing with the service sector's potential for job increase misses one of the most important dimensions of the changes that have taken place in the economy, the increased importance of financial capital. Comparing manufacturing with services involves comparing two broad categories of production according to their types of output; manufacturing produces visible, tangible commodities while the service sector produces invisible, intangible commodities ranging from retailing (the service of selling other commodities) to transport (the service of moving them) to banking services and the 'service of military preparedness' provided by the armed forces. Apart from the fact that the service sector comprises a motley collection of different types of activities, comparing sectors defined in this way misses the point that particular activities are carried out by particular types of capital and that large numbers in the service sector are employed by the state as civil servants or military personnel rather than by private capital. Thus, within the service sector, banks, insurance companies, building societies and the thousands of brokers, jobbers, speculators and firms that cluster around finance comprise a distinct fraction of capital whose basis is either borrowing and lending or dealing in money. This particular interest sets financial capital apart from the capital employed in other parts of the 'service sector' and from the industrial capital employed in manufacturing; and its position in the economy gives financial capital great power over the rest of the economy. Because of this, an assessment of the strength of the financial sector is important for any understanding of the character and structure of British capital. In the next section of this chapter the character, interests and role of financial capital will be examined more closely. For the present I shall indicate its size.

Employment and output are useful measures of the capital involved in manufacturing and services, but the size of the financial sector is best measured by the amount of money under its control. At the end of 1981 banks alone had £332 billion of assets at their disposal. If we add in the assets of the insurance companies (£74 billion), building societies (£62 billion), pension funds (£64 billion), investment and unit trusts (£16 billion) and other institutions, the City controlled assets almost twice as valuable as the whole of the UK's output (gross domestic product) in that year. These assets represented over £10,000 per head of the British population (including children).[6]

The financial sector does not only own and dispose of this mass of already accumulated wealth. Its investments are constantly expanding, fed by the savings and pension contributions of all classes. The net growth of the assets of insurance companies, pension funds and trusts in 1982 was £14 billion and the flow of money into the building societies enabled them to lend £7 billion in that year.[7] Although at the end of the Second World War and for several years afterwards the City was constrained by laws and regulations in the uses to which it could put this money it has consistently and successfully struggled for the abolition of all such restrictions. Its complete victory came in 1979 with the removal of the last restrictions on overseas investment.[8] The City's freedom in manipulating financial assets is the essence of its powerful, central position in the economy (see below pp. 17 to 21).

The third category to exercise great economic power consists of the giant firms in manufacturing, trading, finance, oil and other sectors. Many on the Left see the distinct interests of this group as a conflict between 'big' and 'medium or small' capital, or between 'monopoly' and 'non-monopoly' firms;[9] some see the whole character and development of the economy as determined by the 'degree of monopoly'.[10] Theories about the significance of the giant firms differ, but there is also a conceptual problem in measuring the proportion of economic activity for which they account, for any dividing line between large and small firms drawn on the basis of size of assets, sales, or employment is arbitrary. An alternative is to measure the significance of multinational corporations in the economy; that is, the activities in Britain of corporations which have their headquarters here and subsidiaries and affiliates overseas, and of enterprises in Britain which are the branches or subsidiaries of corporations with headquarters overseas. Effectively all the giant corporations operating in Britain are multinational, but it is not their size alone that distinguishes them, it is the fact that their operations are spread across the globe. These two characteristics give multinationals both interests and power which differ from other companies. British firms with investments in overseas operations have different concerns and interests from those confined to Britain, and foreign firms operating in Britain differ from both.

The British economy has an unusually high proportion of multinational corporations, and the 1960s and 1970s saw a considerable expansion both of such foreign capital in Britain and of British firms with operations abroad. Between 1962 and 1979 UK firms' capital abroad grew fivefold in nominal value to £25.5 billion and the stake of foreign firms in the UK grew almost ninefold to £18.9 billion.[11] If we add together the foreign capital operating in Britain and the overseas capital of British firms to indicate the significance of multinational capital as a whole, it was between 27 per cent and 32 per cent of the UK's annual gross national product in the years from 1962 to 1978.[12] Within the manufacturing sector during the 1960s and 1970s British multinationals invested abroad in industries which did not use a high level of technology whereas foreign multinationals investing in Britain concentrated on technologically advanced sectors, although individual industries such as chemicals were an exception to the rule.[13]

Given the importance of overseas trade to the UK economy, the strategic position of multinational corporations is clearly shown by the high proportion of foreign trade that is in their hands. In 1979 British and foreign multinationals accounted for over 80 per cent of British exports. Of the total, a mere 87 giant enterprises were responsible (in 1976) for over half of British exports.[14] The multinationals' exports and imports are different from those of other corporations for to a large extent they take place within the company itself, as when Ford cars made in Germany are sold under British model names in Britain. The proportions vary but the multinationals with the largest stake in exporting British output generally sell a high proportion within the same company. Thus, in 1979 the largest 56 exporters among US multinationals in Britain, accounting for three-quarters of all such firms' exports, sent two-thirds of their exports to other branches of the same firm.[15]

The figures I have presented give some indication of the magnitude of three important characteristics of capital in Britain: the relative significance of manufacturing capital has declined in recent decades; the size of the capital controlled by financial institutions has increased; and big capital, in the form of multinational enterprises, has a strategic position in industry and trade. Such figures do not give an adequate picture of British capital, however, for it is the way that the different sections *operate*, rather than their mere size, which is important. Let us look at the operation of manufacturing capital, the financial sector and multinational corporations.

III

Instead of examining the way *manufacturing capital* operates in general I shall focus on a specific problem, the factors which have led to its rundown, or 'de-industrialization'. Such a focus permits a more concrete and relevant study of aspects of its operation. The relative loss of position by manufacturing capital has been widely discussed.[16] Explanations have been sought in terms of management's dealings with three forces, often seen by industrialists as part of their external environment: organized labour, the state and international competition.

The most fundamental of these is *labour*. For industry's profits depend upon labour above all else. It is a well-established argument of the right wing that the militancy of the working class, especially in the 1950s, 1960s and early 1970s, is responsible for the decline of manufacturing industry. But left-wing writers refine that view and argue that either labour militancy over wages has pushed down profits or labour's strong workplace organization has hindered the application of new technology and profitable rationalization of industry.[17]

The role of the *state* in the problem of manufacturing industry has been discussed from several perspectives. Self-interest leads that section's capitalists to argue, at every budget time, that taxation has restricted their profits and hence their ability to invest and rationalize. This view has been given an academic rationale by the Right who argue that governmental (non-marketed) services financed by taxes are parasitic,[18] and by the Left who argue that the welfare state has been financed by taxes on profits.[19] Monetarists argue that growth and efficiency have suffered from the state's intervention for it interferes with market forces. On the other hand, during the 1960s when British manufacturing, although booming, was less dynamic than its French, Japanese and other competitors, some Keynesians were arguing that the state was failing industry and, while leaving full scope to market forces, should develop indicative planning following the French model.

International competition has been seen as a source of manufacturing industry's problems in several ways. The argument most frequently taken up by the Right is that low labour productivity and high wages make British manufacturing uncompetitive (an argument which merely repeats the responsibility attached to the labour movement). A different view, emphasizing the impact on Britain of global changes, argues that the growth of new industrialized countries and the enfeeblement of manufacturing in Britain and other advanced capitalist countries are both elements in a changing international division of labour. This view fits well with a Marxist analysis of capital's expansion and internationalization. It has, nevertheless, been adopted and distorted in support of Thatcherite economics and the view that international forces rather than particular fractions of the capitalist class are wholly responsible for British unemployment.

Certainly, labour, the state and international competition have all been relevant to the worsening position of capital employed in British manufacturing. But the views on them that I have summarized here do not all have strong evidence to support them and none is as straightforward as it seems. In contrast to the most commonly accepted views, it is the weakness of organized labour rather than its strength that has characterized British manufacturing. The failure of the state to galvanize industry and the problems created by the changing balance of international competition are real enough, but they themselves have resulted in large measure from the nature of British capital itself and, in particular, from the character of financial capital. In this section I shall discuss the assessment of labour's strength and weakness; in subsequent sections I shall consider the influence of financial capital.

Industrial capital, and particularly manufacturing industry, yielded declining profits for its owners from the early post-war years to the end of the 1970s. The trend was downward with only small interruptions. The rate of return on the capital invested in private manufacturing companies declined from 13 per cent in 1960 to 3 per cent in 1979, and industry as a whole showed a similar trend.[20] This is often taken as an indicator of the progressive weakening of British industry and business interests argue that it is a cause as well as an indicator: if profits were higher, they argue, they would have invested more. But the argument does not stop there, for the low profits themselves are blamed upon workers' militancy.

The view that labour's strength and commitment to class struggle has been the cause of low profitability and industrial decline has had an international dimension which argues that profitability is not only low in absolute terms but low relative to other countries and this has resulted from a uniquely militant strain in British labour. The figures do show that profitability was low relative to other countries. In the UK, the net rate of return on capital in manufacturing industry was lower than that in West Germany, the USA and Canada throughout the period 1955 to 1978. The year 1970 gives a striking illustration: in that year the (gross) rate of return in UK manufacturing industry was 10 per cent as compared with 40 per cent in Japan, 19 per cent in West Germany and 17 per cent in the USA.[21] The comparative weakness of UK profits tempts many to accept that it has been caused by the strength of British trade unions compared with those of other countries. But has it? The short answer is no; but a longer answer is warranted to establish the point.

Trade-union strength could affect profits in two ways: first, by forcing wages up at the expense of profits and, second, by effectively fighting for control of the methods and pace of work thereby limiting productivity (in the extreme, by blocking new technology and working practices). Wage earnings did rise relatively fast and productivity did rise relatively slowly in the UK during the 1970s. The net effect of changes in wage costs (per hour of labour) and changes in productivity (as output per hour of labour) is a change in the wage cost of each unit of output. In the UK wage costs per unit of output went up 15.5 per cent per year between 1970 and 1980, while in West Germany they rose at a rate of only 5.5 per cent, in the USA at 6.2 per cent, and in Japan at 6.6 per cent.[22] Figures like these are used to lend support to the idea that Britain's trade unions have caused low profits but a closer look at the evidence does not support the argument.

First, the data for the previous decade, 1960 to 1970 show that wages increased relatively slowly and productivity relatively fast so that UK wage costs per unit of output went up no faster than other major countries. Yet, as we have seen, UK profit rates were declining throughout the 1960s and they remained low compared to other countries. In the UK wage costs per unit rose at 2.8 per cent per annum in that decade, which was the same rate as Japan and West Germany experienced (2.7 per cent).[23] If labour militancy was the problem, its effect on Britain's comparative performance was not strongly evident in the 1960s even though those were the years when developments such as the powerful shop stewards movement in the car industry were at their height.

Second, there is no reliable evidence identifying trade-union militancy as a cause of either high rates of wage increase or low productivity growth. Given the certainty with which employers, governments and Fleet Street claim that trade unions are at the root of Britain's problems, it is important to be clear on what the evidence does show.

The most entrenched idea which gives credence to the employers' claim is that Britain is very strike prone, and much more so than countries with more successful industries. In fact, in a comparison of working days lost through strikes in 16 major countries, the UK was almost half-way up the league. It ranked seventh in working days lost (average number per thousand employees per year) between 1967 and 1976, while Canada, Italy and USA, Australia, Finland and Ireland lost a greater number of days in strikes.[24] Throughout the period 1964 to 1976 the USA lost many more days in strikes each year than the UK but wage costs per unit of output rose less than in the UK, reflecting lower wage increases or higher productivity growth or both. The figures for annual average days lost per 1,000 employees in 1964–6 were 870 in the USA and 190 in the UK; between 1967–76 they were 1,349 and 788 respectively. Yet in the USA unit wage costs rose only 1.5 per cent per annum from 1960 to 1970 and 6.2 per cent per annum from 1970 to 1980 while in the UK they rose at an annual rate of 2.8 per cent and 15.5 per cent in those periods. Thus, not only has the strike record in the UK not been particularly high, but a comparison of the UK and the USA suggests that there is no direct, simple link between days lost in strikes and industrial performance.

International comparisons of the UK strike record are one way to assess its importance; another is to judge how widespread strikes have been. Strikes in British manufacturing industries have been highly concentrated in a few large firms so that their direct impact on wages and productivity, if any, has not been widespread. Thus, for the period 1971 to 1975 (when union membership and strike activity was rising) the Department of Employment found that 98 per cent of manufacturing establishments employing about 80 per cent of that sector's workforce experienced no official strikes in an average year.[25]

But the strike record is not the only way to judge whether the activities of trade unions have led to excessive wage increases or low productivity growth: trade-union strength could be high even if the number of days lost in strikes is not. Economists have attempted to measure trade-union strength in a variety of more or less arbitrary ways and to calculate statistically whether it relates to either wage increases or productivity growth.[26] These studies have not produced reliable evidence that wage increases have accelerated as a result of trade-union strength or that productivity has been held back by it.[27] Certainly casual impressions held by people who have lived through the changing struggles of the 1970s and 1980s can lead to a feeling that trade-union strength has been a major factor in industry. After all, the high wage increases in the early 1970s coincided with a considerable expansion in trade-union membership, and the declining union membership in industry has coincided with low nominal wage increases. But several statistical studies have now established that changing union membership is the effect of such economic conditions not their cause.[28]

Industrial capital and especially manufacturing industry is relatively weak in the UK and has been in decline. Its condition does depend ultimately on the relation between capital and workers, but this does not imply that the cause of its weakness lies in the workers' strength. Industrial relations should not be seen as a zero-sum game. There is no hard evidence to show that trade-union strength has been the cause of industrial capital's problems. But there are several reasons for thinking that if trade unions had been *more* militant industrial capital would have been forced to be more competitive. Workers in British industry have not won high real wages. They are among the worst paid in the advanced capitalist countries. This is a sign of trade-union docility and it has enabled British industrial capital to persist with old, inefficient plant. Cheap labour has meant that old equipment could continue to generate profits while industrial capital in other countries modernized and eventually came to undercut British products. A militant trade-union movement struggling effectively for high wages would have made labour costly and forced capital to modernize. Such a display of trade-union strength would have involved a struggle for the planned, agreed and controlled implementation of modern technologies.

Thus, a focus on British workers' unique militancy does not help us understand the character and weakness of the industrial fraction of British capital. The weakness of the forms of struggle British workers have adopted is more significant. This, however, is an unusual view. The stylized facts that have dominated the public image of the unions, together with some rigorous research, support the opposite case. The image of workers in the car industry, for example, engaged in demarcation disputes between themselves and in shop-steward-led struggles to wrest control of production from management leads automatically to a view that union strength hinders productivity; why else would an aggressive manager like

Michael Edwardes have had to try to smash that union power in the late 1970s? Similarly, the research which suggests that the increased output achieved from investment in new plant is lower in Britain than elsewhere, is taken to imply that it is not the lack of new machinery but workers' resistance to operating it intensively that is the root of the problem.

But such conclusions are not warranted. The fight to defend demarcation lines and the shop stewards movements were in fact a sign of the fragmentation and weakness of British unions. Their sectional and local strengths were but a symptom of the weakness suffered by the unions when confronting capital at a high level, within the industry, the firm, or such tripartite corporatist bodies as NEDC. Unable to enforce demands at such a level for a high wage economy with rational co-ordinated investment (on French or, in part, Japanese lines) union members were left only with the possibility of defending their position at sectional and local levels. This trend was encouraged by the fact that British management itself has been fragmented, plant-based and oriented to the short-term rather than a force for co-ordinated, rational accumulation of industrial capital. The Edwardes's strategy was not a sign of union strength; rather, his easy victory in labour relations was a sign that what had been presented as workers' strength for decades was in fact very precarious and was lost as soon as the management structure and style that had facilitated it was rationalized.

The relatively low productivity achieved with new plant in British industry is also explained by the general conditions under which capital is accumulated and particularly by the absence of a long-term rational plan for Britain's industrial development. It is not legitimate to attribute it to a single cause such as workers' militancy; indeed, the inability of unions to impose a strategy of high wages and rational accumulation on capital is a major part of the explanation.

The failure of industrial capital to adopt such a strategy is not only a consequence of the character of the labour movement. The form and nature of the British state have also been crucial factors in preventing it from adopting the strategic role played by the French or Japanese states. And the impact upon industry of a separate fraction of British capital, financial capital, or the lack of such an impact compared with West Germany and Japan, has been a major problem in its own right.

IV

The City of London, the shorthand for financial capital in Britain, has had a unique role in the economy and in politics. Speculation on the foreign exchanges and City views on the exchange rate have influenced government policy and affected industry and trade with a power and directness that neither trade unions nor industrial managements could match. So has the City's influence over interest rates. Financial capital has been a leading element in the internationalization of capital. And the most recent mark of its distinctiveness is that the City prospered in the 1970s and 1980s, while industry and trade faltered in the wake of the long post-war boom.

The City's unique role stems from the fact that financial capital operates quite differently from industrial and other forms of capital. Financial capital means the vast amount of capital that takes the form of money, including bank deposits, loans, and investments in stocks and shares, in contrast to capital directly tied up in plant and machinery. In Britain it is controlled by banks, insurance companies, pension funds, building societies and other financial institutions. Its profits come from two types of activity which are distinct but closely intermeshed: one is borrowing and lending in various forms, the other is dealing in money and financial securities, for example buying and selling foreign exchange, or dealing in shares on the stock market. The City's profit which comes to bankers and financiers in the form of interest, dividends, capital gains, or fees for dealing in money and credit, ultimately depends on the profitability of the real economy. The basic drive of financial capital is to try to prevent its ultimate dependence on industry from damaging its own profits, and financiers have attempted to do this in two ways. First, they have attempted to ensure that exchange rates and interest rates exert a discipline over industry and trade and particularly over any class struggle that could threaten profits. For example, when bankers argued during the 1960s against the devaluation of sterling that was forced in 1967, their opposition was partly based on the view that although a high exchange rate increased foreign competition, that itself would stimulate managements and workers to keep wage costs down and strengthen industrial profits.[29] Second, financial strategy has followed a rather different tack as financiers have sought to make their profits as independent as possible of industrial problems. Financial capital has been pushed into foreign investment, loans to the state and investment in real estate at every opportunity, rather than into loans or equity for British industry.[30]

The fact that the operations of financial capital are not dominated by the financing of industry is partly reflected in the 'low gearing' of UK companies. 'Gearing' is a measure of a company's external borrowing as a proportion of the shareholders' own capital; if it is low it broadly suggests that firms finance investments in plant and machinery out of their own profits rather than by borrowing from the financial system. Thus low gearing suggests a relative lack of industrial financing by financiers and bankers, although it is not conclusive on that score since gearing could be low in countries such as West Germany where, unlike Britain, bankers themselves are major owners of shares in industry so that their financing shows up in shareholdings rather than external borrowing. In the UK, gearing varied between about 50 per cent and 60 per cent during the 1970s (on one measure) whereas it was between 300 and 350 per cent in Japan, between 100 and 150 per cent in France, and between 90 and 100 per cent in West Germany. British industry has relied on proportionately less funds from the financial system than firms in other countries apart from the USA. And the financial capital that has been directed into industry has been largely short term in character. Until the 1980s, for example, banks provided mainly overdraft finance to industry rather than committing funds for an eight year period or longer to match the long-term nature of major industrial investment projects.

Another sign of the distance between financial capital and industrial capital is that banks and the big investment institutions, the pension funds and insurance companies, have historically avoided any direct involvement in the running of industry. They have not, as a rule, appointed their own nominees to the boards of companies they have put money into and have not made any systematic arrangements for collaboration between industry and the City on development strategies for production, investment and financing. Moreover, when bankers lend to industry they have looked for security in collateral that will cover them when the firm collapses, and have themselves been the main 'whistle-blowers' calling in the receiver to ensure that they get their money when firms are in trouble, rather than seeking security by agreeing guidelines for the development of the company while it is alive.[31]

The distance between financial and industrial capital in the UK is markedly different from the relationship between them in other countries. The growth of Japanese industry has been founded on close links between the large industrial corporations and the banks. The latter are a major source of finance, as reflected in the high gearing ratio; this is long term in character, and bankers and industrialists are linked in structures that have been the basis for strategic planning. Similarly, in West Germany financiers (and trade unionists) have had a direct involvement in industrial firms.

It is often argued that the City has failed industry and the industrial success of Japan and West Germany with their quite different financial relationships has been interpreted as support for that argument. The distance between the City and industry cannot be doubted, but it does not follow that the City has 'failed' industry in any simple sense. The low amount of industrial financing, its short-term character and the lack of involvement all reflect a complex of forces and cannot be interpreted as industry requiring the greater involvement of financial capital while the City holds back. Rather than seeking to identify one sector of capital as the source of British capital's problems it is more valuable to try to understand the operations of each and the complex forces that have shaped them.

International deals, including overseas investment, have always been a key element in the way financial capital operates and it is increasingly so today. The drive to secure its profits from the risk that would be presented by dependence on British industry has led financial capital to base much of its profits on foreign business and, even there, to ensure that as far as possible, it is one step removed from the enterprises, the factories, plantations and mines, that actually generate the profits except where, as in mining for oil, profits appear almost guaranteed. Thus, the City's foreign business is strongly oriented to lending to states (where, in the ideal situation, interest payments are financed by taxes), lending to banks and other finance houses overseas, buying and selling currencies (that is, operating the foreign exchanges) and arranging credits for a fee, all of which are less risky undertakings than the uncertain prospect of future interest.

Foreign investment is the issue that attracts the greatest attention for it is easy to judge that the high level of foreign investment has diverted funds that would otherwise have gone to UK industry. The City has had a high level of foreign investment at least since the late nineteenth century. This was one element in what Lenin and other Marxists identified as the export of capital that characterized their age.[32] For almost three-quarters of a century it has been believed that at the end of 1913 Britain's net assets overseas were worth £4 billion, of which a high proportion represented the City's exports of financial capital, as distinct from industrial and commercial firms' own foreign assets. These estimates have recently been shown to have been over-estimates of the net position,[33] but the fact that UK financial capital was heavily dependent on foreign investments in the heyday of imperialism is not in doubt.

Foreign investment by the City, the export of financial capital, was restrained during the years following the Second World War by restrictions on financiers' ability to buy dollars for that purpose, but in 1979 one of the first acts of the Thatcher government was to abolish all such controls and financial capital has renewed its basic strong drive in that direction. This export of capital by the City is roughly measured by the flow of 'portfolio investment' overseas. Whereas it was £1 billion in 1978 (and had been zero or negative for most of that decade) it had risen to more than £6 billion by 1982 as a result of the Tory liberalization.[34] The financial institutions leading this outflow were the pension funds and insurance companies whose money comes mainly from individuals' savings for old age, mortgage repayment and other purposes. Thus, whereas pension funds invested 8.7 per cent of their money overseas in 1979 they invested over 28 per cent overseas in 1982, while for insurance companies the overseas proportion rose from 6 per cent to 22 per cent during the same period.[35]

A large part of the City's lending to overseas borrowers, however, does not represent an export of *British* capital in any simple way. Bank loans in foreign currencies, in particular, are part of a process of international lending *and* borrowing: the foreign currencies loaned abroad (or to UK firms) have themselves been borrowed and are likely to have come from overseas. These operations of both borrowing and lending foreign currencies (as distinct from using British capital's pounds to buy foreign currencies to invest abroad) were unrestricted even before 1979 and grew at a fast rate throughout the 1960s and 1970s. They are known as 'Eurodollar' (or 'Eurocurrency') operations. Unlike the US and European governments, but like the Bahamas, British governments (whether Labour or Conservative) have bowed to City pressure and left the banks free from regulation to pursue Eurodollar business. In consequence, London has maintained its position as the world's largest centre for international banking. In 1982 27 per cent of all international bank lending emanated from the UK and 15 per cent from the USA, while in 1980 the gap was even wider at 26 per cent and 9.3 per cent respectively.[36]

London's role as the world's leading centre for Eurodollar banking has dominated the operation of finance capital in many ways in recent years. It illustrates an important fact about financial capital in Britain: its international operation cannot be seen simply as a one-way movement outward. Rather, the growth of Eurodollar business involves money both coming in and going out. Even the overseas portfolio investment that represents an export of British capital is partly offset by investment from overseas. Instead of financial capital being involved in a straightforward exodus, it is best to see it as part of a process of internationalization.

This internationalization has affected not only the operations of financial capital but also the ownership of the institutions that own or control it. Financial capital in the UK is managed by institutions that are themselves increasingly foreign owned. This is most clear in the case of banks. An official report in 1959 found only 40 foreign banks in London,[37] but by the end of 1983 there were about 400. US and Japanese banks have become particularly significant in London. As a result, London's pre-eminence in international bank lending does not imply British banks' pre-eminence: in 1983 only 21 per cent of London's international bank lending emanated from British banks while 20 per cent stemmed from US banks in London and 27 per cent from the City's Japanese banks.

The internationalization of financial capital means that we can no longer conceive UK financial capital as being British owned, but only as operating from a British base.

V

The banks engaged in international finance are multinational in the sense that they have branches and subsidiaries in several countries and transfer resources, staff and capital between them more or less freely in order to maximize profits. Industry and commerce, too, are dominated by multi-national corporations as I indicated above; some are British with overseas

B

networks, others are subsidiaries in Britain of firms with foreign (especially US) headquarters. How does this section of capital differ from other industrial and commercial enterprises?

The most important difference is that these enterprises have a close relationship with financial capital. First, banks and multinational (industrial and commercial) enterprises are interdependent. Second, the largest multinationals in some respects combine both financial and industrial capital in their own hands, for many have large, floating masses of funds with treasury departments whose task is to maximize profits by switching them from one currency and investment to another, unconstrained by considerations of the company's production and trade. Third, the majority, which do not have their own internal banking-type currency operations, have internalized the link between financial and industrial capital. That is, they determine which of their lines, in which countries, are to have the corporation's investment funds allocated to them.

If manufacturing in Britain is relatively unprofitable and manufacturing abroad is relatively profitable, British multinationals will switch their capital towards manufacturing abroad, and foreign multinationals will invest less in the UK. In fact, British multinationals have made higher profits from their subsidiaries abroad than from their plants in the UK, and this margin of extra profitability widened throughout the 1960s and 1970s. Differences in the profits enterprises can obtain by operating in different countries have been the driving force for flows of ('direct') investment by multinationals both out of and into the UK. From 1972 to 1982 (and well before that period) outward direct investment by UK multinationals significantly exceeded inward flows in every year. The result of this net foreign investment and of the historical record of direct investment out of Britain over the previous century and more was that by 1982 the assets of British multinationals abroad amounted to some £51 billion and the assets of foreign multinationals in the UK were £29 billion (including oil industry investments).[38]

Noting that multinationals' investment in production abroad and in the UK depends upon profit rates here and abroad does not take us to the heart of their operation. Multinationals take a world-wide approach to their production and trade. In allocating capital between different countries and different lines it is not simply a question of choosing the country in which production of commodity X would be most profitable; instead, it is a question of how production of one line in one country fits into the overall production of the enterprise world-wide so as to maximize its total profits. This approach typifies particularly the most advanced multinationals who design their production so that the components are manufactured in different countries and assembled elsewhere according to the relative costs and profits in each country. This policy of 'world-wide sourcing' became the prevalent basis of multinationals' production in the 1960s and 1970s.[39]

How does the production of the multinationals within the UK fit into their world-wide operations? Two factors have attracted foreign multinationals into investing in the UK: the profit they are able to extract from modern industries which use relatively advanced technology and are capital intensive, and the relatively low wage rates of British labour (as compared with other European real wages) in industries where labour costs are important. Thus, they have concentrated their activities in high technology industries such as oil on the one hand and in low-skill assembly operations which use cheap labour to put together imported parts to produce cars and other light engineering commodities for the European market on the other. But even in mechanical engineering there is evidence that the cheapness of British labour has been an important element affecting multinationals' inward investment.[40]

There is some evidence that foreign multinationals' plants in the UK are more profitable than British plants in the UK. One study, for example, found that between 1958 and 1961 a majority (51 out of a sample of 80 subsidiaries of US companies in the UK) achieved higher productivity than UK companies in the same industries (and obtained higher profits).[41] Another study found that US subsidiaries in the UK obtained profit rates 20 per cent higher than domestic UK firms in 1970–3 (and 92 per cent higher in 1950–4).[42] The 'superiority' of foreign multinationals' managements in their ability to extract profits within Britain is largely due to their policies toward labour (after allowance is made for the greater capital intensity of these subsidiaries). But adopting foreign policies with regard to labour, with a disregard for traditional union structures, has had a double-edged effect. One study found that labour relations in foreign subsidiaries in Scotland were worse than in comparable UK firms.[43]

In addition to multinational corporations' relations to financial capital and to labour, their relationship with the state has been an important factor in determining their strategy. Multinational corporations in the UK have, in a large number of cases, benefited from a close relationship with the state. In industries such as arms production, the electronics industries and nuclear energy small groups of multinationals have both benefited from state policy and shaped that policy.[44]

VI

The development of multinational enterprises is one element in the increasing concentration and centralization of capital. Many industries are now dominated by a small number of giant firms. The tendency towards

concentration in UK industries has been continuous since the Second
World War. While the big firms have got bigger, the role of small firms has
declined although this decline levelled off and showed a slight reversal in
1970.

An approximate measure of the significance of large firms in an industry
is the 'five firm concentration ratio' which measures the extent to which an
industry's sales are in the hands of the five largest firms. A five firm
concentration ratio of 75 per cent, for example, shows that in that industry
three-quarters of all sales emanate from the five largest firms. The average
level of concentration ratios in UK industries has increased since the 1930s.
Between 1963 and 1975 the number of industries with low concentration
ratios (under 60 per cent) decreased from 46 per cent of all industries to 39
per cent of the total. At the same time the industries with high
concentration ratios (over 80 per cent) increased from 29 per cent of the
total to 35 per cent.[45]

The increase in industrial concentration in the late 1950s and 1970s,
although significant, was modest compared with its rise in one sector
between 1950 and 1970. In those two decades the share of manufacturing
industry's net output accounted for by the 100 largest private manufacturing firms rose from 21 per cent to 40 per cent.[46]

Concentration has increased because of the expansion of giant firms
(especially through mergers in the merger booms of the 1930s and 1960s).
It has been accompanied, for long periods, by a decline in the number of
small firms although in the 1970s that decline was partially reversed. The
scanty data that is available suggests that the number of establishments
with less than ten employees fell from nearly 100,000 in 1930 to under
50,000 in 1970 but then appears to have risen again to 59,000 by 1976.[47]
Similarly, the proportion of manufacturing employment accounted for by
establishments employing less than 200 workers fell from about 32 per cent
in 1963 to about 27 per cent in 1973. It then rose to reach 30 per cent in
1979.[48] Whatever their historical decline, small firms remain important in
trades where technological change has been slow such as building and some
professions and in sectors such as retailing (the corner shop).[49] Thus, in
1976 small firms accounted for 49 per cent of employment in construction,
48 per cent in professional and scientific services and 39 per cent in the
distribution trades.

Politicians from both Right and Left have emphasized the importance of
small firms to the economy. Although there was a major official report on
small firms in 1971,[50] their value has been argued for on the basis of little
knowledge. It has been argued that they are labour intensive thereby
contributing more to employment than large firms; indeed, in manufacturing industry the level of investment per person is lower the smaller
the firm. Another claim has been that small firms have greater flexibility
and ability to innovate and are therefore crucial for the development of

new industries. In fact, a 1971 study found that small firms have a proportionately lower input of resources into research and development than medium and large firms and, on the whole, have made fewer innovations per employee.[52] In Tory ideology the belief in the innovative powers of small firms is linked to the view that redundant workers can, unless work shy, become capitalists themselves and that a prosperous capitalism can be founded upon workers making money for themselves in their own small firms. The evidence has not supported such views, for small firms have proved to be very fragile. The Department of Trade and Industry commissioned a report on the performance of almost three years of its loan guarantee scheme for small businesses. It was found that one-third of the 150 firms surveyed had been so unviable that they had gone into liquidation and that the small firms suffered acutely from poor financial management and administration.[53]

The special character of capital in small firms lies not only in the fragility of the firms, but in the way the labour process is organized. The prevalent type of operation is one where, with low capital intensity, profits depend on cheap and intensive labour. As a result, small firms have a strong resistance to the unionization of their workers, and unions are further hindered by the dispersed and relatively isolated labour force. The low unionization of this sector provides an extreme version of the problem I discussed above in the context of manufacturing as a whole. Weak trade unionism enables small firm capital to obtain profits from cheap labour without innovating; it therefore generates stagnation rather than dynamism and reinforces small firms' standing as the most backward form of capital.

VII

The main driving force in the development of capital is privately-owned capital, but since the Second World War much of the British economy has been controlled by the state. Part of the state sector of the economy, the nationalized industries, has increasingly been run in the same way as private capital; another part, the welfare services such as health, education and pensions, has not. The state has, however, increasingly attempted to make these services emulate capital by administrative methods of achieving efficiency and productivity gains, and the state has undermined their position by encouraging private health care and private pension provision. A third part of state economic activity, typified by arms spending, is not itself capitalist production, but is strongly intertwined with the interests of a few multinational corporations whose development depends on it.[54] Because the nationalized industries are so much an element of capital, they cannot be omitted from this chapter.

Nationalization occurred in two main waves. The first, by the 1945–51 Labour government, took into state hands the coal industry, electricity generation, gas, rail, air and road transport, steel and the Bank of England. Thus, with the exception of steel and the central bank, the transport and energy industries were the sectors nationalized in this wave.

Under the Tories, steel and road transport were returned to private capital in the 1950s. The second wave, under both Labour and Tory governments from the mid-1960s to 1976 nationalized manufacturing industries in the main, including the renationalization of the largest steel manufacturers. In this period, Rolls Royce aero engines were nationalized, as were British Leyland, the shipbuilding and most ship-repairing industries, the largest machine tool manufacturers (Alfred Herbert) and the aircraft and missile industry (which was brought into British Aerospace).

By the completion of the second wave of post-war nationalization the publicly-owned industries (including the Post Office) employed about 8 per cent of UK workers, and produced about 11 per cent of the country's gross domestic product. In terms of employment the largest nationalized industry was the Post Office (400,000 in 1979) while the National Coal Board employed 300,000 and British Rail over 200,000.

Except in the case of steel and road haulage, the first wave of post-war nationalization involved relatively little political conflict over public ownership itself. The labour movement wanted nationalization for a variety of reasons: state ownership was seen by some as an essential prerequisite for a socialist planned economy; by others as a means of securing and improving their own conditions and wages; and by the right of the labour movement as a key to the rational administration of a tamed capitalism. Capitalists were able to support nationalization in order to rationalize energy and transport, part of the economic infrastructure on which their capital depended, especially since these sectors had become inefficient and unprofitable under private ownership. Their owners were able to secure their wealth by giving up their shares in unprofitable industries in return for secure government bonds.

But although there was a partial alliance between labour and capital in favour of these nationalizations, socialist and capitalist conceptions of the nationalized industries' role and operations differed sharply. The capitalist notion that they should not operate at a loss and require subsidies out of tax revenues (which come from private capital) has become increasingly entrenched despite the interest of some energy-intensive or transport-intensive industries in obtaining cheap supplies from subsidized public industries. In fact, the basic capitalist principle of excluding workers from the management of the industries was won at the beginning in the Acts which established the Public Corporations to run them. Thereafter, White Papers in 1961, 1967 and 1978 established financial criteria that increasingly simulated those of private industry. The 1967 White Paper made nationalized industries' future investment plans dependent on whether they would yield at least the same profit as capital used in the private sector and the policy of setting such financial targets was refined by the 1978 White Paper. But even before such policy landmarks, 'efficiency', 'productivity' and 'reduction in overmanning' had become the watchwords of the nationalized industries and were symbolized by Dr Beeching's destruction of much of the railway network to cut losses.

The imposition of these rules and associated rules on pricing and the sources of finance has been a means of restoring capitalist ways of working to industries, such as coal, where capital's dynamism and control had effectively and fundamentally broken down. The industries nationalized in the second wave were also unprofitable but in a less fundamental sense and there the rationale was more straightforwardly to apply capitalist methods more effectively (the best example being the Edwardes regime at BL) rather than construct new forms of control to recreate capitalist operating methods.

The main argument in support of these policies toward the nationalized industries has been that they are inherently less efficient than private industry and hence a drain on the latter. In fact, between 1963 and 1968 the nationalized industries showed an overall profit; and between 1969 and 1974 seven of the major industries showed a profit which was offset by the losses of British Rail and the National Coal Board. But although comparing the profit of the state-owned and private industries is an exercise with a strong political appeal, it is not a meaningful exercise, for some items included in nationalized industries' costs should not be, whereas others that are not included in their profits should be.[55]

The thrust in the development of the nationalized industries has been towards operating them in similar ways to private capital. However, they have also been subject to the ruling ideologies on the state's overall economic role. Thus, when Keynesianism was the basis of economic policy, the nationalized industries' investment plans were manipulated as part of the state's regulation of aggregate demand throughout the economy and control of their prices and wages was given a leading role in anti-inflation policy. Under the monetarist policies pursued most vigorously since 1979, cash limits on the nationalized industries have been used to restrict their workers' wages, closure of unprofitable and profitable plants (in steel and coal especially) has been used to cut back their role in the economy, and the aim of cutting back the state's economic impact has achieved its highest expression in 'privatization', selling off the most profitable sectors to private capital.

VIII

Thus, while capital in manufacturing industry has declined and been weakened, financial capital has increased its strength by changing its operations and internationalizing in new ways, and state industries have been forced into the same paths as private industry. At the same time, industry and finance have become increasingly dominated by giant multinational corporations. These trends are interrelated. One key to them all has been the state's emphasis on supporting and creating the operation of market forces throughout the economy rather than using state power for either socialist planning or (as in Japan and other capitalist countries) for the rational direction of capitalism. Industrial capital has, in effect, lost place to financial capital. Putting socialist planning on the agenda would involve the state in taking control over and restructuring the relations between the different sectors of capital in Britain.

2

The British Upper Class

JOHN SCOTT

The upper class is rarely seen as an important issue in political debates. Socialists have often succumbed to the popular viewpoint that the upper class is marginal to political and economic affairs because it consists simply of a declining, decaying 'aristocracy' or 'peerage'. This image of the upper class is associated with the view that class differences are essentially differences in speech, dress, attitudes, and life style. But the reality of class is significantly different from this popular image. British society, like all capitalist societies, is divided into a hierarchical structure of inequality. Each level in the hierarchy is marked by a similarity of life chances; a similarity of condition and opportunity among those located at that level. The inequalities of wealth, power, and prestige which generate these differential life chances are formed into a system of social strata which lie one above the other to make the social pyramid. The dominant stratum in any society constitutes an upper class when its members have a distinct class situation, different from the class situation of those below them, and when the features of their class situation result in distinctive forms of social consciousness.

Britain today has such an upper class. Its class situation is rooted in the ownership and/or control of property which can be used as capital and which, thereby, generates a substantial income. Its members share a common 'market situation', in so far as the use of capital depends upon the existence of a market for capital. The crucial element in their class situation, therefore, is their relationship to capital, considered as a productive resource. This market situation is the material basis for a specific life style and for the ability of the class to exercise a degree of social closure. An upper class consists of intermarrying families, and the life chances and life style of its members are reflected in the strategies used by these families to close off opportunities for access to its own ranks.

This argument runs counter to the idea of the so-called 'managerial revolution', which has been influential in the development of Labour Party policy. The thesis of the managerial revolution holds that changes in the pattern of property ownership – the dispersal of share ownership to a larger and larger pool of people – has led to major changes in the stratification systems of industrial societies. It is claimed that the old style capitalists have disappeared and that power has devolved to executive managers who form part of a large, open, meritocratic 'middle class'. I will show in this chapter that this view is far from the truth. Power has not passed to neutral technocrats; it remains in the hands of a capitalist upper class. Those changes in property ownership which have taken place have resulted not in the demise of the capitalist class but in its internal transformation. Personal ownership of a business enterprise or a landed estate is no longer a necessary condition for upper-class membership. Instead, membership is dependent upon the opportunities available to people for participating and benefiting in the use of capital. Large personal shareholdings are monopolized by a class whose members are no longer tied to the particular enterprises in which they hold shares. The members of the upper class participate and benefit in class-wide property.

In this chapter I shall give an overview of the formation of this upper class as a necessary prelude to an investigation of the patterns of ownership which constitute its economic anatomy. The social closure effected by this class – its ability to reproduce itself as an upper class – will be documented, and this will be related to its participation in political rule. Finally, I shall make some suggestions about an appropriate socialist strategy for dismantling the upper class.

The making of the British upper class

The British upper class of today is the outcome of a long process of historical development in which successive upper classes have fused, split, and allied themselves in a variety of ways. Capitalist development began early in England. From the twelfth century monetary payments and monetary measurements spread through the agrarian system of production and transformed its 'feudal' relations into proto-'capitalist' relations. The sale of agricultural surpluses at town and country markets tied the landlords who controlled the production into a system of commercial relations connecting the villages into a nexus of trading relations. The 'national' system of markets which emerged around the large urban centres was itself controlled by a large group of merchants stretching from small, local 'burghers' to the wealthy international financiers of London.

By the sixteenth century there were three overlapping upper classes — magnates, gentry, and bourgeoisie — and all were distinctly capitalist classes. The landed magnates, the major landowners, dominated the country nationally and locally, determining the framework within which gentry and bourgeoisie acted. The landed gentry consisted of smaller land-owners, generally with land in one part of the country only and often dependent upon the magnates who held land in the same area. They had grown considerably in importance as the prosperity of the magnates faltered in the agricultural crisis of the fifteenth century and as a consequence of the Tudor disposals of church lands. The gentry were actively involved in the running of their estates, and the relatively smaller size of their estates made them more dependent than the magnates on the rational and profitable use of their land. The merchant bourgeoisie was based in London, and its members were formed into syndicates and companies which monopolized the import and export trade and were crucial supports of government finance. Especially important to the bourgeoisie were its close links with the Low Countries and other financial centres of Europe, which made it an autonomous and assertive force. Although having a distinct class position, the merchants were also recruited from the younger sons of the gentry – and the more prosperous merchants bought landed estates of their own. The bourgeoisie and gentry together could be considered as in the vanguard of capitalist development.

The major feudal baronies evolved into massive estates owned by the magnates, rather than being held as tenants of the crown. A magnate estate consisted of blocks of land in various parts of the country, the whole being operated as a single unit of capitalist production. The estate was the basis of a leisured and luxurious life style; the support of power and privilege. As *rentiers*, living on rents earned from tenant farming, the landed magnates remained sharply divided from the gentry and bougeoisie in terms of wealth, power, and status. This relationship gradually changed. By the eighteenth century the spread of capitalist relations of production had forged magnates and gentry into a unified class of landed *rentiers*. As landowners enclosed more and more of the old open fields and common land, agricultural labourers lost the immediate, day-to-day possession of the means of production which they had retained from the feudal period. At the same time, the landowners rented out more and more of their land to tenant farmers. Although formed into magnate and gentry fractions, the *rentier* class had achieved an economic and social unity. Extension of the market for land and the 'agricultural revolution' of the eighteenth century led to a concentration of the ownership and control of land in the hands of the *rentiers*. In both financial and technical terms, agricultural production became more concentrated; and the enlarged estates remained subject to family strategies aimed at ensuring the continuity of the family estate and perpetuating the wealth and power of the landed family.

Separate from the landed class in the eighteenth century was a commercial class of financiers and merchants, centred on London and based too in such areas as Glasgow, Bristol, and Liverpool. The dominant element in this class was the 'monied interest' of financiers involved in the Bank of England and public finance, but the class was complex and diversified into specialist merchants, bankers, bullion traders, and so on. A major transformation in the class structure occurred in the nineteenth century, when the new manufacturing class began to rival the financiers and the *rentiers*.

Manufacturing accounted for a relatively small proportion of economic activity prior to the eighteenth century, but the Industrial Revolution created an increasingly powerful class of manufacturers based in the North and the Midlands. Based on family enterprise and family capital, the manufacturing firms grew in size during the nineteenth century and were associated with the development of new forms of control over the labour process in the new factories. The manufacturers increasingly came into confrontation with the landed class. A relative decline in the returns from agriculture led many landowners to diversify their wealth into mineral exploitation, urban development, railways, and overseas ventures, and late in the century some began to take directorships in the larger industrial enterprises. As the scale of industrial production increased, so the links between the City financiers and the manufacturers were strengthened: the capital requirements of the large enterprises were met by the formation of joint stock companies, and the City played an important role in determining the availability of this capital. 'City' and 'industry', however, tended to remain distinct at the national level. The three upper classes – landed, financial, and manufacturing – moved closer together, yet did not fuse into a single capitalist upper class.

The changing pattern of upper classes in British society is illustrated in figure 2.1. By the First World War the three upper classes had begun to fuse into a unified 'business class', and the fusion was completed in the inter-war period. The core of the class consisted of the active participants in the ownership and control of the major units of capital which make up the modern capitalist economy – whether these units were primarily land, money, or productive assets. Indeed a major trend was for the various forms of capital to lose their distinctiveness and to become entwined as units of finance capital. The nature of this process will be examined in the following section, but it is necessary first to document some aspects of the political participation of the upper classes.

Upper-class politics have frequently been discussed in terms of the concept of a 'ruling class', assuming that there is some direct, immediate, one-to-one relationship between economic dominance and political power. More particularly, the concept of a ruling class presents an image of monolithic class hegemony. The failure of this concept to grasp concrete historical patterns of class power has been associated with the popularity of so-called 'elite' analyses. The notion of 'elite' emerged as an ahistorical alternative to the more specific and determinate concepts of varying forms

Figure 2.1   Upper-class formation

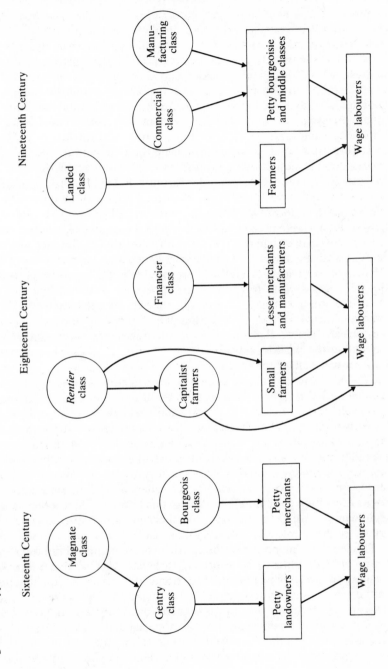

Sixteenth Century

Magnate class → Gentry class

Bourgeois class

Gentry class → Petty landowners

Bourgeois class → Petty merchants

Petty landowners → Wage labourers

Petty merchants → Wage labourers

Eighteenth Century

Rentier class → Capitalist farmers

Financier class

Rentier class → Small farmers

Capitalist farmers → Small farmers

Capitalist farmers → Wage labourers

Small farmers → Wage labourers

Financier class → Lesser merchants and manufacturers

Lesser merchants and manufacturers → Wage labourers

Nineteenth Century

Landed class

Commercial class

Manu-facturing class

Landed class → Farmers

Commercial class → Petty bourgeoisie and middle classes

Manu-facturing class → Petty bourgeoisie and middle classes

Farmers → Wage labourers

Petty bourgeoisie and middle classes → Wage labourers

of class domination. Much elite analysis remains empty and formal, and material collected by elite analysts has to be related to the dynamics of class relations prevailing in British society. Neither 'ruling class' nor 'elite' is satisfactory as a concept for understanding class power in Britain. Miliband has correctly argued that whether a state actually serves the interests of the dominant class depends crucially upon the creation of a 'partnership' between class and state, a partnership which involves the continuing lobbying of the state by organized interests and the upper-class monopolization of key political positions, as well as the constraints imposed on any state which operates in a capitalist society.[1] The creation and maintenance of such a partnership is a precarious and uncertain process, and it should not be assumed that all stages of British history – or the history of any other society for that matter – will be characterized by a unified and cohesive ruling class. Historical patterns of class domination are best understood as sequences in which specific power blocs are able to hold sway, each power bloc representing a specific alliance of class forces.[2]

The power bloc which dominated the British state in the eighteenth century was an alliance of landed magnates and leading financiers, an alliance of large-scale capitalist interests. The policies and interests which that bloc was able to force upon the state have to be understood in the context of the conflicting interests of the landed and commercial classes and their various fractions. A few hundred families formed this bloc, which was able to ensure that the state pursued an aggressive policy aimed at expanding the wealth and power of the ruling group itself. The leading families were allied by intermarriage, though this rarely extended across the divide between land and trade, and maintained the support of the other members of their classes and of the subordinate classes by their use of a vast web of patronage which extended throughout the whole society. Government offices, parliamentary seats, pensions, church livings, tutorships, and positions in domestic service were all dependent upon the power exercised by patrons: *who* you knew was more important than *what* you knew. A network of social contacts had to be mobilized if entry to important social positions was to be achieved, and therefore chains of dependence tied people to the existing social order. The whole system was legitimated through a hierarchy of social honours stretching from the 'mere' gentleman to the dukes, princes, and the monarchy itself.

This legitimating notion of the 'gentleman' remained important through the nineteenth century, the reformed public schools playing a key role in its inculcation and transmission. The patrician politics of the eighteenth century were accommodated to the political power of manufacturing industry by ensuring that the manufacturers were thoroughly socialized into the gentlemanly norms of the landed value system. The 'Establishment', a dominant status group drawn from all three dominant classes, monopolized political power. This monopolistic power bloc operated through the party opposition of Liberals and Conservatives. The party system which prevailed through the phase of entrepreneurial capitalism which spanned the nineteenth century was forged during the 1840s and 1850s. The first part of this period was one of Liberal dominance: although there was a continuous decline in Liberal electoral support, the Conservative vote was lower than that of the Liberals (or Whigs) in 12 out of 13 general elections.[3] Gradually, however, the Conservative Party became the unified voice of the Establishment, the party of Queen, Empire, and 'One Nation'. From its heartland in the South and in the English country seats, the Party's electoral machine built up support in the North West, the Midlands, and the metropolitan areas. By 1886 an electoral coalition sustained a power bloc drawn from all classes. Within this bloc the Establishment predominated, but its members were particularly drawn from the expanding 'middle class' of managers and clerks, from small businessmen and shopkeepers, and from skilled manual workers. A period of almost unchallenged Conservative government began.

In these ways the entry of the industrialists to the national political scene was contained within the shell of the old ideas of deference and *noblesse oblige*. The bonds of patronage were subtly transformed into a structure of sponsorship organized through the major public schools and Oxbridge colleges. Access to top positions depended not so much on who you knew as on attendance at the 'right' school or college. The Establishment remained at the heart of the state until well into the twentieth century. The 'old boy network' dominated government and parliament, the civil service, the church, the military, the law, and other top positions until the First World War, and it was the central feature of the British political process until the 1950s. The phase of Establishment power and influence ran in parallel with the phase of Conservative dominance in the party system. The power of the Establishment has been sustained by economic prosperity, and both the Establishment and the Conservative Party have declined as prosperity has become less certain. The Conservative share of the vote has crumbled since the 1930s, and has been especially rapid from the 1960s. The unbalanced development of the British economy since the 1870s – its dependence on overseas investment and the role of the City in international trade – is integrally linked with the position of the Establishment as the dominant power bloc in British society. This is the key to the claim that British economic decline is to be related to the archaic features of the British state.[4]

Economic anatomy of the upper class today

Just as many people have equated the upper class with a residual

'aristocracy' or 'peerage', so many commentators on the modern economy
have talked of abstractions such as 'capital'. The central argument of this
chapter is that workers and others never actually confront 'capital'; they
confront those who own or control capital and those who exercise
delegated authority on behalf of the owners and controllers. Our images of
these owners and controllers, however, rely heavily upon the picture of the
nineteenth century entrepreneurial capitalists, and many people experience a difficulty in describing contemporary class relations without
resorting to either inaccurate stereotypes or economic abstractions. It is
argued here that the contemporary upper class is a capitalist class and must
be understood in relation to the structure of British capitalism as it exists
today. A description of the forms taken by property ownership will provide
the basis for a picture of the actual groups which go to make up the upper
class.

The upper class is a business class, but it is not simply a class of *rentiers:*
the transformation of property ownership means that the class privileges of
the propertied depend upon their active participation in the use of that
property. The core of the class consists of those who run the major units of

Table 2.1 Twenty largest estates (1970–2 and 1980–2)

1970–72		1980–82	
Name	Estate (£)	Name	Estate (£)
Felix D. Fenston	12,670,566	Count Antoine Seilern	30,836,261
Chas L. Arnold	5,829,618	10th Earl Fitzwilliam	11,776,401
7th Earl of Radnor	4,552,599	Chas. A. R. Harpur-Crewe	8,127,801
Harold K. Salvesen	4,115,701	Dow. Countess of Sefton	7,607,168
Fredk. G. D. Colman	2,291,372	Sir Richard J. Boughey	5,956,143
Sir Thos. R. Merton	1,920,337	Joseph Sunlight	5,714,422
Gilbert C. Felce	1,909,399	Barbara Green	5,559,614
Paul Rosefield	1,907,768	Eileen C. M. Walton	5,510,651
Diana Gubbay	1,713,682	Sir Mark Tatton-Sykes	4,800,697
Elkan M. Jackson	1,660,432	Robert W. Houchin	4,136,118
Alan R. D. Pilkington	1,548,944	Erich Markus	4,120,438
Wm. W. Macfarlane	1,536,621	Viscount Rothermere	4,072,870
Countess of Seafield	1,477,068	Thomas C. Morss	4,046,343
4th Earl Sondes	1,440,330	Edward H. Goulburn	3,834,362
Jacob Green	1,337,363	Hon. Michael Astor	3,794,442
Sir Cecil Tollemache	1,309,644	Rowland Smith	3,681,326
Leslie H. Wilson	1,266,401	Denise E. G. Delaney	3,604,881
Richard J. Pinto	1,249,386	6th Baron Brownlow	3,524,587
Sir Allen Lane	1,216,474	Jeffery Coryton	3,441,573
Dermot H. B. McCalmont	1,216,401	Thomas Freer	3,163,974

Source: Daily Mail Yearbooks. The figures show the gross value of the estate, i.e. before tax.

capital which comprise the British economy. Around the core are propertied families who have retired from business or whose members are pursuing careers outside of business, though who remain dependent on the core for the survival of the wealth which their property represents. An intergenerational and intragenerational exchange of personnel between the core and its outer circles expresses the economic unity of the class as an inter-marrying social class of propertied families.

The extent of the wealth of the wealthy – perhaps the 100,000 people who make up 0.2 per cent of the population – has been documented in other places.[5] Although their share in national income and wealth may have declined somewhat since the 1930s, their share remains high. Strategies of tax minimization and income diversification have been major features of the ability of the upper class to perpetuate and enhance its inherited wealth. Studies have shown that the sources of wealth among the very rich have become increasingly diversified. Landowners diversified into commerce and industry during the nineteenth century, and those who made their fortunes in manufacturing have shown a persistent tendency to buy land. More important than this, however, is the fact that the wealth of a family increasingly comes not from one particular family enterprise, but from a portfolio of investments in a great number of large enterprises. Some of these trends can be illustrated from the selection of wealthy individuals listed in table 2.1. In each year a large number of people of great wealth die, and table 2.1 shows some of the largest fortunes for two recent periods. The increase in the average fortune which is apparent from the table is due to the increase in the rate of inflation over the course of the 1970s. While approximately 50 people every year left half a million pounds in 1970–2, there are now about 50 millionaires dying each year. The list for 1970–2, shows a number of large landowners and some names which are associated with the products of their businesses: Colman's mustard and Allen Lane books (Penguin) being the most obvious. The majority of the millionaires, however, are unknown to the general public, even when their wealth comes from large, well-known enterprises: Jackson made his fortune with the London Rubber Company, Green from drapery, Macfarlane from biscuits, and Salvesen from whaling and transport. Millionaire estates falling just outside the 'top 20' included those based in Lebus furniture, Decca records, and Tizer. The situation in 1980–2 was similar. Rothermere (the *Daily Mail*) and Astor are famous names, while Green (sister of impresario Larry Parnes), Walton (greengrocery), Edgar (H Samuel, jewellers), and Freer (electrics) are unfamiliar to most people. Millionaire estates falling just outside the 'top 20' for 1980–2 included Sir Cyril Kleinwort (merchant banking) and John Lennon (who left £2.5 million). Of course, tax minimization and tax avoidance means that many of these estates underestimate the real wealth of their families, and many wealthy families successfully redistribute their wealth among themselves before the head of the family dies. But the lists given in table 2.1 give an indication of the nature and type of 'millionaires' to be found in Britain today.

Table 2.2   The trend in share ownership (1963–1981)

| | % of market value held | | |
	1963	1975	1981
Personal	54	38	28
Insurance companies	10	16	21
Pension funds	6	17	27
Unit and investment trusts	11	14	10
Others[a]	19	15	14
Totals	100	100	100

Note:
a Includes banks, other companies, stockbrokers, charities, etc.
Sources: J. Scott, *Corporations, Classes, and Capitalism,* London, Hutchinson, 1979, p.78; *Financial Times,* 15 November 1983.

The economic basis for this diversification of family wealth is the 'depersonalization' of property which has occurred in the twentieth century. There has been no 'managerial revolution'. Share dispersal has enabled personal shareholders to exercise control over companies with ever-smaller percentage shareholdings, and an increasing proportion of shares has passed into the hands of financial companies. The concentration of economic activity in a relatively small number of enterprises was furthered around the turn of the century with the creation of a number of large national monopolies, but the process has been most rapid since the Second World War. Alongside this concentration of output, employment, and market shares there has been a rising concentration in share ownership. Insurance companies, unit trusts, and pension funds have become the major holders of company shares, and much of the remaining family wealth is managed by bank executor and trustee departments. Table 2.2 shows some recent trends. The proportion of shares held by individuals fell from more than a half to just over a quarter between 1963 and 1981. The proportion held by the three main types of intermediary increased from just over a quarter to over a half in the same period, the increase being greatest among pension funds. These financial intermediaries are, in turn, subject to the same pattern of ownership. The resulting network of intercorporate relations comprises a circle of control which ties most of the largest companies together. The business class consists of those who are beneficiaries of both their own property and the vast complex of 'institutional' property, and the core of the class consists of those who are actively involved in the management of this property. This core group has control over the flow of funds within the economy and is therefore able to determine the shape and rate of capital accumulation.

Table 2.3 Family ownership and control (1976)

Family name	Company controlled
1 Majority Ownership	
Baring	Baring Brothers
Cayzer*	British and Commonwealth Shipping
Fleming	Robert Fleming
Forte*	Trust House Forte
Gestetner	Gestetner Holdings
Hambro	Hambros
Laing	John Laing
McAlpine	Newarthill
Mitchell	Geo. Wimpey
Moores	Littlewoods
Rank*	Rank Organisation
Ronson	Heron Corporation
Rook	C. Czarnikow
Rothschild	N. M. Rothschild
Sainsbury	J. Sainsbury
Salmon, Gluckstein	J. Lyons
Stenhouse	Stenhouse Holdings
Vestey	Union International
Weston	Associated British Foods
Whitbread*	Whitbread
Wolfson	Great Universal Stores
2 Minority control	
Al Fayed	Costain Group
Anderson	Guthrie Corporation
Borthwick	Thomas Borthwick
Cohen	Tesco Stores
Guinness	Arthur Guinness
Kleinwort	Kleinwort Benson Lonsdale
Laing	United Biscuits
Lever*	Unilever
McAlpine	Marchwiel
Mackay	Inchcape
Pearson	S. Pearson
Rowntree*	Rowntree Mackintosh
Schroder	Schroders
Smith	W. H. Smith
Stein	Ladbroke
Sunley*	Blackwood Hodge

3   Limited and shared minority

Aisher	Marley
Broackes	Trafalgar House
Bunzl	Bunzl Pulp
Chinn	Lex Service Group
Pilkington	Pilkington Brothers
Richards	Woodhall Trust
Rowland	Lonrho
Samuel	Hill Samuel
Samuel	Land Securities Investment
Thorn	Thorn Electrical Industries
Warburg	Mercury Securities

Source: Company Records. Companies in which foundations unconnected with particular families are in control have been excluded. An asterisk marks those companies in which families control with or through a foundation or similar body. In some of these cases, family control is exercised jointly with unnamed trustees.

The privileges and wealth of the whole of the upper class depend on the activities of its core members who run the large business enterprises. This core consists of three interrelated groups: entrepreneurial capitalists, internal capitalists, and finance capitalists. Entrepreneurial capitalists are based around a continuing substantial stake in their own companies. Family enterprises which survive from the past and newer enterprises built up by tycoons ensure a continual flow of entrepreneurial capitalists into the core of the class, despite a continual loss of family firms in takeovers. Such capitalists are particularly prominent in retailing, property, construction, and merchant banking, and are to be found in large numbers in medium-sized companies. The distinguishing characteristic of this group is that, like the entrepreneur of the nineteenth century, its members are substantially dependent on the success or failure of a particular enterprise.

Tables 2.3 and 2.4 give an indication of the major entrepreneurial capitalists in Britain today. In table 2.3 are shown the names of families and individuals who held controlling positions in Britain's 250 largest companies in 1976. A total of 48 companies were controlled in this way. The largest category, 21 companies, consisted of those in which a particular family, or close group of intermarried families, owned a majority of the shares. Seven of these companies operated in retail distribution, hotels, leisure, and related areas, three others were food or drink producers, two were in construction, and four were in finance. Those subject to minority control – where the family was the largest shareholder and could not easily be challenged by outsiders – showed a similar concentration in certain economic sectors: five in food or drink, three in retail distribution and leisure, three in construction, and two in finance. The final category of limited and shared minority control refers to situations where a family is the largest shareholder and is represented on the board but can be outvoted by other shareholders or must share its controlling position.[6] Companies in this category were rather more diverse, but four of them were to be found in construction and related industries. Clearly, entrepreneurial capitalists are concentrated in certain industrial sectors.

Table 2.4   Family shareholders in large companies (1976)

Family name	Company name
Aston	S. and W. Berisford
Baxter	Brooke Bond Liebig
Berni	Grand Metropolitan
Bird	Legal and General Assurance
Bowring	C. T. Bowring
Brooke	Brooke Bond Leibig
Cadbury	Cadbury Schweppes
Caine	Guinness Peat
Chambers	Brooke Bond Liebig
Clark	Plessey
Clore	Sears Holdings
Colman	Reckitt and Colman
Danny	Eagle Star Insurance
Eveson	C. T. Bowring
Fitch	Fitch Lovell
Forrester	Babcock and Wilcox
Gribbin	Northern Foods
Hanson	Hanson Trust
Harper	Harrisons and Crossfield
Hatch	Glaxo
Heathcoat Amory	Coats Patons
Holloway	Powell Duffryn
Holt	Ocean Transport and Trading
Horsley	Northern Foods
Joseph	Grand Metropolitan
Katz	Unigate
King	Babcock and Wilcox
Kissin	Guinness Peat
Lambourne	Fitch Lovell
Lister	Associated Dairies
Lyons	UDS Group
Mackenzie	London and Northern Group
Margulies	S. and W. Berisford
Marks	Marks and Spencer
Mountain	Eagle Star Insurance
Peake	Harrisons and Crossfield
Percival	S. and W. Berisford
Pybus	AAH

Rank	Rank Hovis McDougall
Reckitt	Reckitt and Colman
Richmond	Northern Foods
Robinson	Dickinson Robinson
Sainer	Sears Holdings
Simon	Simon Engineering
Stockdale	Associated Dairies
Tyler	AAH
Vestey	Gerrard and National Discount
Ward	Thomas W. Ward
Watts	British Electric Traction
Weinstock	General Electric
Wills	Imperial Group
Younger	Scottish and Newcastle Breweries
Ziegler	Associated Dairies

Source: Company records. Some family names refer to holdings of wide extended families covering several surnames.

The entrepreneurial capitalists are also to be found as large shareholders in companies where most of the shares are held by financial intermediaries. It has already been argued that many of the largest companies have no single dominant shareholder, but are tied into a circle of interweaving shareholdings. In a significant number of these companies families or individuals appear among the controlling shareholders. An analysis of the 20 largest shareholders in each of the top 250 companies which were not subject to majority or minority control showed that 35 companies had families as influential shareholders. The names of these families are given in table 2.4.

It can be seen that 53 families were discovered. Over a half of these were true entrepreneurial capitalists, being represented on the boards of the companies in which they were large shareholders, and a number of others had retired from positions within the companies. Many of the families were founders of the companies concerned or had run businesses taken over by these companies, as is apparent from their names: Baxter's butchers, Berni steak houses, Cadbury's chocolate, Colman's mustard, Marks and Spencer stores, Reckitt's starch, Wills tobacoo, Younger's beer, and so on. It is clear, therefore, that entrepreneurial capitalists are an influential group in the upper class of today, having control or significant influence in 83 of the top 250 companies.

Internal capitalists are bureaucratic executives who owe their privileges to their position within the administrative hierarchy of a particular enterprise rather than to any shares which they may own in that company. As the class as a whole diversifies its wealth, the role of internal capitalist becomes the characteristic business career open to members of the upper class – though it is also a channel of social mobility into the upper class from below. This group has been at the centre of the idea of the 'managerial revolution', and so it is important to emphasize that a major gulf exists between those executives who participate at the highest levels of decision-making, and those whose activities are confined to day-to-day operational matters. There is no significant devolution of power to a managerial 'technostructure'.

Table 2.5   *The top 27 finance capitalists (1976)*

Name	No of directorships in top 250
Sir David H. Barran	5
John A. F. Binny	4
Sir George S. Bishop	4
Viscount Caldecote	4
E. Philip Chappell	4
Sir Robert A. Clark	5
Earl of Cromer (Baring family)	4
Ian J. Fraser	5
Sir Reay Geddes	4
Baron Greenhill	6
Barrie Heath	4
John F. C. Hull	4
Earl of Inchcape (Mackay family)	5
Sir Peter A. Matthews	4
Daniel Meinertzhagen	4
Baron Netherthorpe (Turner family)	5
Sir David L. Nicolson	5
Sir Anthony Part	4
Sir John Partridge	5
Lord Pritchard	4
Baron Remnant	4
Baron Robens	5
Sir Eric Roll	4
Sir Francis E. P. Sandilands	6
Philip Shelbourne	5
Harry Smith	4
Sir Gerald B. Thorley	4
Total	121

Source: Directory of Directors, Stock Exchange Yearbook, Company records.

The third group within the core of the upper class, the finance capitalists, is also the smallest group. It consists of those who are recruited from among the internal and entrepreneurial capitalists to the boards of directors of enterprises other than those in which they began their careers. Many of them may be recruited from politics, the civil service, and other areas outside the world of business. Such people, therefore, hold directorships in two or more enterprises in various sectors of the economy and they play a key role in co-ordinating the operations of the business system as a whole. They are the co-ordinating controllers of monopoly capital. Table 2.5 lists the 27 finance capitalists who sat on four or more boards among the top 250 companies of 1976. All but seven of these men had some kind of title – hereditary peerages, life peerages, and knighthoods. They can be considered as the 'elder statesmen' of the business system. Through their directorships the finance capitalists link many of the large companies.

These 'interlocking directorships' tie together the diverse capitalist interests and provide a basis for some degree of co-ordination in their activities. This is illustrated in figure 2.2, which shows the links created by the men with the largest number of directorships in table 2.5. The 11 people with five or six directorships held a total of 57 directorships in the top 250, and many others in their subsidiaries and in smaller companies. The directorships of nine of the 11 people could be linked together into a single chain of connections.[7] Nine people thus carried a network of 39 large companies. This is, of course, only illustrative. The network in figure 2.2 is merely an arbitrary segment of a larger network generated by the directorships of all the finance capitalists. Nevertheless, the diagram illustrates the degree and density of connection typical of large companies and it shows the opportunities that finance capitalists have for utilizing network linkages. An analysis of the larger network itself has shown it to have been organized around the four big banks, the Bank of England, Hill Samuel merchant bank, ICI, and Commercial Union Assurance – and the 11 people discussed above sat on all but one of these companies. The finance capitalists have sometimes been regarded as a financial oligarchy of fat men with fat cigars, and have been identified with the upper class as a whole. This is far from the truth. Despite the importance of the few hundred people involved, they are only one element in the core of the class. The increase in economic concentration and the creation of extensive bonds of influence and control between enterprises has been the material basis for the emergence of this narrower group of finance capitalists. The increased interdependence of companies created the need for a group which could express and articulate that interdependence.

At this point it is necessary to investigate the relationship between the City and industry. Although there is considerable evidence that the commercial practices of the enterprises based in the City of London are sharply distinguishable from the practices followed by other enterprises and that the voice of the City has been particularly influential in government policy-

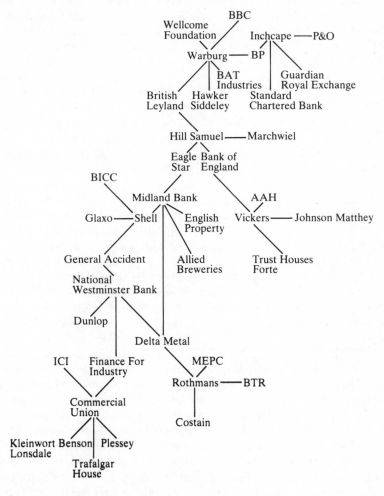

Figure 2.2   Top company links (1976)

making, this does not mean that the basic division in the economy is that between City and industry. The division which did exist prior to the First World War has gradually been removed. In terms of both ownership and control, banks, traders and producers have come closer together over the last 60 years. The major enterprises have increasingly diversified their activities to cover a wide spread of business interests, and today are units of 'finance capital' in which manufacturing, banking, and commerce are combined in varying mixtures. The entrepreneurial, internal, and finance capitalists of the class core are all tending to be involved in such units of finance capital, though large landowners remain somewhat apart. The upper class today is more unified in economic terms than was the case earlier this century.

The reproduction of the upper class

It has been emphasized that the upper class is a class of intermarrying families encompassing a core of active business leaders and an outer circle of people active outside the business world in such areas as the law, the army, the universities, politics, and so on. The unity and cohesion of the class and its ability to reproduce itself and its privileges over the generations depends upon the strategies of closure and integration which are pursued by its members. It is through these strategies that the class avoids being simply a collection of holders of 'elite' occupational positions and becomes a collective entity capable of sustaining organized action in the pursuit of class interests. The study of the upper class, like the study of any social class, cannot simply consist of the pigeon-holing method of attempting to allocate this or that person to the upper class. Classes are dynamic, historical entities and must be studied in all their complexity through the strategies of reproduction which they follow in 'making' themselves.

The central mechanism of upper-class reproduction has always been the direct inheritance of capital, but this is no longer necessary nor always sufficient for upper-class membership. The growth of shareholding by financial intermediaries reduces the chances for movement into particular family firms, and promotion through the executive hierarchy opens up new possibilities for mobility. Active business leaders must increasingly draw upon resources other than personal wealth. While inheritance continues to be important for the benefits which it gives, its role in corporate ownership and control has altered. Participation in control involves the conversion of inherited economic assets into social and cultural assets: contacts and credentials. Such social and cultural assets have always been important alongside the ownership of capital, but the economic trends described above have enhanced their role. Formal training and the possession of educational credentials are important supplements to the more informal assets of the old boy network and the 'right' school. The public school and Oxbridge route therefore survives as a central feature of the reproduction of the upper class, and the purchasing of private education is a crucial means for the conversion of inherited wealth into social and cultural assets.

The mechanisms of class reproduction and the privileges of the upper class are masked and legitimated by two contradictory phenomena: the social imagery of an extensive, meritocratic middle class and the 'gentlemanly' values embodied in the traditional social hierarchy and public school education. The desire to avoid the language of privilege and class division leads many members of the upper class to project an image of themselves as members of a large middle class. This middle class is defined as consisting of those with school and university qualifications who have been able to enter and climb the bureaucratic and professional hierarchies. The incomes received by members of this middle class are legitimated by their status as meritocrats. But it is important to distinguish between those whose class situation depends solely on the service role in bureaucratic and professional hierarchies, and those whose class situation is rooted in the ownership and control of capital.[8] The latter, the upper class, must be clearly distinguished from the true middle class. The disappearance of many features of the extravagant life style followed by earlier upper classes – leisure and conspicuous consumption – made this class distinction less obvious and gave some semblance of truth to the claim that 'we are all middle class now'. The highest levels of the upper class, however, retain a social and cultural distinctiveness which sets them apart from the 'mere' middle class and serves to legitimate the privileges of the whole upper class. The Establishment retains its distinctiveness as a status group on the basis of the remnants of the old 'gentleman' ideal.

Central to this remains the system of titles and honours, within which the superior titles legitimate the great privileges of Establishment members and the inferior honours tie members of the middle class to the established social order. In the public services the many honours and lower titles are used as mechanisms of social control, as the award of honours is linked to career progression. But in business, too, the receipt of knighthoods and peerages has become more routinized and predictable. In particular, those who progress to become finance capitalists are likely to receive, or already to have received, such honours. Those who receive life peerages are involved in a process that goes beyond legitimation, as this gives them the right to a seat in parliament and, therefore, to participation at the national level of politics. Life peerages tend to be awarded to those holders of knighthoods who have been publicly active beyond the narrow confines of their career and have proved themselves to be politically useful and dependable. As in the past, the honours system is deliberately used for political purposes and as a means of social control and legitimation.

The political representation of upper-class interests

For much of the twentieth century the Establishment has provided a means of political representation for upper-class interests. The public schools and Oxbridge have been the main recruitment mechanisms for those positions in politics, the civil service, the military, business, and other areas which are monopolized by members of the Establishment. The unity and cohesiveness of the upper class are ensured by the high level of similarity in the education and social background of its members. Although there are church families, army families, political families, and so on, these families are linked over the generations and within each generation by their similar background, by an interchange of personnel, and by their common dependence upon the success of the corporate system. Tables 2.6 and 2.7 show the continuing significance of the public schools and Oxbridge in a number of top occupational positions.

Table 2.6   Public school background (1939–70)

| | % from public schools | | | |
	1939	1950	1960	1970
Top civil servants	85	59	65	62
Ambassadors	74	73	83	83
Top judiciary	80	85	83	80
Top naval officers	19	15	21	38
Top army officers	64	71	83	86
Top RAF officers	67	59	58	63
Bishops	71	75	69	67

Source: D. Boyd, *Elites and Their Education*, London, NFER, 1973, ch. 5.

Table 2.6 shows that the proportion of public school entrances to each of a number of top occupational positions has been uniformly high over a period of 30 years. Only in the case of the senior naval officers did the proportion fall below a half, and a high proportion of the later cohorts were educated at Dartmouth, the navy's own public school. The army shows an increase in the significance of the public schools, the proportion

Table 2.7   Oxford and Cambridge background (1939–70)

| | % from Oxbridge colleges | | | |
	1939	1950	1960	1970
Top civil servants	77	56	70	69
Ambassadors	49	66	84	80
Top judiciary	78	74	75	85
Top army officers	3	9	12	24
Top RAF officers	18	14	19	18
Bishops	90	85	77	78

Source: D. Boyd, *Elites and their Education*, London, NFER, 1973, ch. 5.

rising steadily from 64 per cent to 86 per cent, while the civil service shows an overall but irregular fall. The judiciary, ambassadors, air force officers, and bishops all showed no sign of any significant decline in the salience of public school education. It can be seen from table 2.7 that there was a high degree of stability in the level of recruitment from Oxford and Cambridge for most of the occupations, though bishops showed a slight opening of recruitment and ambassadors showed a marked move towards greater closure. The Oxbridge background of military officers was lower than for other groups, as each service had its specialist officer colleges.

Table 2.8   Occupational background of Conservative MPs

			% from each occupational group		
	1945	*1955*	*1966*	*1974*	*1979*
Business	47	46	48	45	41
Law	19	21	24	20	24
Military	14	11	4	1	6
Civil service	5	4	6	3	4
Other	15	18	18	30	25

Sources: Figures for 1945–74 from J. Scott, *The Upper Classes*, London, Macmillan, 1982, p.175. Figures for 1979 from J. Ross, *Thatcher and Friends*, London, Pluto Press, 1983, p.20. Notes: The figures for business include land ownership and farming, and the 1979 figure for law includes accountancy. The 1979 data relate to MPs elected at the October election.

In considering patterns of upper-class interest representation it is clearly important to pay special attention to the ways in which these interests are politically organized in the Conservative Party. The parliamentary party, as shown in table 2.8, is drawn heavily from business, the business-related professions, and the military, all being occupations permeated by the public school and Oxbridge products. Outside parliament Conservative activists follow the same occupations, with the small business sector being relatively more important. The core of support has been encased within a shell of landed wealth and traditional values. Before the First World War this landed section predominated within the Party, a predominance reflected in the number of members of the House of Lords who held government office. Since that time the landed interest has remained an important influence in the Party and the government. Public school representation among Conservative MPs has run at a consistent level of between three-quarters and four-fifths for the whole of the period from 1906 to 1979. Over a half of the post-war MPs went to Oxford or Cambridge. Those from the public schools and Oxbridge tend to sit for the safest seats, 'outsiders' being drawn in to parliament mainly when the Party wins enough marginal seats to form a government. At the cabinet level itself, the public school proportion has been between four-fifths and nine-tenths. Even the original Thatcher cabinet of 1983 had four-fifths of its members drawn from the public schools, with one-third from Eton and Winchester alone. These figures reflect the fact that the 'old boys', with the safest seats, tend to have had the longest political careers.

These facts about the social composition of the Conservative Party must be placed in the context of the weakening of the Establishment and the crumbling of the Conservative vote, as all these processes have had an impact on policy-making within the Party. Electoral decline meant that the task of building a secure electoral coalition, and therefore of creating a firm 'partnership' of state and class, became more and more difficult for the leadership. The economic conditions of the 1950s facilitated the task of the Conservative leadership in securing a parliamentary majority and drawing on the widely-based consensus around the welfare state project initiated by the post-war Labour government. 'Keynesian' economic policies of demand management rested upon a continued acceptance of traditional norms and values. The goals of economic policy were formulated and clarified within the Establishment, and specific policy proposals were drawn up and implemented by the public school and Oxbridge graduates who filled all the key positions in the Treasury and the Bank of England.[9] This policy embodied an outlook on economic policy which reflected the international constraints on British capitalism, and not the dominance of a distinct City fraction of capital. This viewpoint was an important element in post-war Keynesianism, determining its appearance as a series of stop-go phases as economic expansion was repeatedly brought to a halt in order to avoid balance of payments problems.

Keynesianism, therefore, depended on the survival of traditional authority, of popular attitudes of deference and respect, and on a willingness to accept, or at least tolerate, the authority of political and economic decision-makers. As the supports of this authority weakened, so the task of political and economic management came to involve more calculative strategies aimed at meeting the increased economistic demands of organized labour. This attempt to buy-off dissent generated higher levels of inflation, and the consequent fiscal problems of the state led to responses such as incomes policies and demands for 'restraint'. Macmillan, who had overseen much of the heyday of British Keynesianism, was able to use the relative economic success of the period to perform the difficult task of maintaining parliamentary support for Conservative government. His resignation opened up the whole issue of the nature of the party and of the the kind of electoral support which it should try to build. The choice of the leader, from Home to Heath to Thatcher, reflected the party's uncertainties and equivocations over policy: patrician 'one nation' Toryism, radical technocratic modernization, or *petit bourgeois* self-help and self-interest. The choice of Thatcher promised a new climate of economic competition and ruthless restructuring, but her leadership coincided with a world recession that proved more important in determining the trends of that period than has formal government policy. Indeed, the shifts in Conservative Party policy throughout the whole post-war period reflected the undermining of Keynesianism and its social supports.

An upper class may succeed in forming a power bloc in which it holds a hegemonic position, but this dominance rests on concessions to other strata and classes and, therefore, on a balance of conflicting class interests. The power bloc built up in British society, headed by the Establishment and having its political expression in the Conservative Party, represented just such a compromise of class interests. Its difficulties in the post-war period show that any power bloc must operate within the constraints imposed by the way in which capitalist relations of production are structured in a particular national economy. A dominant class is not an all-powerful class, but must accommodate to the interests of other classes and to the constraints imposed by the social structure in which it operates. For this reason the dominance and success of any power bloc is inherently unstable.

The international decline of Britain in economic and political terms, the collapse of traditional authority, and the growing power and assertiveness of trade unions can be seen as the immediate causes of the undermining of the conditions which buttressed the already declining power of the Establishment.[10] But the underlying causes are to be found in economic changes dating from the 1930s and earlier: rising concentration, the unification of manufacturing, commerce, and banking, the growth of institutional shareholdings, and rising state intervention resulted in a restructuring of the political economy in a direction which undermined the personal and informal mechanisms through which the Establishment operated. The Conservative electoral coalition crumbled, and economic policy from the late 1950s and early 1960s, in both Labour and Conservative governments, became more supportive and directive towards big business as deliberate strategies of rationalization, modernization, and planning were pursued. The NEDC, prices and incomes controls, attempts at legal regulation of industrial relations, the IRC, NEB, Social Contract, industrial rescues, planning agreements, and proposals for the direction of investment funds were all mechanisms of interest representation and economic intervention which ran counter to all the tenets of Keynesian policy. Such mechanisms, however, have remained weak by comparison with established practices, and so the decline of the Establishment has not been matched by the rise of a coherent alternative means of representing upper-class interests. Recent governments have failed to create the kind of partnership between state and capital which is necessary for the effective dominance of upper-class interests. Neither corporatist nor social market doctrines have succeeded in achieving the kind of hegemony achieved by Keynesianism and the associated welfare state project. Instead, *ad hoc* mechanisms have been adopted, extended, and dropped, without any coherent system emerging.

The power of any bloc is determined by a web of personal connections and formal structures, within the constraints set by a capitalist national economy. As the Establishment and its power bloc have declined, so the personal connections on which it depended have been weakened. The interests of the core members of the upper class are no longer represented in the state simply because of the existence of a common social background (of kinship, education, and clubs) among economic and political decision-makers. More formal mechanisms of interest representation have increasingly had to be adopted. The main formal mechanisms through which business interests are represented in government and party are the system of party finances and the business lobby. Important mediators in both mechanisms are such organizations as the Economic League, British United Industrialists (BUI), and Aims. The Economic League was formed just after the First World War by the former head of Naval Intelligence and rapidly became a prominent force in propaganda for 'free enterprise'. A particularly important aspect of its activities was, and continues to be, the operating of a blacklisting service, whereby employers can obtain information on the Communist and other 'subversive' activities of potential employees. The League has always had close connections with the intelligence and security services, and has been involved in a two-way exchange of information with them. While fundraising for the Conservative Party is one aspect of Economic League operations, BUI is almost solely concerned with raising Party funds. Formed after the Second World War, BUI publishes some propaganda sheets but concerns itself mainly with the transfer of the funds which it collects to the Conservative Party and the Economic League. Aims, formerly called Aims of Industry, was formed specifically to counter the post-war Labour government's nationalization policies. Its major campaign was the Mr Cube campaign directed against the nationalization of the Tate and Lyle sugar company. Its recent activities have been general free enterprise propaganda, and it has been associated with many anti-union activities.

These and similar bodies, such as the Confederation of British Industry (CBI) are headed by finance capitalists and other prominent businessmen, and while they attempt to lobby whichever government is in power, they exercise a continuous influence over Conservative Party policy-making. One of the main channels of such influence is the provision of party funds. Corporate financing of the party began in the 1920s and 1930s. Before this party funds had come mainly from individual donations, and this change was a reflection of the transformation of property ownership from the entrepreneurial system to impersonal, institutional ownership. Over a quarter of the top 200 companies today give directly to the party, and many others give to BUI, the Economic League, and Aims. The main base of party financial support is the large firms in banking, insurance, food, drink, and construction, these sectors accounting for almost half of all corporate donations. Donations to the Economic League and BUI are strongly structural in character: support comes from the *largest* companies and from those which are well *connected* to other companies. Donations to the party itself are far less structural: they come from a variety of companies, fluctuate from year to year, and depend on performance in government and opposition. This makes the party heavily dependent upon the role played by political 'brokers' in mobilizing party funds. The merchant banks are especially important in this. As well as being important donors themselves, they mobilize funds from the companies with which they are associated. Directors of these same merchant banks are frequently active within the party and the various organizations of the business lobby.

The abolition of the upper class

As has been shown in the earlier parts of this chapter, the existence of an upper class is not simply a matter of accent, dress, or life style. Members of the upper class are the beneficiaries of a highly unequal society rooted in property ownership, they ensure the perpetuation of their privileges through strategies of social closure rooted in the educational system, and the whole inegalitarian system is legitimated through the persistence of traditional norms and values. The question of the abolition of the upper class, therefore, must come to grips with all these conditions of existence.

A strategy of abolition must initially direct itself to the removal of the normative patterns which legitimate the system. Destruction of the archaic cultural shell within which upper-class privilege is encased will reveal the structure of privilege itself for what it is: the grotesque product of an inegalitarian society. The traditional norms and values, however, are not susceptible to legislative removal. No single act of parliament can effectively destroy the cultural accretions of the past. The system of honours and titles must, of course, be abolished, but the large number of titled persons already in existence may continue to use those titles – as in France, Italy, and other countries which have abolished such honours – and the very scarcity of the remaining titles may actually enhance their social exclusiveness. It is, therefore, necessary to attack the social and cultural exclusiveness of the class more directly. The heart of this exclusiveness is the private educational system, and this is where a successful strategy should be focused. Educational reforms would have to be associated with radical reforms of the recruitment practices of the major institutions monopolized by the Establishment: the civil service, the military, the law, and, above all, the business world itself.

The creation of a meritocracy, however, is not the end of a socialist strategy, it is only one aspect of a strategy aimed at the abolition of the upper class. Indeed, the reforms outlined above could be successful only if they were themselves part of a wider strategy. One major part of such a strategy must be reforms aimed at a restructuring of the state and the exercise of political power. A successful democratization of the state would further restrict the opportunities available for the disproportionate political representation of members of the upper class.

Within a national and local state system which is undergoing a process of democratization, members of the upper class would still have superior chances of access and influence to those of the mass of the population because their continuing economic power could still be translated into political power. It is here, therefore, that a socialist strategy comes to the heart of the whole matter of abolition: the economic power of the upper class must be directly attacked. The economy must itself be socialized and democratized. This would involve reforms in share ownership, pension funds, and an extension of the co-operative principle, and the goal of the policy should be to encourage opportunities for maximizing popular participation in the enterprises which make up the heartland of the British economy. An important element in furthering the socialization of the economy would be state ownership itself, not simply outright nationalization but also substantial minority and majority holdings in key enterprises. In this way, the state could exercise a major influence in all markets, alongside those enterprises in which worker pension funds, worker co-operatives, and other forms of ownership prevail.

An additional set of reforms must be concerned with direct controls over the individual benefits gained from participation in the corporate system. Limitations on inheritance and maximum salaries must be established through effective taxation. This issue has to be seen as central to the abolition of the upper class. The myth that socialists aim at a levelling out of all social differences should hardly need refutation, but socialists must concern themselves with such issues as the extent of inequality in income and wealth which is compatible with the maintenance of a socialist society.

The abolition of the upper class is not a task which can be achieved by a series of discrete reforms. The upper class is an integral part of a capitalist society, and its abolition is intimately linked with those reforms which are aimed at the abolition of capitalism itself. These political issues have to go beyond mere slogans to confront the detailed questions of the particular measures necessary to move British society in a socialist direction: questions which concern not only utopian blueprints for the future, but also concrete proposals for countering the inevitable responses of the upper class itself.

3

The Class Structure

JOHN URRY

In this examination of the class structure of modern Britain I shall consider the following questions:

● What is the nature of social class: just what is meant by the idea of class, is it still a useful notion, to what levels of society does it apply?
● What is meant by talking of the class *structure*: what is structured by what and what are the consequences of the structure?
● What are the patterns of social inequality in contemporary Britain: how are income, property, educational opportunities and other resources distributed between people? Are there systematic divisions along the lines of class, occupation, gender, race, age or religion?
● Do these inequalities persist and get handed on from one generation to another: what are the possibilities of individuals 'escaping' from their social background and experiencing social mobility either upwards or downwards?
● If there is mobility between classes does this mean that such classes are no longer of importance?
● What are the main changes occurring within the patterns of social inequality in Britain: are divisions based on class becoming more or less significant than other social divisions within society?

Broadly speaking, Britain is still a class society, and in particular the divisions generated within capitalist production are of central importance in its overall structure. However, it is not possible to demonstrate that all aspects of the anatomy of Britain are the direct and simple product of its capitalist structure. For even if we concentrate, as in the main I will, upon class differences which are economically generated there are considerable problems as to which are the key aspects that need investigation. The

Marxist analysis of class concentrates upon the divisions between capital (and capitalists) and labour (and wage-labourers) and on the fundamental relations of exploitation between them. The central division here is between those who own and control capital, and those who do not and have therefore nothing to sell but their labour power. This means that if we consider all those within a given occupation, such as 'plumber', this will contain members of different classes, namely wage-labourers, the petty bourgeoisie (the self-employed) *and* capitalist employers. This Marxist distinction between capital and wage-labour is one pertaining to the underlying social relations of capitalist production and it then expresses itself within a multiple diversity of occupations, incomes and status groups. These in turn give rise to various attempts to resist capital and result in new divisions within labour, such as that between craftworkers, the 'labour aristocracy', and the less skilled; and between male workers and female workers who are 'crowded' into less skilled occupations through the exclusionary practices of certain male-dominated trade unions.[1] Moreover, there are important forms of social inequality, particularly those of patriarchy and racism, which are not simply identical with class relations. So although there are profoundly significant and enduring forms of social inequality in Britain, these cannot be simply reduced to the class relations between capital and wage-labour. In this chapter I shall consider these various forms of social inequality, beginning with their effects upon the distribution of income and wealth.

But before considering that in detail, let me deal first with one obvious difficulty in discussing the class structure of modern Britain. In much popular discussion Britain is said to be a peculiarly class-ridden society, because of the importance apparently attached to distinctions based upon accent, dress, manners, schooling, and so forth. It is maintained that these distinctions of rank are of especial importance and that they transcend obvious divisions of economic interest. Indeed, it is said that there is a strong cultural bias in British society which de-emphasizes the simple making of money, profit maximization and indeed, in some versions, work itself. It is also, however, part of conventional wisdom that in this sense, class has declined in significance in recent years. Britain, it is *now* said, is a much less class-ridden society since these sorts of distinctions no longer function to separate off different groups. The growth of the media and mass culture, the expanded entry into higher education, the declining significance of private, family ownership of land and the heightened value placed on work, profit maximisation and monetary success, have all weakened the power of these conventional class distinctions.

What in a socialist analysis of class should be made of these arguments? First, there is no doubt whatsoever that this view of class is strongly held and that many people do genuinely associate class with these kinds of 'status' distinction. Furthermore, there is very little doubt that there is something distinctive about class relations in Britain, that they have been peculiarly mediated by these distinctions of status, by conceptions of snobbery, and by a set of exclusionary social practices revolving around public schools, Oxbridge, London clubs, the London season, country houses, the ownership and pleasurable use of land, the Royal Family, and so on.[2] Indeed there is much to be said for the view that capitalism was established in Britain in a strangely compromised form. So although there is no doubt whatsoever about the extraordinary changes brought about by the widespread development of industrial capitalism in Britain (by factories, new massive cities, steam power and so on), the effects of all of these on political and cultural life were rather less marked. Indeed amongst the industrial capitalists of Britain there has been a process of what Martin Wiener calls 'the gentrification of the industrialists'.[3] He maintains that 'leaders of industry and commerce in England over the past century have accommodated themselves to an elite culture blended of pre-industrial aristocratic and religious values that inhibited their quest for expansion, productivity and profit'.[4]

One response to this thesis on the Left is to reassert that Britain remains a fundamentally capitalist society in which the basic relationship between the capitalist class and the working classes is the central class relationship without any particular peculiarities.[5] However, this 'fundamentalist' position cannot itself be accepted without qualification. In the following I shall presume that the class structure in Britain has in fact been shaped in such a way that these status distinctions (as sociologists generally call them) have been of considerable importance; and that a crucial feature of twentieth century British politics has involved the fight against class *in this sense*, against what used to be called the Establishment.[6] In recent years there has been some diminution in the importance of such an Establishment and of the related social practices of snobbery, rank and status evaluation (partly because of Labour Party politics). This does not of course mean that class in a more straightforward 'economic' sense is not of tremendous significance in Britain as we shall see. But it does mean that such class relationships may not generate quite the same kind and intensity of political opposition and conflict as fundamentalists would expect.

Income and wealth in Britain

There are some difficulties in analysing this distinction, not least because of the problems entailed in measuring wealth held in the form of land, houses, shares, factories and durable possessions. It is almost impossible to conduct a survey of such wealth, and so in consequence the best estimates of its distribution are based on the values of the estates declared for death duty. And even these contain considerable inaccuracies as families try to minimize their declarations and hence their liability for paying such duties. There is also much debate as to what counts as wealth, for example, whether it should be taken to include occupational pension rights or a house bought on a mortgage which many employees now 'own' and which make the distribution of wealth less uneven. A further difficulty is raised by the unit under consideration. Should we consider the individual or the family as the unit of investigation? The former would seem right in relation to the study of income distribution since otherwise we would be adopting sexist assumptions about the organization of families and of the role of the family breadwinner. However, in relationship to the distribution of wealth we have already seen above that the families play an absolutely central role, especially through inheritance and the provisions of more diffuse educational, social and cultural attributes in the reproduction of the British ruling class.[7] And indeed 'family' here does not mean the 'modern' nuclear family but the much wider 'extended' families which through the mechanism described by Scott have been able to sustain their extraordinary concentrations of wealth. Table 3.1 presents a list of the wealthiest families in Britain.

Table 3.1   Britain's wealthiest families[8]

Family	No. of half-millionaires in last 150 years	Origins of family fortune
Rothschild	21	finance
Wills	21	tobacco
Coats	16	textiles
Colman	10	food
Palmer	10	food
Morrison	9	commerce
Ralli	9	commerce
Gosling	7	banking
Baird	6	iron
Courtauld	6	textiles
Garton	6	sugar
Guinness	6	brewing
Joicey	6	coal
Pilkington	6	glass
Ratcliff	6	brewing
Reckitt	6	starch
Tate	6	sugar
Watney	6	brewing
Wilson	6	shipping
Sebag-Montefiore	6	finance
Dukes of Northumberland	6	coal/land

There is however considerable controversy about the role that inheritance plays in accounting for the distribution of wealth in Britain. Indeed there has been a marked tendency for inherited wealth to be thoroughly criticized and the object of political change, while self-made wealth is viewed as less reprehensible especially if it is not passed on through inheritance. The evidence suggests that although there was some increase in the numbers of self-made millionaires during the 1950s and 1960s, it is still true that 'inheritance is the major determinant of wealth inequality'.[9] Harcourt and Hitchens suggest that inheritance accounts for between 60 and 80 per cent of the fortunes of very wealthy men and women. Indeed while a quarter of such men were in some sense self-made, only about 5 per cent of women were. Women inherited money both from their parents and from their husbands and there were high rates of intermarriage amongst the very rich.

Table 3.2 Share in total personal wealth, England and Wales, 1923-72[10]

	Top 1%	Top 5%	Top 10%	Top 20%
1923	60.9	82.0	89.1	94.2
1924	59.9	81.5	88.1	93.8
1925	61.0	82.1	88.4	93.8
1926	57.3	79.9	87.4	93.2
1927	59.8	81.4	88.3	93.8
1928	57.0	79.6	87.2	93.1
1929	55.5	78.9	86.3	92.6
1930	57.9	79.2	86.6	92.6
1936	54.2	77.4	85.7	92.0
1938	55.0	76.9	85.0	91.2
1950	47.2	74.3	—	—
1951	45.8	73.6	—	—
1952	43.0	70.2	—	—
1953	43.6	71.1	—	—
1954	45.3	71.8	—	—
1955	44.5	71.1	—	—
1956	44.5	71.3	—	—
1957	43.4	68.7	—	—
1958	41.4	67.8	—	—
1959	41.4	67.6	—	—
1960	33.9	59.4	71.5	83.1
1961	36.5	60.6	71.7	83.3
1962	31.4	54.8	67.3	80.2
1963	Not available			
1964	34.5	58.6	71.4	84.3
1965	33.0	58.1	71.7	85.5

BRIGHTON POLYTECHNIC LEARNiNG RESOURCES

1966	30.6	55.5	69.2	83.8
1967	31.4	56.0	70.0	84.5
1968	33.6	58.3	71.6	85.1
1969	31.1	56.1	67.7	83.3
1970	29.7	53.6	68.7	84.5
1971	28.4	52.3	67.6	84.2
1972	31.7	56.0	70.4	84.9

The significance of these patterns of redistribution of wealth *within* families is also of great importance interpreting table 3.2. On the face of it this would appear to support the claim that there has been a substantial reduction in inherited wealth over this period. However, this is not necessarily the case partly because of the problems involved in what counts as wealth, but also because the apparent decline in inequality mainly reflects a pattern of redistribution *amongst* the members of wealthy families. This view is supported by table 3.3 which has been adapted from table 3.2. Thus, while the share of personal wealth held by the top 1 per cent of wealth holders fell from about 60 per cent to 30 per cent over this 50-year period, the next 4 per cent increased their share from about one-fifth to one-quarter, while the next 5 per cent doubled their share from about 7 per cent to 14/15 per cent and the next 10 per cent tripled theirs from 5 per cent to 15 per cent. Atkinson maintains that the redistribution of wealth over this century has not been between the rich and poor but between successive generations of the same family and between husbands and wives.[11] This means that age and gender inequalities of wealth have been reduced within households and the wider families of the rich, but there has been relatively little redistribution from the moderately rich to the average and to the poor. Four-fifths of people share about 15 per cent of total wealth.

Table 3.3 Share in total personal wealth, England and Wales, 1923–72, selected years[12]

	Top 1%	*Next 4%*	*Next 5%*	*Next 10%*
1923	60.9	21.1	7.1	5.1
1924	59.9	21.6	6.3	5.4
1925	61.0	21.1	6.3	5.4
1930	57.9	21.3	7.4	6.0
1936	54.2	23.2	8.3	6.3
1950	47.2	27.1	—	—
1951	45.8	27.8	—	—
1952	43.0	27.2	—	—
1960	33.9	25.5	12.1	11.6

1961	36.5	24.1	11.1	11.6
1962	31.4	23.4	12.5	12.9
1970	29.7	23.9	15.1	15.8
1971	28.4	23.9	15.3	16.6
1972	31.7	24.3	14.4	14.5

It is important to examine the distribution of wealth because it is much more unequally distributed than earned income, while for some households it provides extremely significant resources which are or can be realized as income. It is important to note that top wealth holders are not necessarily top earned income recipients or vice versa. This is well shown in table 3.4 which is based on Townsend's survey which provided the basis for *Poverty in the United Kingdom*, although the table also shows that the bulk of the population (64 per cent) are in the lower 80 per cent of both wealth holding and income.

Table 3.4   Proportions of households in various combinations of income and wealth[13]

Assets	Net Disposable Income			
	Top 5%	6–10%	11–20%	Bottom 80%
Top 5%	2.0	0.6	0.6	1.9
6–10%	0.9	0.8	1.2	1.9
11–20%	1.2	1.6	1.4	7.0
Bottom 80%	1.4	4.0	9.2	64.3

Nevertheless, the unequal distribution of wealth is in general a major source of unequal income. The greater the wealth, the more significant is shareholding, and hence the greater the 'unearned' income that accrues. Most people receive no investment income (except indirectly through pension fund holdings), while 1 per cent receive over a third of all investment income.[14] Such 'unearned' income is very important to the wealthy, providing between a quarter to one-half of their income.[15] This particularly stems from the ownership of shares which are very unequally distributed; about 300,000 people owning more than half the personally held shares in Britain in the early 1970s.[16]

Turning now to the distribution of income, the Royal Commission on the Distribution of Income and Wealth suggested that there were about 65,000 very highly paid employees in the mid-1970s.[17] The Commission concluded that 70 per cent of these were managers, and the rest consisted of those in legal, financial, medical and academic professions as well as senior civil servants, entertainers and sportsmen.[18] There were approximately similar numbers of high-earning self-employed, mainly in the professions and commerce.[19] The most distinctive feature, however, was the extraordinarily low representation of women amongst these high-earnings groups. The Commission concluded that only 2 per cent of the high earners were women.[20]

Table 3.5   Distribution of income in the UK before and after tax, 1949–1978/9[21]

| | *Percentage share of total income* | | | | | |
| | *Before tax* | | | *After tax* | | |
	Top 10%	*Next 60%*	*Bottom 30%*	*Top 10%*	*Next 60%*	*Bottom 30%*
1949	33.2	54.1	12.7	27.1	58.3	14.6
1954	29.8	59.3	10.9	24.8	63.1	12.1
1959	29.4	60.9	9.7	25.2	63.5	11.2
1964	29.0	61.4	9.6	25.1	63.5	10.8
1967	28.0	61.6	10.4	24.3	64.1	12.0
1973/4	26.8	62.3	10.9	23.6	63.7	12.8
1978/9	26.1	63.5	10.4	23.4	64.5	12.1

Let us now look at the overall distribution of income in Britain. First, table 3.5 presents some of the broad changes in the percentage share of total income over the post-war period. There are a number of points to note here:

1   The main period of reduced income inequality was in the early parts of the post-war period and has not increased much more recently.[22]
2   To the extent that there was income redistribution this took place mainly between the top 10 per cent and the next 60 per cent, while the share of the bottom 30 per cent has remained almost constant.[23]
3   Income tax does not effect a major redistribution of income from the top 10 per cent to the bottom 30 per cent, indeed the proportions received by the different income groups remain fairly similar before and after tax. Moreover, if we consider table 3.6 we can see that it is also necessary to consider the net effects of both taxes paid to the state *and* benefits received from the state. Clearly this does produce some significant changes, but after all these apparently redistributive measures are taken into account, the top 20 per cent of households still receive four times the income of the bottom 20 per cent and over three times that of the bottom 40 per cent.
4   One important reason why the redistribution is not more substantial

Table 3.6   Redistribution of income through taxes and benefits, 1980[24]

	United Kingdom				£s per year and numbers	
	Quintile groups of households					
	ranked by original income					
	Bottom 20%	Next 20%	Middle 20%	Next 20%	Top 20%	All house-holds
Average per household (£s per year)						
Original income	170	2,170	5,910	8,540	14,440	6,350
+ Benefits in cash						
Age related	1,250	800	200	100	100	490
Child related	60	120	230	230	190	170
Income related	480	210	80	60	60	180
Other benefits in cash	180	180	90	70	50	110
Gross income	2,140	4,030	6,500	8,990	14,840	7,300
− Direct taxes	10	420	1,170	1,790	3,280	1,330
Disposable income	2,130	3,610	5,340	7,200	11,560	5,970
− Indirect taxes	540	1,020	1,420	1,780	2,530	1,460
+ Benefits in kind						
Education	190	310	510	600	630	450
Nat. Health Service	560	500	460	430	440	480
Welfare foods	20	20	30	20	20	20
Housing subsidy	180	140	130	100	70	120
Other allocated benefits	10	30	50	70	110	50
Final income	2,550	3,580	5,090	6,640	10,300	5,630
Average per household (nos.)						
Adults	1.4	1.7	2.0	2.2	2.7	2.0
Children	0.3	0.5	1.0	1.0	0.8	0.7
Workers	0.1	0.9	1.5	1.9	2.4	1.4
Retired people	1.0	0.6	0.2	0.1	0.1	0.4
No. of households in sample	1,389	1,389	1,388	1,389	1,389	6,944

is because if we consider the effects of all taxes the proportions paid at different income levels do not vary very greatly. This is shown in table 3.7. Apart then from the bottom 20 per cent of households, who receive most of their income in the form of cash benefits (86 per cent in 1980), all other households lose between 30 and 40 per cent of their income in direct and indirect taxation. The effect of indirect taxation is thus substantially to neutralize the moderately progressive effects of direct taxation. It should be noted that these figures relate to 1979 and relate therefore to a period before the effect of Conservative budget changes

Table 3.7   The proportions paid in taxation by each decile of households, 1979[25]

| | Decile Groups | | | | | | | | | |
| | Bottom | | | | | | | | | Top |
	1	2	3	4	5	6	7	8	9	10
Proportion of income* paid in all direct and indirect taxes	21.9	24.2	29.7	35.9	38.9	38.4	38.8	38.8	38.6	38.6

Note:
* includes direct tax benefits

(which decreased the progressive element of income tax) came fully into operation. It should also be noted that income tax has become less progressive as the range of incomes on which tax is paid has expanded to include most wage-earners. This has been necessary because of the fall in the take from corporation tax throughout the 1970s.[26]

5   The most dramatic consequence of these patterns of social inequality is that a considerable proportion of the British population live in a state of poverty. According to Townsend's definition, which is based on the absence or inadequacy of those diets, amenities, standards, services, and activities which are common or customary in modern Britain, 25 per cent of households and 23 per cent of persons were in poverty.[27] Or, to put it another way, more than half of the population in Britain will experience poverty at some point in their lives.[28] Poverty is more likely to be experienced by women than by men, by the fairly young and the old, by those with larger families, by those with, or dependent on those with, unskilled, manual occupations, by those with no assets or negative assets, by those who have experienced unemployment in the previous year, by immigrants, by those in one-parent families and by those disabled.[29]

6   The significance of occupation for the location of a household in the patterning of income inequality is clearly shown in table 3.8. However, if we consider the main developments over the course of this century there have been some considerable changes in the structure of earnings *between* different occupational classes. Table 3.9 presents some relevant data for the period 1913–14 to 1978. Amongst men, there clearly has been a substantial reduction in the relative incomes of 'higher professionals/managers' over the course of the century, although as the Royal Commission pointed out there has been a sizeable growth of various 'fringe benefits' which partly compensate for this fall in relative incomes.[30] It should also be noted that while the number of employers fell between 1911 and 1971 by 20 per cent, the number of higher

Table 3.8 The distribution of income and head of household's occupation[31]

| | Decile group of household income distribution | | | | | | | | | | |
	Bottom 10%	9th 10%	8th 10%	7th 10%	6th 10%	5th 10%	4th 10%	3rd 10%	2nd 10%	Top 10%	All incomes
Occupational grouping of head of Household											
Employee											
Professional, technical, administrative and managerial	3	6	30	53	75	93	162	215	264	346	1,247
Other non-manual	13	27	50	68	73	90	101	100	99	103	724
Manual	62	106	219	324	385	407	352	340	281	183	2,659
Self-employed	19	35	48	77	78	57	62	46	54	88	564
Retired	358	396	291	145	83	67	51	39	36	22	1,488
Unoccupied	298	183	114	85	59	38	24	13	19	10	843

professionals and managers increased three times between 1911 and 1971, and hence brought down the average income for these occupational classes.[32] It is also clear from this table how the relative income of male clerks fell considerably in relationship to that of male manual workers, a point noted in much of the literature on the so-called 'proletarianization' of 'deskilled white-collar workers'.[33]

Table 3.9 Occupational class averages as percentages of the mean for all occupational classes, men and women (pounds)[34]

	1913–14	1922–4	1935–6	1955–6	1960	1970	1978	Multiple of 1913–14
Men								
1 Professional								
A Higher	405	372	392	290	289	211	209	0.5
B Lower	191	204	190	115	120	136	137	0.7
2B Managers etc	247	307	272	279	263	245	203	0.8
3 Clerks	122	116	119	98	97	97	93	0.8
4 Foremen	152	171	169	148	144	121	118	0.8
Manual								
5 Skilled	131	115	121	117	113	104	110	0.8
6 Semi-skilled	85	80	83	88	83	93	97	1.1
7 Unskilled	78	82	80	82	76	83	86	1.1
Men's average (current weights)	116	114	115	119	120	123	121	1.0
Women								
1 Professional								
A Higher	—	—	—	(218)	(217)	178	169	—
B Lower	110	137	130	82	86	88	98	0.9
2B Managers etc	99	102	104	151	142	135	128	1.3
3 Clerks	56	68	61	60	61	61	69	1.2
4 Forewomen	70	98	96	90	86	73	81	1.2
Manual								
5 Skilled	54	56	53	60	56	49	57	1.1
6 Semi-skilled	62	63	62	51	48	47	59	1.0
7 Unskilled	35	47	45	43	40	44	57	1.6
Women's average (current weights)	62	66	64	60	59	59	68	1.1

7   The inequality between men's income and women's income is also very clear in table 3.9. Female earnings are consistently lower than those for men and there has been relatively little change over this whole period, except perhaps during the 1970s.[35] Moreover, if we ignore the

Table 3.10   The percentage distribution of ethnic groups in different occupational categories, 1981 (GB)[36]

	White	Ethnic Group W. Indian/ Guyanese	Indian/Pakistani/ Bangladeshi
Males			
Professionals	6	2	8
Employers and managers	16	4	12
Intermediate, junior non-manual	18	7	14
Skilled manual	38	49	35
Semi-skilled manual/ personal service	16	27	25
Unskilled manual	5	11	6
Females			
Professionals	1	0	3
Employers and managers	7	2	4
Intermediate, junior non-manual	53	50	41
Skilled manual	7	4	13
Semi-skilled manual/ personal service	23	34	35
Unskilled manual	8	8	3

tiny number of women in 'higher professional' and managerial classes then the incomes of women are more evenly distributed than those for men.[37]

8   Black workers, like women, are 'crowded' into less well-paid occupations, although as can be seen from table 3.10 this effect applies more to black men than to black women. The inequalities in earnings from paid employment which this generates are substantial but need to be considered in different ways. First, the average earnings of white men are considerably higher than those of black men.[38] Second, the differences between the earnings of white and black men vary with regard to the occupational level being considered. Thus, in 1974, white non-manual males earned 29 per cent more than black non-manual males, while skilled manual workers earned 10 per cent more, while semi-skilled and unskilled workers earned the same.[39] Third, these differences are not found with respect to females where the median weekly earnings of black and white women are more or less identical.[40] Fourth, there is practically no information about ethnic variations in the ownership of wealth. Perhaps, however, one significant point should be noted and that is the high proportion of immigrants owning their own homes (80 per cent of Indians for example) although many of these are in poor inner-city areas.[41]

So far we have only considered a number of snapshots of British society that, at different points in time, reveal particular patterns of social inequality. We have also tried to identify some of the changes that occurred between these different snapshots. However, little of this discussion really gets at the notion of class as sets of social *relations* both within a class and between one class and another. Nor does it account for the manner in which classes are formed and reformed over time. It also does not take account of how classes are experienced as such by the members of a class – whether they feel and act as class members, or as members of other social groups (for example, as women, blacks etc.), or as separate, relatively isolated individuals. These all involve enormous issues which can only be briefly discussed here.

Social and geographical mobility

The best-known academic research which relates to these issues is the study of social mobility. The basic idea behind such work has been summarized by Giddens as that of 'structuration'.[42] By this he suggests that the more that mobility chances are closed off (the greater the structuration) the more this facilitates the formation of identifiable classes. This is because the lack of intergenerational and intragenerational mobility provides for the continuation of common experience for all members of a given class. Conversely where mobility in and out of a given class is high then that class is relatively weakly formed, people will not feel much class identity, and few effective class organizations are likely to develop. The lower the mobility chances in a society the greater the degree of class structuration.

It was commonly thought in Britain following research just after the Second World War that social mobility was relatively restricted. This was because, although a third of the (male) sample had been mobile out of the class they had begun in, the range of this mobility was fairly limited.[43] There was a buffer zone of lower white-collar and skilled manual occupations beyond which those from the upper class or working class did not pass as they moved downwards or upwards. Overall, this research suggested that the British class structure was fairly highly structurated, that the majority of men would have an occupation which was the same as, or close to, that of their fathers. In particular, there was very little chance whatsoever of a working-class boy (defined in occupational terms) becoming a capitalist employer, a manager, or a 'higher professional'.

Later research has, however, partly modified this analysis. The Nuffield mobility project surveyed 10,309 men aged between 20 and 64 in 1972 and found, *inter alia*, that there was more long-range mobility than had previously been thought; that there was little in the way of a buffer zone between the working class and the service class (approximately professionals, managers, employers); that there was a fair amount of work-life mobility from the working class into the intermediate class and from the intermediate class into both the service and the working classes; that only about 25 per cent of the service class was self-recruited and indeed was recruited from all the other classes in roughly similar proportions; and that the working class was largely self-recruited.[44]

Many commentators would argue that the main reason for these changes lay in the expansion of, and improved access to, the education system over the past 40 years or so. However, the Nuffield researchers concluded that 'school inequalities of opportunity have been remarkably stable'; they endorsed Tawney's comment, orginally made in 1931, that the 'hereditary curse upon English education is its organization upon lines of social class'.[45] Halsey, Heath and Ridge show that the gap in educational opportunity between the service class and the working class is dramatic; so that by the minimum school-leaving age three-quarters of the working class had left school, while three-quarters of the service class stayed on. However, this disparity between the two classes becomes less marked the higher the level of education. Thus, *'for those who survive*, inequalities of opportunity are much reduced'.[46] Yet this applies of course to a relatively tiny proportion of working-class boys (less than one in 40 passed one A level in the sample). One good indicator of this is the fact that the difference between the age at which the service-class boys and working-class boys took up their first job slightly *increased* between the First World War and the later 1940s.[47] Likewise the relative class chances of access to university were more or less constant over the period studied, but the absolute gains for the service class were massive compared with those for the working class.[48]

Overall then educational changes merely facilitated the changing patterns of service-class recruitment in Britain. What explains these patterns is the changing occupational structure as it affected men over the period in question. Goldthorpe maintains that the most significant factor affecting class structure 'has been [the shift] chiefly from manual occupations to those of a higher professional, administrative and managerial character'.[49] The service class has in a sense been 'forced' to take in some sizeable proportion of men from other classes – its expansion could only be met by a considerable recruitment from below. It is this relatively contingent factor which led to the expansion of what is termed absolute mobility. Relative mobility rates (those rates after abstracting out such occupational changes) remained more or less unaltered and indicated no substantial increases in the openness of British society.

There are two other points to note about this analysis of social mobility in Britain. First, it is also necessary to consider how these overall patterns of mobility affect individuals and groups living in local areas. The class structure is rarely experienced at the national level but is organized on a sub-national basis. In the past there were numbers of such areas in which a highly divided local or national class structure generated persistent patterns of trade-union militancy and support for the Labour Party, and in some cases sustained red bases or 'Little Moscows'.[50] These areas were generally ones with a dominance of heavy industry or transportation and where there was a strongly developed and reinforced 'occupational community'. Examples include coalmining, shipbuilding, the railways, automobiles and engineering. Other areas, including some even with concentrations of heavy industry, were much less militant and less structured along lines of class, although they still exhibited many other features of 'traditional working-class communities', namely, emphases upon community and neighbourliness, the importance of kin, the central role of the 'mother', the importance of ascribed rather than achieved position, and so on.[51]

However, even where traditional working-class communities have provided the basis for particular forms of class experience, there have been some important economic and demographic changes which have partly undermined them in recent years.[52] Such changes include: (a) the rapid decline in employment in manufacturing industry, from 8.5 million in 1961 to 5.5 million in 1983; (b) the dramatic fall in employment in heavy industry: between 1973 and 1983 the numbers in metal manufacture fell by almost one-half, those in engineering by over one-quarter, and those in mining by over 15 per cent; (c) substantial increases in employment in the service industry until at least 1981, from 10.5 million in 1961 to 12.75 million in 1983; (d) increases in the heterogeneity of the labour force, with the public sector now accounting for one-third of all employment, and with women constituting 43 per cent of the British labour force; (e) the decline in the population living in conurbations; the numbers in the six largest falling by two million between 1961 and 1981; and (f) high rates of residence change so that about five million people move *each* year.

Changes in the labour process

Broadly speaking the main process at work here can be described as the 'deskilling' of labour. This has been elucidated by Braverman who argues that the organization of the labour process is fundamentally determined by the accumulation of capital.[53] In particular, he suggests that there is in all capitalist societies a tendency for labour to become progressively fragmented and deskilled and for conception (thinking out and planning work) to be separated off from execution (the actual carrying out of the work) and to be embodied within separate structures of management. These developments occur because of the tremendous savings available in the cost of labour that can be obtained. In particular the fragmentation of work tasks (the growth of what Marx calls the 'detail division of labour') enables capital to obtain *precisely* those quantities and qualities of labour it requires and ensures that more expensive skilled workers do not have to waste their time and their employers' money in doing less skilled work which could be done by cheaper labour. The growth of complex managerial structures both reduces the skill level and hence the relative pay of workers, and undermines the knowledge that workers possess of the labour process, which is one crucially significant source of strength that they previously enjoyed. The effect of these processes is that most manual workers in Britain do jobs in which they have little opportunity to exercise their aptitudes and abilities. Most workers will exercise more skill in driving to and from work than in the actual work they do when they get there.[54]

There are, however, three further points that need to be made here. First, there has not been a simple extension of direct managerial control throughout all British industry since, say, 1900. Rather there have been two other strategies that employers have used to control labour, those of 'paternalism' and 'responsible autonomy'; the former resulting from the persistence of familial control in much of British industry, the latter involving a reliance upon semi-autonomous but constrained work groups to regulate and police workers.[55] Second, new forms of management and of deskilling in Britain have always lagged behind the USA and, to some extent, behind West Germany as well. Indeed in Britain the craft unions at the turn of the century were able to prevent some forms of deskilling and the growth of attempts to develop 'scientific management'. New systems of management only developed in the 1930s with the growth of new industries, particularly those established in the South East with previously non-unionized labour. Some craft unions have been able, even where their work has been technically deskilled, to maintain their skilled status in the face of massive attempts to rationalize and restructure the labour process. Finally, new forms and sources of skill are continuously being created in the economy, the most obvious in recent years being those associated with the electrical, computing and microelectronics industries. And even in cases where deskilling might occur as a result, such as in the use of numerical controlled machines in engineering, this does not occur automatically or universally. The effects on the distribution of skills seem to vary considerably from one enterprise to another.[56]

In recent years in Britain deskilling has particularly affected non-manual work, in part because labour costs represent a particularly high proportion of total costs in such work. Thus, for example, in the insurance industry, the issuing of a policy, previously handled by a single 'skilled' underwriter, is now handled by several clerks each working to a closely specified set of separate routines. As units of administration become larger, specialization and subdivision make it possible to concentrate activities in large pools of labour.[57] While this may at one time have been only true of typing, it is now true of many facets of office work. Furthermore, with the introduction of increasingly expensive equipment such as word processors, it becomes necessary to concentrate similar activities in order to make economic use of the machines. A familiar consequence of fragmentation of the labour process is the greater control that accrues to management because each worker has control over a smaller part of the whole. The smaller the task performed, the greater the loss in independence. Typists operating electric typewriters can set their work out in their own way and can, to some extent, pace themselves. This reorganization and rationalization of office work and the reduction of employee autonomy with the growth of managerial control are all related to the increasing mechanization of clerical work. Machines have been introduced into almost all areas. The pace of work is increasingly dictated by the machine which also demands very accurate input, particularly where computers are concerned. Deskilled white-collar workers become like workers on a production line. Typists working to telephone dictation, for example, will move on to the next piece of work as soon as they have finished their current one, since the equipment can store dictations.

Although this is clearly a very important development in the British class structure it does not necessarily follow that the deskilling of white-collar labour will make such employees take up common cause with workers. This is for two main reasons; first, because collectively white-collar employees organize workers and generally have a better 'work situation';[58] and second, because three-quarters of such workers are female and hence gender differences may partly undermine common class actions.

Gender, race and the class structure

The most important point in this context is that class, gender and race are not to be viewed as dimensions of inequality which are separate and discrete. People experience or live social class through their experience as black or white, male or female. People engage in forms of struggle which are structured by class, but the way those struggles materialize depends upon their relationship to these other structures of gender and racial oppression. Moreover, central to these processes is the working of the British state, which does not just embody some extra aspect of 'political' inequality, but is centrally and systematically involved in the very constitution of the forms and limits of such struggles.

However, it is also crucial to note that the effects of these struggles do not simply produce a systematic challenge to the overall class structure and the British state. This can be seen most clearly in the patterns of institutionalized racism or sexism found within the working class, forms which do not merely make working-class struggles difficult, but which actually serve in part to *structure* race and gender relations in Britain. For example, the ways in which certain British trade unions prevented black workers from joining partly forced black workers into less unionized, less skilled jobs often located in inner-city areas. Having established themselves within such areas, black workers have been particularly affected by the dramatic and devastating collapse of especially manufacturing employment in these areas. They have in a sense been left to fight the 'class struggle' but in a situation where they are deprived of the indigenous organizational resources, especially of powerful trade unions, to do so.[59] In the same way skilled workers have partly conducted their struggles against capital through systematically preventing women from joining their unions and by using the state to exclude women from such employment. As a result relations of gender oppression are partly the consequence of trade-union practices and policies of a broadly patriarchal kind. Indeed it has been suggested that the relatively high rates of female participation in the labour force in Britain result from the strength of the male-dominated trade unions who have been able, through various exclusionary practices, to crowd women into lower level jobs with poorer wages and conditions than is the case in some other Western European countries.

Two other reasons why both women and black workers receive systematically inferior income are, first, that even when they are doing the 'same' job white men are often on higher rates of pay because of longer service and faster promotion because of 'discrimination' etc. Second, women and black workers are concentrated within certain occupations which tend to be subordinate to those in which white men operate — there is in other words a high degree of vertical segregation.[60] One very clear area in which this can be seen is in deskilled white-collar work where three-quarters of the workers are female. Male white-collar workers have fairly good opportunities for promotion into 'management' but the female workers concentrated within subordinate positions do not.[61] Thus the class division between male white-collar workers who are being trained for management, and female 'proletarianized' white-collar workers, overlaps with the gender division.[62]

Black struggles have often materialized around the defence of a 'community' against, in particular, white police but also against other elements of the state. This defence, which is in a sense simultaneously cultural and political, has then led back into the workplace and heightened the degree of apparently 'class' struggle.[63] At the same time there are class divisions among both women and blacks but these divisions are unlikely except in the most extreme forms to generate class-based struggles.

Depersonalization of capital

In the same way as I have shown that major changes are occurring in various subordinate classes within modern Britain, there are also changes taking place which affect the organisation of capital. Firstly, as John Scott argued earlier, it is less and less the case that firms are wholly or largely owned by individuals or families; they are increasingly owned, potentially at least, by very many people through the institution of share ownership.[64] Modern capitalism is therefore becoming 'depersonalized' particularly from the viewpoint of wealthy families whose property interests are now spread widely across numbers of enterprises. At the same time, ownership is reconcentrated as financial institutions, pension funds, insurance companies and banks come to hold large proportions of company shares. This does not represent any return to personal ownership, since these institutions are similarly owned impersonally or are managed by boards of trustees. However, the nature of capitalism as such has not been fundamentally altered by these changes in ownership. Institutional ownership often gives a wide measure of control, and control in an institutionally owned firm may mean much the same as in a personally owned firm. The spreading of ownership has also produced a fair degree of mutual ownership between financial and industrial or commercial institutions. Even pension funds, often celebrated as people's capitalism, are essentially financial institutions and, especially where external fund managers are used, they are inserted into a systematic profit-making structure.

However, although forms of control and the relationship between ownership and control have not greatly changed, the depersonalization of ownership does have consequences for the constitution of the capitalist class. Of course, the reorganization of property interests has not made propertied persons less wealthy; but as there is an increasing separation of possession, economic ownership and legal ownership the work situation of the capitalist class is becoming increasingly less distinguishable from that of the service class. In sum, the members of the service class are increasingly functionaries for capital, not for capitalists; services are not to such an extent performed for a distinct capitalist class which owns and controls specific identifiable companies.

Conclusion

I have tried to detail the main features of the contemporary British class structure; namely, the maintenance of high rates of inequality of income and wealth between men and women, and between whites and blacks; the increases in social mobility for men because of the large-scale growth of the service class but the failure of British society to become otherwise more 'open'; economic and demographic changes which in part undermine 'solidaristic' working-class localities; the tendencies for both manual and clerical work to become 'deskilled' but not necessarily for such workers to become part of a common 'proletarian' mass; the increased feminization of the labour force and its effects upon class formation; the growth of a substantial black 'underclass'; and the depersonalization of the capitalist class and its increasing interconnections with the service class. Later chapters explore some of the struggles which have developed in response to these changing but nevertheless systematically generated forms of social inequality within Britain.

4

Geography and Class

DOREEN MASSEY

History

There are some well-established images of the geography of inequality in the United Kingdom.[1] Mention 'the regional problem' and immediately there is conjured up a picture of narrow streets and terraced houses, of half-demolished shipyards, pitheads and steelworks, and of bleak industrial estates. That, certainly, is the image of 'the regional problem' held particularly by people living in the South. And yet we know that there is more to it than that. For one thing, there is more to geographical inequality than that classic form of the regional problem. In the 1970s and 1980s the decline and dereliction of the inner cities have pushed their way even more prominently onto the political agenda. For another thing, the form and shape of geographical inequality changes quite rapidly over time. The classic regional problem of South Wales, the North East of England and central Scotland, which now seems so irremovable and eternal, did not exist a century ago. For much of the nineteenth century these were the industrial boom areas of the country.

Geographical differences within the UK are more complex than is sometimes realized. They also change, both in their form and in their underlying causes, from one historical period to another. I would also argue that they are of some political importance, although the *way* in which they are important changes between different periods.

Between the wars

It was the period after the First World War, the 1920s and the 1930s, which saw the first full emergence of the regional problem as we have come to know it. There is no need here to document its horror. Memories of it still colour strongly (too strongly, some might say) the collective reminiscences of the labour movement. There are some important points to be made about the nature and causes of this most well-known aspect of British geographical inequality.

● It was measured primarily in terms of unemployment levels, and in disparities in unemployment levels between different regions of the country.
● Indeed, it was measured primarily in terms of *male* unemployment levels.
● The high levels of unemployment had their immediate cause in the collapse of jobs in one or two particular industries – coal, shipbuilding, iron and steel, for instance – which were highly concentrated into a few parts of the country, and dominated those regions' employment structure.
● This collapse in its turn was due to the ending of the UK's role as the internationally dominant economy – in other words to a change in the international division of labour. The new industries which were growing in this period were far more geared to the domestic economy. This, along with their different technological and labour requirements, led to their location in the South East and Midlands of England. The 'problem' of the decaying heavy industry areas of the North and West of the country was, in other words, the result of a wider context of change, both at an international level and in the overall balance of industries within the country.
● It also went along with a shift in the balance of size and power between trade unions. While numbers fell in the industry based unions of the North and West, they grew apace in the general unions for semi-skilled workers in the Midlands and South East.

The post-war boom

The geography of inequality received little attention during the 1950s. This was not because it had disappeared – unemployment in the North and West of the UK was still far higher than that elsewhere. But absolute levels of unemployment were everywhere low – even in the North and West. The labour movement was quiescent on the issue; the Left hardly mentioned it. It was a period of apparently easy growth, and many chose to ignore the unstable foundations and underlying structural weaknesses of that growth. This was as true for the questions of geographical inequality and the regional problem as it was for the economy as a whole. On both fronts, the 1950s in Britain was a decade of coasting along and storing up trouble. First in the late 1950s, and then in 1963, trouble hit. The end of the long boom was announced in the UK by the dramatic reappearance of 'the regional problem'. Coal and shipbuilding, in particular, went once again into decline.

There is a serious lesson to be learned by the Left from this decade: the lack of attention paid to geographical inequalities by the Left in the 1950s was a result of the fact that it considered the issue to be one simply of spatial distribution, one to which no attention need be paid until the symptoms showed.

The fruits of this neglect have been evident ever since. Since the early 1960s geographical inequality has once again been high on the political agendas of governments, trade unions, and, occasionally, the Left.

Since the mid-1960s manufacturing employment has been in almost continuous decline in the UK, the national economy has moved from relative to absolute decline and we have undergone a series of different political strategies for dragging the economy out of recession. Integral to all this has been a major restructuring of British industrial and social geography. For the purpose of this rapid survey, we can divide the period into two, the first from the early 1960s to the early 1970s, the second from the late 1970s until the mid-1980s, separated by the mid-1970s, years of vacillation and transition. The two periods form a sharp contrast in terms of the world economic context, the specifically British economic situation, and the ruling political strategies. The combination of these differences mean that in each period the patterns of geographical variation in this country were refashioned in a very different way.

The situation which we face now, in the mid-1980s, is a result of the combination of the long-term inheritance of the classic regional problem together with the dramatic, and very different, geographical effects of each of these two periods.

The 1960s and early 1970s

With the world economy still growing, but with Britain's economy in relative decline, this was the period of 'modernization', rising productivity, restructuring and the White Heat; it was a period of the rapid concentration of capital, of public sector growth, and also of a very active regional policy.

All this had very distinct geographical implications. The decline of jobs for men in the old industrial Development Areas continued. One strand of the 1964–70 Labour government's modernization strategy was the rationalization of the old basic industries, many of them nationalized or to be nationalized. It is a point to remember that the level of job loss in many of these industries, but especially coalmining, was extremely high during this period (see table 4.1). In effect, in terms of relative unemployment, this meant the potential continuation of the old form of the regional problem. At the same time, however, a number of industries were establishing new plants in 'the regions'. In each case the location in the regions was a response to the need to cut costs, often in the face of intensifying competition. Among these industries were clothing, parts of the service sector, electronics and even the central state. In each case, however, the new jobs in the regions were primarily in branch plants and the employment they offered was low paid, of low skill status and quite often part-time. The attraction of the regions was a reserve of green labour (in this case mainly women) further cheapened by regional policy.

Table 4.1   Job loss in mining and quarrying, 1961–71: the results of 'modernization'

Region	Employment levels (Male) 1961	1971	Employment loss
North	146,810	61,940	84,870
Wales	101,490	49,790	51,700
Scotland	84,340	35,620	48,720
Totals	332,640	147,350	185,290

Source: C. H. Lee, *British Regional Employment Statistics 1841–1971*, Cambridge, Cambridge University Press, 1979.

The higher-status and better-paid employment – the research and development in electronics, the headquarters in clothing, the higher levels of departments of the state – did not move out to the regions but remained in London or in the outer South East. If such activities did decentralize they remained in this part of the country. It was during this period that the M4 corridor began to attract attention. This emerging new pattern was reinforced by the effects of the rapid concentration of capital during this period. For economic concentration went along with an increased geographical concentration of headquarters in London and the South East at the same time as elements of production itself were being decentralized. There are many different ways of measuring this geographical concentration of headquarters, but to take one straightforward index: in 1982 out of the 'top' 50 companies by size in the UK, only three had their headquarters outside London and its surrounding area in the South East. In other words, control over the process of accumulation is overwhelmingly exercised from one part of the country, and the upper-echelon managerial personnel is, therefore, located there too. Some aspects of the processes outlined above are indicated in figure 4.1.

It should be noticed that the only counter to this trend, the only instance where the jobs going out to the regions, or being established in the regions, were skilled and well-paid, was in the then growing local authority and

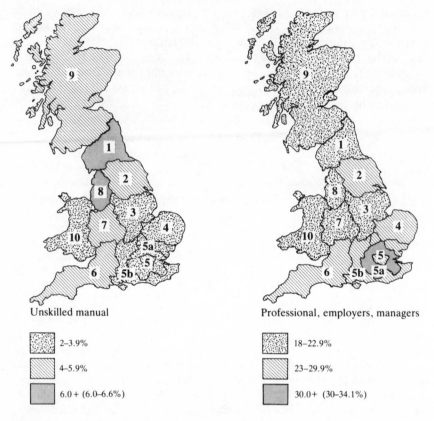

Figure 4.1   Aspects of the new spatial division of labour
Data: Socio-Economic Group (of economically-active 'heads of households' only), 1982.
Source: General Household Survey; Special Tabulations.
Key:

1 North	5 South East	7 West Midlands
2 Yorkshire and Humberside	5a Outer Metropolitan Area	8 North West
3 East Midlands	5b Outer South East	9 Central Clydeside conurbation
4 East Anglia	6 South West	

welfare state sector. This is particularly true of jobs for women. Apart from all the other damage they will do, therefore, cuts in local authority and welfare spending will also reduce one of the few sources of skilled jobs for women in the regions.

So the 1960s present a complete contrast with the preceding decade. There was a major change in the spatial organization of the economy and it took place in the context of considerable state intervention in the forms of a strong regional policy. What was the result? And what can be learned?

The first and best-remembered result of this period was that there was some statistical narrowing of the relative differentials in unemployment rates between the Development Areas and the rest of the country. It was immediately claimed that the regional problem was being solved, and that regional policy was responsible for its solution. Neither of these things was true. To take the second point first, although regional policy had been one element in steering the decentralization of some jobs to the regions, it was by no means the only one. Much wider causes deriving from increased international competition, changing technology and the changing geographical availability of female labour were significant in structuring the whole situation. But anyway, to return to the first point, it was not even the case that the regional problem was being solved. What was pre-eminently going on during this period, in spite of the relatively minor and in any case temporary convergence of unemployment rates (around a national average which itself was rapidly rising) was not the end of geographical inequality, but its emergence in a new form, a new spatial division of labour (see figure 4.1).

During the 1960s geographical inequality and differentiation were functional to both capital and the state in the attempts made to improve profits. The National Plan saw half its projected 'manpower' gap being bridged by the simple expedient of using the reserves of labour in the regions. And when the Plan fast proved an optimistic dead letter, a geographical shift to regions of high unemployment and/or to new labour forces was central to British capital's attempts tò hold down wages. The promise of regional policy assistance seems also to have been an important quid pro quo for the rationalization of the old, basic sectors, especially coal.

The 1970s and 1980s

In the context of a slowdown in the world capitalist economy, and the dominance of a very different political and economic strategy, the changing geography of this period has been moulded above all by the pattern of de-industrialization.

The geographical distribution of the loss of manufacturing jobs has been more general than was the collapse of the nineteenth century basic sectors in the 1930s. But de-industrialization has nonetheless had a clear geographical progression and pattern. It began in the cities, especially London, but included all the major conurbations (see table 4.2). This straightforward loss of manufacturing jobs is at the heart of present-day urban decline and 'the inner-city problem'.

From the cities, as de-industrialization accelerated, it spread to whole regions, especially the engineering-based regions of the West Midlands and the North West (see table 4.2). The West Midlands, from having been a boom region in the 1950s, by the mid-1980s had a shattered economic base.

Table 4.2   The loss of manufacturing employment in the conurbations 1960–81

Conurbations†	1960–78*		1978–81**	
	Number of manufacturing jobs lost	(%)	Number of manufacturing jobs lost	(%)
London	−569,000	(−42.5)	− 91,191	(−11.9)
West Midlands	−176,000	(−24.3)	−149,117	(−23.4)
Merseyside	− 46,000	(−21.2)	− 50,108	(−24.6)
Manchester	−178,000	(−30.7)	− 98,628	(−22.4)
Tyneside	− 27,000	(−18.6)	− 33,478	(−20.7)
Clydeside	−100,000	(−28.0)	na	na
West Yorkshire	− 78,000	(−30.1)	− 64,855	(−19.3)

Notes:
* Adapted from S. Fothergill, M. Kitson, and S. Monk, 'The Impact of the New and Expanded Town Programmes on Industrial Location in Britain, 1960–78' *Regional Studies*, August 1983, p.258.
† Definitions of conurbations vary slightly over the time period. The 1960–78 reference to Tyneside excludes Sunderland and the West Midlands excludes Coventry.
** Based on Metropolitan County boundaries.
Source: Regional Trends, 1980, 1983, 1984; Department of Employment.

What the de-industrialization of this period has done is to create a new map of unemployment (see figure 4.2). To the old industrial areas [where high unemployment, worsened now by the closure of some of the new investments of the 1960s, continues] have been added new regions. And within each region of the country there are the unemployment blackspots of the inner cities. The collapse of the inner cities, and of the economies of the West Midlands and the North West, is not just the result of the geographical redistribution of jobs. It is, once again, related to a shift in the UK's place in the international division of labour and the British state's (changing) political response to that. The regional problem we inherited from the 1920s and 1930s was the result of the collapse of British nineteenth century world economic dominance. The new spatial division of labour of the 1960s and early 1970s was the geographical face of a particular political attempt to 'modernize' the British economy. The new problem regions and the inner cities of today reflect above all the collapse of the UK's international manufacturing role.

In this context, the regional policy of the 1960s can have little effect – there is little mobile investment for the incentives to attract. Moreover, the long history of granting some form of assisted status to areas likely to spawn social unrest as a result of economic decline has led to an enormous, and largely *ad hoc*, range and complexity of assisted areas. As well as places having regional policy status, there are partnership areas in inner

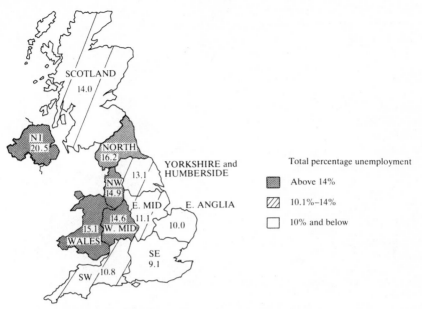

A Total unemployment: the regional pattern. October 1983

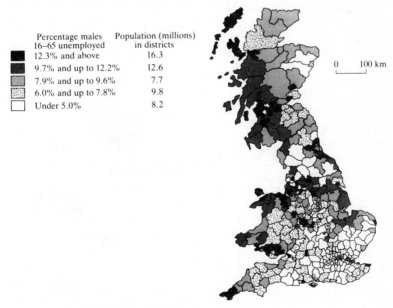

B Male unemployment: the local pattern. *Source* OPCS (1983)

Figure 4.2 The new geography of unemployment in the UK

Figure 4.2 (contd)

C Differences in levels of male unemployment between different types of area. *Source* OPCS (1983)

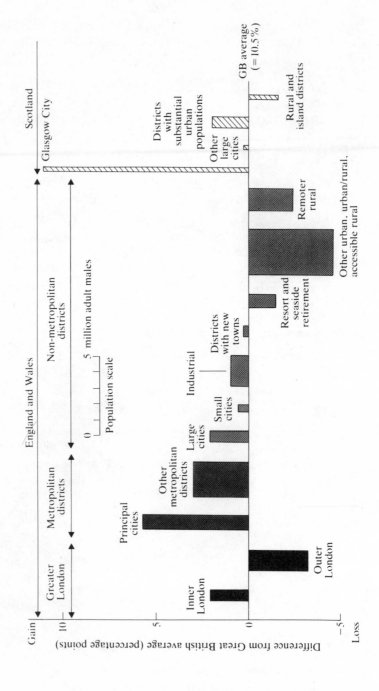

cities, science parks, Enterprise Zones, Development Corporation areas, and so on. The net result, apart from ideological effects, such as the use of Enterprise Zones in the attempt to demonstrate that planning and all forms of state intervention are a constraint on growth, is heightened competition between areas for the fewer jobs to go around. And once again this has to be seen in an international context – it seems likely that the main economic effectivity of regional policy incentives at the moment is in the international competition within Europe for investment by multinational, and multinationally mobile, corporations.

The significance for the Left

Why, however should all this matter to the Left? How does it intersect with wider socialist policies? From the history just outlined a whole range of lessons can be drawn.

Most obviously, geographical inequality can be used against the labour movement. Capitalism develops unevenly. One aspect of that unevenness is geographical. And as with other forms of unevenness, the inequality and differentiation created in one period are used as part of the conditions for further growth in the next. The geographical reorganization of British capital, nationally and internationally, has been fundamental to all its attempts since the early 1960s to increase its competitiveness, hold wages down, and generally restructure itself out of crisis. It has also been important in undermining the strength of the trade union movement. Over the last 20 years two of the major geographical bases of the movement – the old industrial Development Areas and the cities – have been severely eroded.

In other and more obvious ways geographical differences are used divisively. Individual companies play one plant off against another, or close down in a well-organized area and open up with green labour somewhere else. Such tactics were particularly frequent in the relatively mobile and technologically changing 1960s. In the 1970s the inner cities and the regions competed with each other over regional aid. In the 1980s, with so little new or mobile investment around, local communities are pitted against each other in a struggle to attract aid. And a large part of that competition involves advertising an available, and docile, labour force (see figure 4.3).

The labour movement lost hands down over regional policy in the 1960s

D

There's a skilled and stable workforce in Warrington-Runcorn.

Here's the proof.

An independent survey by PA Management Consultants of companies in Warrington-Runcorn showed that employers were full of praise for their workers. They praised their high productivity levels, their attitude to work, and their low rate of absenteeism.

Most of all, however, employers were impressed by the advanced skills, and strike-free record of their work force.

Engineering firms rely heavily on their work-force for business success, and now we can prove there's a workforce you can rely on in Warrington-Runcorn.

I'd like a free copy of the Warrington-Runcorn workforce survey, and details of ready built factory units from 500 to 50,000 sq.ft.

Name _____

Position _____

Company _____

Address _____

_____ Tel: _____

Post to: The Development Corporation, P.O. Box 49, Warrington, Cheshire WA1 2LF

Ring Eileen Bilton ☎ **(0925) 33334**
24 HOUR NUMBER

WARRINGTON-RUNCORN
The right move for engineering

Figure 4.3   The wonders of Warrington

and 1970s. Most obviously, it was divided. Workers in Development Areas called for increased grants while workers in the then relatively prosperous regions of the Midlands and South East were blaming the same policy for the obvious signs of erosion which were beginning to show in their relative prosperity. Neither side won. In the Development Areas workers accepted redundancy from older industries only to find that the jobs in incoming industries went to other people. In the South and East the attack was focused on policies of spatial redistribution (regional policy) when the real cause of the increasingly apparent decline lay at national level and in the beginnings of de-industrialization. Attention was diverted while British capital successfully used regional inequality and difference as one means of cutting wages and undermining bargaining strength. The geography of jobs is not just the *outcome* of changes in the national economy, it is an important element in determining how that economy will grow and change, and an important component therefore in the battle between capital and labour.

In exactly the same way, 'social geography' is not just a reflection of the changing national social structure; it is also an element in its formation. Since the 1960s the primarily sectoral basis of regional economic differentiation has been giving way before a differentiation based rather on a distinction of functions within individual industries. Increasingly conception is spatially separated from execution, upper management from lower management and production, 'strategic' decision-making and control from day-to-day administration. Geographical differentiation can reinforce the social distance which already exists between these functions. In Britain the upper echelons of managerial, technical, financial and state administrative strata tend to live well away from the main centres of actual production; and it is reinforcing their social status to do so.

Geographical separation and difference can reinforce social separation. The formation and functioning of both the economy and the social structure of the country are affected by their geographical organization. At any one time people in different parts of the country are experiencing different kinds of changes. To be sure, there are few geographical areas of the country which are unaffected by decline. But that decline varies from place to place and is experienced differently by the labour movement in different areas. In some the collapse of manufacturing jobs is going on in a context of rapid growth in professional and technical jobs, and population, a fact which must reinforce the sense of loss for those marginalized by the different labour demands of the new growth. In some areas which not so long ago had very few jobs in industry there is now actual expansion of such employment. Elsewhere people who live in places which 20 (even 10) years ago they thought of as boom towns are now having to cope with rates of unemployment which rank among the country's highest. And the labour movement faces up to these changes and challenges with traditions of

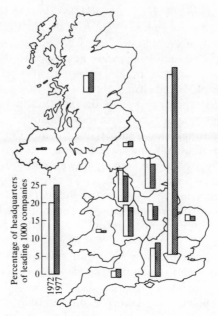

Figure 4.4   The regional distribution of the headquarters of the leading 1,000
companies in the United Kingdom, 1972 and 1977 (calculated from data in
J. B. Goddard and I. J. Smith 'Changes in corporate control in the British urban
system, 1972–1977' *Environment and Planning* A., 10, 1978, table 1)
Source: R. J. Johnston and J. C. Doornkamp (eds) *The Changing Geography of the United
Kingdom*, London, Methuen, 1982, p.193.

organization, and experiences of history, which are distinct from place to
place. Both the impact of the crisis and the political conditions for
organizing against it, vary from one part of the country to another.

Geographical differences in Britain today

The social and economic geography of the UK today is thus the result of a
long history, the overlay of the many different ways in which capital has
made use of, and abandoned, the British space. If you put together figures
4.1 and 4.2, the one showing the new geography of unemployment, the
other illustrating an important aspect of the geography of the jobs that are
left, you will get a broad picture of the spatial structure of economic
activity in the UK of the 1980s. It is important to remember that this is not
just a pattern of jobs and joblessness: what it represents is an underlying
geography of the relations of capitalist production – of control over
investment, control over the labour process, skilled jobs and deskilled

jobs, the use of new, 'green' labour reserves, and the abandonment of previous skills.

Of course such differences between parts of the country extend beyond the sphere of employment into all aspects of life. In maps 1 to 5 (see pp. 91–95) I have picked out just one or two key indicators of ways of life and 'standards of living'. Each of the maps can be viewed separately, but perhaps more important are the general points which emerge from them as a group. The position of Northern Ireland stands out as quite uniquely bad. Either statistics are unavailable or the situation they represent is far worse than that in Wales, Scotland or any of the English regions. On all the maps there is indeed considerable variation between regions. And looking at regional averages *reduces* the overall level of variation. In the South East of England, for instance, Bexley is averaged out with Bethnal Green. For this reason on some maps intraregional variation has been indicated by listing the 'best' and 'worst' cases within each region.

Taking the maps of standard of living (ownership of consumer goods, health, income) it is clear that there is a better performance on all indices in the South and East of England, in particular in East Anglia, the South West and the South East. It is important, however, to remember the last point – for there are local variations within each of these regions: parts of London itself are the most obvious examples, but the car ownership figures also point to low levels in Plymouth and Norwich, for example. The figures for the geography of council housing mirror fairly closely those for the material standard of living. Overall, though, it is clear that a South/North gradation persists, with, in general, the West Midlands now being part of the North, and with considerable variations within each region.

So there are both persistent and new geographical differences within the United Kingdom which affect political strategy. The maps have been deliberately selected to examine some of the indicators usually reckoned to be 'key' to the changing social face of Britain; they show changes which it is argued should be the basis of the way the political strategy of the labour movement should also change. Nationally, it is true that there is a rapidly growing 'new middle class', that owner-occupation is a majority tenure, that there is access to a whole range of consumer goods, and so forth. That is the national picture. The maps for all these things, however, bring out the consistency of their geographical variation. North of a line from the Mersey to the Humber almost half of the households do *not* have a car. In the northern region (which includes far more than the industrial North-East), 40 per cent of households live in council-owned property, 48 per cent of them do not have a car, less than a third own the full range of 'selected consumer durables' and, as a proportion of the population, the 'new middle class' is only just over half as important as it is in the South East. The social and occupational structure of the country is certainly changing, but the way that change is happening, and its degree, varies radically from place to place. Any politics must be sensitive to such different experiences.

Problems and possibilities

There is no doubt that the recent changes in the industrial and social geography of the United Kingdom present new difficulties and a range of new issues and problems. Major geographical centres of labour movement strength have been reduced. The new geography of industry, in particular the increasing importance of less urban locations, presents whole new problems for organizing, problems which are exacerbated by the fact that it is often not just a new location, but also a new green workforce which must learn to organize. Even more significantly the plant may be part of a multinational empire, leaving workers vulnerable to competition with other plants and often faced with negotiating with a management which transmits decisions rather than formulates them. The feeling of isolation and powerlessness can be strong. And there is potential for isolation in another way, too. With such a desperate need for jobs in so many parts of the country, it is all too easy for policies for local economic growth to degenerate into simple bribery of capital through 'incentives' and competition between areas – competition, in other words, between workers.

It may be, however, that these major changes can themselves form a context for radically new kinds of initiative. It is such a radical break that is needed. The policies pursued in recent decades, and often supported by at least sections of the labour movement, are inadequate. Some of the problems of existing forms of regional policy have been indicated above. In the inner cities policy has so far patently failed to reverse the catastrophe. In this context every new initiative, however small, is important and a number of foci can be discerned.

There are 'new militancies'. When in the 1960s and 1970s many companies decentralized to the Development Areas of declining heavy industry they often employed, as we have seen, the new green workforce of women rather than the newly-redundant men. The hope was that this would be docile labour. But as subsequent struggles have shown, new bases of strength and resistance are being constructed. As we bemoan the decline of the 'old working class' the level of organization and politicization amongst many sections of white-collar workers, particularly public sector workers, is growing. There are also the beginnings of attempts to get to grips with the international aspects of capital's geographical organization. The recent joint meetings of Kodak workers from France and the UK, together with representatives of their respective local authorities, is an example which might open up new possibilities.

There is also an increasing interest in 'local politics' in the widest sense, not as a substitute for national level politics but as a response to the different articulation of the present crisis in different places. One aspect of this new interest has been the production of a wide range of 'local studies' of the local economy, local social structure, and the politics of the local state. Such studies are important resources. And the process of their production is often itself a political and politicizing exercise, bringing together the knowledge, skills, interests and concerns of a wide range of different people in the local community. One of the opportunities offered by local level organization in general is that of linking different spheres of action, the politics of workplace with the politics of community for instance, of building bridges between previously separated groups and concerns. In such a context new alliances can be built. The clearest example of this is in the inner areas of some of the largest and most derelict cities. As the old bases of the labour movement are under attack from industrial restructuring and geographical reorganization, new bases are being constructed.

Finally, and perhaps more important, I should like to return to a theme which has underlain the whole of this article. Questions of economic and social geography, 'the regional problem' and 'the inner-city problem', must *not* be seen purely as questions of geographical distribution. This is to miss their significance. For they are in fact related to wider questions of the organization of production itself, and thereby also to a much wider politics. To take just one example: it is a fact that in the new geography of jobs most of the high-level, high-status and well-paid research, technical and development functions are situated in the South and East of England. This is one element contributing to the geography of 'the new middle class' in figure 4.1. It is also a case where geography – the clustering of this class in the outer metropolitan area and beyond and in many cases well away from production itself – contributes to the social status which is attached to these jobs. The M4 corridor is often regarded as a success story and people in other areas ask what is wrong with them that they have not achieved the same thing. But the story of the M4 corridor is only in the narrowest sense a success. And certainly it could not be emulated by a whole series of other areas. For the concentration in this area of a particular kind of job means that there will be only production and assembly jobs in other areas. The difference between the M4 corridor and other areas of the country is a reflection of a division of labour within production itself. Without that division there could not be such geographical disparities, disparities reinforced by geography itself. Any serious challenge to questions of geographical disparity must involve not only policies of spatial redistribution, as they have in the past, but also a challenge to the underlying social relations on which they are based.

Map 1   Personal disposable income in 1981, as % of UK average
Source: Regional Trends.

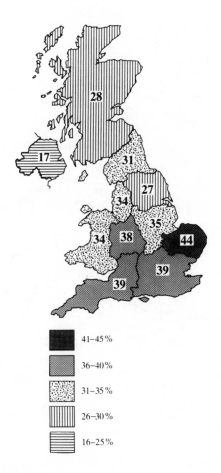

Map 2   The consumer society?: the regional pattern of ownership of selected
        consumer-durables, 1981

Source: Family Expenditure Survey, 1981.

Note: The figures represent the percentage of households in the region which have all of the
following: car, central heating, washing machine, fridge, TV and telephone.

% households *without* a car (+ range between constituencies)

Map 3   The mobile society?: the regional pattern of car-ownership, 1981
Source: CSO, 1983.

Scotland
Edinburgh Central 8.8
Glasgow Provan 93.3

53

Northern
Ireland
?

37

North
Penrith and the Border 17.6
Jarrow 65.3

40

Yorkshire and Humberside
Sheffield Hallam 10.3
Sheffield Brightside 68.8

North West
Southport 6.7
Wythenshawe 75.8

33

30

East Midlands
Harborough 13.6
Nottingham North 66.2

West Midlands
Sutton Coldfield 12.1
West Bromwich West 62

28

East Anglia
mid Norfolk 16.5
Norwich South 47.3

28

33

26

Wales
Cardiff Central 11.4
Torfaen 55.8

26

South East
Old Bexley and Sidcup ⎱ 8.8
Sutton and Cheam ⎰
Bow and Poplar 84.4

21

South West
Bournemouth East 7.4
Plymouth Devonport 46.1

Map 4   The geography of council housing, 1980 (+ the range between
constituencies)

Note: These figures do *not* imply that all other housing is owner-occupied. There are also
other categories – eg. private rental. So, in Glasgow Provan only 2.6% of the housing is
owner-occupied, in Bow and Poplar 5.6%.

Sources: CSO, 1983; OPCS, 1983.

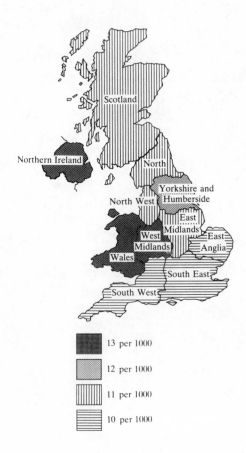

Map 5   Infant mortality
Source: CSO, 1983.

Part 2
The Constituency of the Left

5

Class Struggle and the Trade Union Movement

RICHARD HYMAN

In Britain today, one employee out of two is a trade-union member: a lower percentage than in Scandinavia, where unionization is almost complete, but higher than in most other European countries and roughly double the rate in North America. Roughly one trade unionist in ten is likely to go on strike in any single year. In what sense, then, can unions be regarded as agencies of class struggle, of resistance to capitalism? There can be no straightforward answer to this question, for trade unionism itself is deeply ambiguous and contradictory. The aim of this brief survey is to illuminate some of the complexities of union organization and action.

With very few exceptions, 'progressive' employers are happy to declare their support for 'responsible' trade unionism. The conclusion of the Royal Commission on Labour in 1894 was that strong organizations of workers and employers meeting regularly across the negotiating table were a source of order and stability in industry: strikes became less likely, and when they did occur were better disciplined and more easily settled than when unions were weak and unrecognized. For most of the present century, state policy has endorsed this view and has encouraged the development of collective bargaining. At times of crisis, the traditional response has been to seek to draw unions into a spirit of national unity in defence of the state and social order. During both world wars, union representatives participated in a multiplicity of committees at both national and local levels; the government's aim was that unions should encourage workers to support the war effort, prevent social unrest over the hardships involved, aid recruitment to the armed forces, and increase industrial productivity. In more recent times, as British capital has faced grave problems of international competitiveness, similar efforts have been made to win union support for policies of controlling labour costs and increasing management's control over the labour process. The National Economic Development Council (NEDC), set up by a Tory government in 1962, is the most prominent of several hundred tripartite bodies currently functioning. The view of British unions as a sober and respectable component of national life was symbolized in 1968 by the issue of a special postage stamp to mark the centenary of the TUC.

Yet a totally contrary theme has always formed part of ruling-class opinion: that trade unions are dangerous, disruptive and subversive. Judges, hard-line employers and right-wing politicians and newspapers have always been hostile, and anti-unionism now dominates Tory party policy. Through the 1970s, 'trade union power' was increasingly defined as a central political issue: unions enjoyed legal privileges, restricted individual freedom, obstructed management efficiency, interfered with the working of the labour market, exerted undue political influence.[1] Keith Joseph set out this position in a pamphlet written shortly before the 1979 election entitled *Solving the Union Problem Is the Key to Britain's Recovery*, a position emphasized in the Tory manifesto. The philosophy of weakening the unions clearly inspired the Employment Acts of 1980 and 1982 as well as the proposals for further legislation.

This contradictory mixture of ruling-class attitudes is mirrored on the Left. When Engels first encountered the British labour movement at the height of the Chartist upsurge he declared that 'these Unions contribute greatly to nourish the bitter hatred of the workers against the property-holding class . . . As schools of war, the Unions are unexcelled.'[2] In the *Communist Manifesto*, Marx and Engels described the formation of trade unions as an important stage in the development of revolutionary consciousness within the working class. Yet they were soon to recognize that trade unions could serve merely as vehicles through which groups of workers who were relatively protected from the disruptive force of labour market competition could defend their own sectional interests through the routines of collective bargaining. 'Too exclusively bent upon the local and immediate struggles with capital, the trade unions have not yet fully understood their power of acting against the system of wage slavery itself,' complained Marx in 1866.[3] 'They therefore kept too much aloof from general social and political movements.' Later, Engels recognized the limited import of even militant unionism in Britain: 'caught up in a narrow circle of strikes for higher wages and shorter hours without finding a solution'.[4] Reviewing his early impressions after the changes of 40 years, he went on in 1885 to stress how ruling-class attitudes to unions had altered: they 'were now petted and patronised as perfectly legitimate institutions, and as useful means of spreading sound economical doctrines amongst the workers'. Most of the strongest unions represented an elite of skilled men: 'they form an aristocracy among the working-class; they have succeeded in enforcing for themselves a relatively comfortable position, and they accept it as final.'[5] And Marx himself complained that the emerging caste of full-time officials seemed to have been bought off by the ruling class: 'the leadership of the working class of England has wholly passed into the hands of the corrupted leaders of the trade unions and the professional agitators.'[6]

The approaches of the Left in the twentieth century have reiterated the ambiguous character of trade unionism. Lenin's argument has been widely endorsed: that industrial struggle alone merely generates a 'trade union consciousness', reflected in sectional pressure for limited improvements. The notion that unions display inherent bureaucratic tendencies – as argued by Michels in his 'iron law of oligarchy' – underlines strategies built upon autonomous rank-and-file organizations and action. Yet does spontaneous grassroots initiative reinforce the tendencies to 'economism' – the preoccupation with narrow short-term gains which led some to call trade unionism 'the capitalism of the proletariat'? Socialists who identify production relations as the heart of capitalist exploitation normally treat industrial struggle as a key element in their political perspectives. Likewise, any attempt to win mass working-class support for a socialist programme must be conditioned by the fact of workers' current organized attachment to trade unions. So it is clear that an understanding of trade unionism must figure prominently in any conception of socialist transformation. But are unions part of the problems of capitalism, or part of the solution?

Capitalism and the labour process

Trade unions are historical products of the relationship between wage labour and capital. Under capitalism, work is organized on the basis of a market relationship. Work is equated with employment, with 'earning a living' (and hence unpaid labour, such as the household tasks which are overwhelmingly performed by women outside the employment relationship, is not regarded as 'real work' either in popular perception or in official economic accounting). The prospective worker must find an employer willing to pay a wage or salary in return for the disposal of her or his skill, knowledge or physical strength. It is in the employer's interest to secure labour at the lowest possible cost, and to retain workers in employment only so long as they generate a profit. A fall in the price of the goods or services produced, or the development of new techniques allowing these to be produced more cheaply, may at any moment result in managerial decisions which throw men and women out of their jobs. Within private capitalism, the forces of competition sustain the pressure to economize on labour costs, to draw ever-increased production out of fewer workers, to undermine any basis of security and stability in the employment relationship. Socialists have often assumed that within state employment the situation must be very different; but it has become all too

BRIGHTON POLYTECHNIC
LEARNING RESOURCES

clear that within the framework of a capitalist economy, very similar pressures operate, and that the strategies and actions of managements differ very little between public and private sectors. Under Thatcher, indeed, state managers have often proved *more* ruthless than their private capitalist counterparts.

Under capitalism, labour is in one sense a commodity like any other; but in a different sense it is quite unique. The employment contract may lay down the wages which the worker receives, but does not define precisely what will be provided in return. The worker does not undertake to sell an exact quantity of labour; for work cannot be measured like potatoes, and in any case most employers cannot predict exactly their day-to-day labour requirements. They want to be able to make flexible use of their labour force as circumstances dictate; and the law supports their interests, since the employment contract imposes on workers an open-ended obligation. In return for their wages, employees surrender their *capacity to work*;[7] and it is the function of management, through its hierarchy of control, to transform this potential into profitably productive activity.

In two distinct respects, conflict is thus central to employment. The sale of labour power – the fixing of the worker's income, and hence the employer's labour costs – necessarily involves an opposition of interests. Some would say that this antagonism is resolved impersonally through the operation of market forces; but market relationships are never neutral. The superficial equality of buyer and seller conceals underlying inequalities of market power which underpin the terms of trade; markets are media of control just as much as they are media of exchange. This is particularly true of the labour market, where the employer represents the concentrated power of capital whereas workers participate in the employment contract as vulnerable individuals. Combination in trade unions is, most simply, a means of partially offsetting this built-in inequality.

Conflict over the sale of labour power is discontinuous and intermittent. In unionized firms, annual wage and salary negotiations have become the norm. Non-union employers either follow agreements elsewhere, or else fix pay rates unilaterally and alter them infrequently, responding either to shortages of particular grades of labour or to the individual bargaining of particularly valued employees. Payment by results systems may offer scope for more frequent changes; a decade ago, some manufacturing firms in Britain were the scene of regular bargaining over individual piece-rates, often involving strike action. But management efforts to 'rationalize' payment systems have made such situations increasingly uncommon.

By contrast, the second main area of conflict – the control of the labour process – is often far more unstable. As Marx wrote, management control 'is rooted in the unavoidable antagonism between the exploiter and the living and labouring raw material that he exploits'.[8] To maintain profitability in the face of competition, employers must seek constantly to cut costs, intensify work pressure, introduce new techniques and technologies, make existing employees 'redundant'. An authoritarian structure of discipline and command – more smoothly and more usually known simply as 'management' – is necessary to sustain this drive for profit (or the analogous drive for economy within the public sector).

Conflict is therefore inherent in work under capitalism. Yet in most work situations it is remarkable how *rarely* this antagonism erupts to the surface of industrial relations. In part this is because the capitalist labour process is at one and the same time both conflictual and co-operative. The diverse activities which are fragmented by the capitalist division of labour must be integrated; different phases of the production cycle must be co-ordinated; machines appropriate for the various operations must be procured and maintained in working order; materials and components must be available at the correct time and place; finished products must be despatched. Because capitalism divides and confines workers' understanding of the overall process of production, management with all its disciplinary controls and material privileges nevertheless performs an indispensable productive function. Management's role is thus necessarily contradictory, and workers' response no less so. And because people who work together – whether as equals or as superiors and subordinates – usually attempt (if only to make life easier for themselves) to avoid undue unpleasantness and antagonism, it is often management's function as co-ordinator of a complex and often baffling productive operation which is most clearly perceived.

There are of course strong ideological pressures to regard management as a neutral force performing functions which would be technically necessary with any social system, rather than as a vehicle of class oppression. There are also powerful traditional notions such as 'a fair day's wage for a fair day's work' which in practice have usually encouraged workers to accept low pay for hard effort. But there are other reasons why conflict is normally contained. In any situation, a dense network of unique and detailed relationships influences how far the conflictual or the co-operative aspects of management-worker relations predominate. A continuous process of experience and adaptation affects perceptions of management control as legitimate or illegitimate, reasonable or unreasonable, technically necessary or arbitrary. Some sociologists have talked about a universal tendency towards 'negotiation of order': whether or not a workplace is unionized, working relationships involve a large amount of give-and-take, of tacit and informal bargaining, which smooths some of the rough edges of management discipline and control. Even when there are some four million unemployed, few managers attempt to control simply by wielding the threat of the sack: the inevitable outcome would be bloody-minded resentment and active or passive sabotage. Sophisticated employers want to obtain at least some degree of 'voluntary' co-operation and self-discipline. By exercising control 'humanely' they hope to limit the degree of worker resistance.

Informal negotiation over the 'frontier of control' has been an important feature of British industry for over a century.[9] The 'custom and practice' which is so widely applied in shopfloor industrial relations may be viewed as the product of continuous trade-offs between first-line managers, themselves under pressure to achieve production targets, and workers conscious of their own ability to frustrate the employers' objectives in the day-to-day work process. Many factors influence the character and outcome of such bargaining: employer sophistication and determination, the vulnerability of production to workers' actions or omissions, workers' own collective cohesion and consciousness of their power. But in every situation where capital employs wage-labour, the terms of the relationship involve a constant process of negotiation with antagonistic implications which are often suppressed but at times erupt into open conflict.

Trade unions and class struggle

This background is necessary for a proper understanding of trade unionism. It is common to equate the 'organization' of workers with unionization. But workers are organized by capital itself, and collective identity and action are both logically and historically prior to membership of a trade union. Unionism is a particular organizational form for collective action – and a necessary form for struggle involving more than minimal scope, continuity and strategic sophistication. But trade unions need to be recognized, not as a prerequisite for struggle but as merely one of a range of possible vehicles or expressions of collective worker action.

The central contradiction of trade unionism is that, at the same time as it makes possible the consolidation and increased effectiveness of workers' resistance to capitalism, it also makes this resistance more manageable and predictable and can even serve to suppress struggle. Moreover, struggle tends to be channelled into conflicts over issues on which compromise is possible through collective bargaining; hence 'economic' demands are encouraged and 'control' demands discouraged. A persistent theme in the history of trade unionism has been the conflict between union members and their officials and representatives which such tendencies have provoked – particularly since the creation of national collective bargaining procedures and more bureaucratic trade union hierarchies around the turn of the century.

A further paradox is that while trade unions unite workers, they also divide them. Though some socialists have dreamed of establishing 'one big union', trade unionism has in practice always involved a multiplicity of diverse and often competing organizations. Most workers regard themselves, first and foremost, not as members of a general working class but as a clerk or coal-miner, electrician or civil servant, employee of Ford or the health service; and union structure reflects such narrower identities rather than class membership. In embracing particular categories of workers as members and excluding others, each union gives institutional reinforcement to certain perceptions of common interest while presenting obstacles to alternative contours of solidarity.

Historically, British trade unionism has comprised a vast number of mainly tiny organizations. In 1893, when the first reliable official statistics were compiled,[10] 1,279 separate unions were recorded; their average membership was little more than a thousand, and the largest at the time, the Amalgamated Society of Engineers, had only 73,000 members. Since then the number of trade unionists, in both absolute terms and as a proportion of the labour force, has risen substantially (see table 5.1). There were major phases of expansion in the years 1910–20, 1935–50, and most recently 1969–79. But the trend has not been consistently upwards: mass unemployment caused a considerable loss of membership between the wars, and has had similar effects since 1980.

Table 5.1 Aggregate union membership and density in the United Kingdom: selected years, 1892–1982

	Union membership		Potential union membership		Union density	
	Number (000s)	Annual % change	Number (000s)	Annual % change	Level (%)	Annual % change
1892	1,576		14,803		10·6	
1900	2,022		15,957		12·7	
1910	2,565		17,596		14·6	
1913	4,135		17,920		23·1	
1917	5,499		18,234		30·2	
1920	8,348		18,469		45·2	
1921	6,633		18,548		35·8	
1926	5,219		18,446		28·3	
1933	4,392		19,422		22·6	
1938	6,053		19,829		30·5	
1945	7,875		20,400		38·6	
1948	9,363		20,732		45·2	
1949	9,318	−0·5	20,782	+0.2	44·8	−0·9
1950	9,289	−0·3	21,055	+0·3	44·1	−1·6
1951	9,530	+2·6	21,177	+0·6	45·0	+2·0
1952	9,588	+0·6	21,252	+0·4	45·1	+0·2
1953	9,527	−0·6	21,352	+0·5	44·6	−1·1

1954	9,566	+0·4	21,658	+1·4	44·2	−0·9
1955	9,741	+1·8	21,913	+1·2	44·5	+0·7
1956	9,778	+0·4	22,180	+1·2	44·1	−0·9
1957	9,829	+0·5	22,334	+0·7	44·0	−0·2
1958	9,639	−1·9	22,290	−0·2	43·2	−1·8
1959	9,623	−0·2	21,866	−1·9	44·0	+1·9
1960	9,835	+2·2	22,229	+1·7	44·2	+0·5
1961	9,916	+0·8	22,527	+1·3	44·0	−0·5
1962	10,014	+1·0	22,879	+1·6	43·8	−0·5
1963	10,067	+0·5	23,021	+0·6	43·7	−0·2
1964	10,218	+1·5	23,166	+0·6	44·1	+0·9
1965	10,325	+1·0	23,385	+0·9	44·2	+0·2
1966	10,259	−0·6	23,545	+0·7	43·6	−1·4
1967	10,194	−0·6	23,347	−0·8	43·7	+0·2
1968	10,200	+0·1	23,203	−0·6	44·0	+0·7
1969	10,479	+2·7	23,153	−0·2	45·3	+3·0
1970	11,187	+6·8	23,050	−0·4	48·5	+7·1
1971	11,135	−0·5	22,884	−0·7	48·7	+0·4
1972	11,359	+2·0	22,961	+0·3	49·5	+1·6
1973	11,456	+0·9	23,244	+1·2	49·3	−0·4
1974	11,764	+2·7	23,229	+0·4	50·4	+2·2
1975	12,026	+2·2	23,587	+1·1	51·0	+1·2
1976	12,386	+3·0	23,871	+1·2	51·9	+1·8
1977	12,846	+3·7	24,069	+0·8	53·4	+2·9
1978	13,112	+2·1	24,203	+0·6	54·2	+1·5
1979	13,447	+2·6	24,264	+0·3	55·4	+2·2
1980	12,947	−3·7	24,171	−0·4	53·6	−3·2
1981	12,182	−5·9	24,102	−0·3	50·5	−5·6
1982	11,445	−5·5	23,836	−1·1	48·0	−5·0

Source: George Bain and Robert Price, 'Union Growth' in Bain, *Industrial Relations in Britain*, Oxford, Basil Blackwell, 1983 (updated).

The earliest British unions, dating back some two centuries, were local societies of apprenticed men in such industries as printing and building, each distinct trade maintaining its separate organization. In the mass industries of British capitalism – cotton, coal, iron and steel – unionization developed mainly in the second half of the nineteenth century. Around the turn of the century there was a major extension of unionization, associated with the rise of modern 'general unions'. Finally, recent organizational development has mainly involved the growth of white-collar unionism. The early unions were almost exclusively male institutions, and at the outset of the present century well under a tenth of trade unionists were women; but today the proportion is three in ten (see table 5.2). White-collar unionists constitute over 40 per cent of total membership (table 5.3); while the industrial distribution of trade unionism has shifted from the staple industries of nineteenth century capitalism towards the public services (table 5.4).

Table 5.2 Union membership and density by sex in Great Britain*

	Male Potential			Female Potential		
	Union membership (000s)	Union membership (000s)	Union density (%)	Union membership (000s)	Union membership (000s)	Union density (%)
1896	1,356	9,652	14.0	116	4,230	2.7
1910	2,330	11,326	20·6	275	4,935	5·6
1911	2,799	11,436	24·5	331	5,002	6·6
1920	6,937	11,891	58·3	1,316	5,227	25·2
1933	3,637	13,040	27·9	713	5,915	12·1
1948	7,468	13,485	55·4	1,650	6,785	24·3
1965	7,610	14,777	51·5	2,132	8,119	26·3
1968	7,428	14,452	51·4	2,265	8,251	27·5
1970	7,994	14,177	56·4	2,634	8,363	31·5
1973	8,036	13,945	57·6	2,899	8,790	33·0
1974	8,151	13,809	59·0	3,062	9,010	34·0
1975	8,272	13,920	59·4	3,329	9,122	36·5
1976	8,492	14,069	60·4	3,462	9,257	37·4
1977	8,675	14,085	61·6	3,608	9,431	38·3
1978	8,940	14,074	63·5	3,639	9,561	38·1
1979	8,866	13,979	63·4	3,837	9,708	39.5

Note:
* i.e. excluding Northern Ireland; the totals therefore differ from table 5.1.
Source: Bain and Price, 'Union Growth'.

Table 5.3 Manual and white-collar union membership and density in Great Britain

	Manual Potential			White-collar Potential		
	Union membership (000s)	Union membership (000s)	Union density (%)	Union membership (000s)	Union membership (000s)	Union density (%)
1911	2,730·9	13,141	20·8	398·3	3,297	12·1
1920	7,124·1	13,271	53·7	1,129·2	3,847	29·4
1931	3,544·0	14,157	25·0	1,025·4	4,639	22·1
1948	7,055·7	14,027	50·3	2,062·1	6,243	33·0
1968	6,636·9	13,322	49·8	3,056·0	9,381	32·6
1970	7,095·0	12,852	55·2	3,533·0	9,688	36·5

1973	6,968·9	12,468	55·9	3,966·3	10,266	38·6
1974	7,082·3	12,362	57·3	4,130·8	10,458	39·5
1975	7,112·1	12,327	57·7	4,488·8	10,715	41·9
1976	7,321·6	12,322	59·4	4,632·3	11,004	42·1
1977	7,445·3	12,265	60·7	4,837·9	11,251	43·0
1978	7,549·7	12,168	62·0	5,029·1	11,467	43·9
1979	7,577·5	12,035	63·0	5,124·7	11,652	44·0

Source: Bain and Price, 'Union Growth'.

While the number of trade unionists has increased roughly tenfold during the past century, the number of separate unions has actually declined. This was at first a gradual process – in 1940 there were still a thousand organizations officially recorded – but has become more rapid; the number has now fallen to 400. The average size of just under 30,000 members represents a massive variation between different unions. As can be seen from table 5.5, over half the unions have less than a thousand members; together they account for under half of one per cent of total membership. At the other extreme, the seven largest unions accounted for over half the total; while the 22 with over 100,000 members together contained 80 per cent of all trade unionists.[11]

This concentration of membership in a declining number of unions reflects a process of merger and amalgamation which has become particularly rapid in recent years: partly because the legal requirements have been eased, partly because of financial pressures encouraging rationalization, partly because of empire building on the part of union leaders. Historically, the earliest amalgamations mainly involved the combination of local societies into national organizations. Then followed a series of mergers of unions catering for cognate occupational groups, often within a single industry or sector. Finally there have emerged a number of 'conglomerates' covering a diverse array of industries and occupations.

It is common to distinguish between 'craft', 'industrial' and 'general' unions, but few of the largest organizations (see tables 5.6 and 5.7) comfortably fit within these categories. A brief consideration of the 'top ten' demonstrates their complexity. Thus the TGWU derives from an amalgamation in 1921 of some 20 unions of dockers and road transport workers; but it subsequently acquired a major base in manufacturing and recruited extensively in national and local government services. In the past two decades it has attracted many smaller unions into merger, including sizeable bodies such as the Chemical Workers, the Plasterers, the Vehicle Builders and the Agricultural Workers. The other main general union, the GMBATU, was formed in 1924 from the merger of three unions with their roots respectively among gasworkers, labourers in northern shipyards, and local authority manual workers; one of the component bodies had

Table 5.4   Union membership and density in Great Britain by sector

	1948			1968			1979		
	Union membership (000s)	Potential Union membership (000s)	Union density (%)	Union membership (000s)	Potential Union membership (000s)	Union density (%)	Union membership (000s)	Potential Union membership (000s)	Union density (%)
Public sector*	3,278·5	4,637·4	70·7	3,661·0	5,536·9	66·1	5,189·9	6,297·2	82·4
Manufacturing	3,270·1	7,290·4	51·0	4,138·4	8,285·9	49·9	5,157·4	7,385·8	69·8
Manual	3,566·5	6,123·9	58·2	3,808·1	6,139·9	62·0	4,234·6	5,273·5	80·3
White-collar	153·6	1,166·5	13·2	330·3	2,146·0	15·4	922·8	2,112·3	43·7
Construction	611·2	1,325·8	46·1	472·0	1,570·7	30·1	519·7	1,415·2	36·7
Agriculture, forestry and fishing	224·4	988·9	22·7	131·1	516·8	25·4	85·8	378·3	22·7
Private services†	664·8	4,578·4	14·5	767·5	6,042·0	12·7	1,214·5	7,283·6	16·7

Notes: Road transport and sea transport are not included in any of the sectors.
* Comprises national government; local government and education; health services; post and telecommunications; air transport; port and inland water transport; railways; gas, electricity and water; and coalmining. The nationalized iron and steel industry is included in manufacturing.
† Comprises insurance, banking, and finance; entertainment; distribution; and miscellaneous services.
Source: Bain and Price, 'Union Growth'.

Table 5.5   Trade unions – numbers and membership, end 1982

Number of members	Number of unions	All membership (thousand)	Percentage of	
			Number of unions	Membership of all unions
Under 100	78	4	19·5	0·0
100– 499	101	25	25·2	0·2
500– 999	46	33	11·5	0·3
1,000– 2,499	48	74	12·0	0·6
2,500– 4,999	37	127	9·2	1·1
5,000– 9,999	22	147	5·5	1·3
10,000– 14,999	3	44	0·7	0·4
15,000– 24,999	16	330	4·0	2·9
25,000– 49,999	15	546	3·7	4·8
50,000– 99,999	13	983	3·2	8·6
100,000–249,999	11	1,868	2·7	16·3
250,000 and more	11	7,265	2·7	63·5
All members	401	11,445	100·0	100·0

Source: Employment Gazette.

Table 5.6   Major British unions, 1960

Transport & General Workers' Union (TGWU)	1,302,000
Amalgamated Engineering Union (AEU)	973,000
General & Municipal Workers' Union (GMWU)	796,000
National Union of Mineworkers (NUM)	586,000
Union of Shop Distributive & Allied Workers (USDAW)	355,000
National Union of Railwaymen (NUR)	334,000
National Association of Local Government Officers (NALGO)	274,000
National Union of Teachers (NUT)	245,000
Electrical Trades Union (ETU)	243,000
National Union of Public Employees (NUPE)	200,000
Amalgamated Society of Woodworkers (ASW)	192,000
Union of Post Office Workers (UPW)	166,000
National Union of Printing, Bookbinding & Paper Workers (NUPBPW)	158,000
Civil Service Clerical Association (CSCA)	140,000
National Union of Agricultural Workers (NUAW)	135,000
Iron and Steel Trades Confederation (ISTC)	117,000
National Union of Tailors & Garment Workers (NUTGW)	116,000

Source: TUC Report 1961 or individual organizations.

Table 5.7   Major British unions, 1982

TGWU	1,503,991
Amalgamated Union of Engineering Workers – Engineering Section (AUEW–E) (previously AEU)	1,001,000
General, Municipal, Boilermakers and Allied Trades Union (GMBATU) (previously GMWU)	825,385
NALGO	784,297
NUPE	702,159
USDAW	417,241
Association of Scientific Technical & Managerial Staffs (ASTMS)	410,000
Electrical Electronic Telecommunication and Plumbing Union (EETPU)	380,000
Union of Construction Allied Trades & Technicians (UCATT)	261,489
NUM	245,000
Confederation of Health Service Employees (COHSE)	231,504
Society of Graphical & Allied Trades (SOGAT 82)	225,155
NUT	221,511
Civil & Public Services Association (CPSA) (previously CSCA)	198,935
Union of Communication Workers (UCW) (previously UPW)	198,374
AUEW – Technical & Supervisory Section (AUEW–TASS)	172,256
Banking Insurance & Finance Union (BIFU)	151,985
NUR	150,214
Post Office Engineering Union (POEU)	136,551
National Graphical Association (NGA)	131,690
National Association of Schoolmasters & Union of Women Teachers (NAS/UWT)	120,241
GMBATU – Boilermakers Section	114,927
Association of Professional Executive Clerical & Computer Staff (APEX)	109,155

Source: TUC Report 1983

Table 5.8   British strike statistics: annual averages, 1900–83

	Number of strikes	Workers involved ('000)	Strike-days ('000)
1900–10	529	240	4,576
1911–13	1,074	1,034	20,908
1914–18	844	632	5,292
1919–21	1,241	2,108	49,053
1922–5	629	503	11,968
1926	323	2,734	162,233
1927–32	379	344	4,740
1933–9	735	295	1,694

1940–4	1,491	499	1,816
1945–54	1,791	545	2,073
1955–64	2,521	1,116	3,889
1965–9	2,380	1,208	3,951
1970	3,906	1,793	10,980
1971	2,228	1,171	13,551
1972	2,497	1,722	23,909
1973	2,873	1,513	7,197
1974	2,922	1,622	14,750
1975	2,282	789	6,012
1976	2,016	666	3,284
1977	2,703	1,155	10,142
1978	2,471	1,001	9,405
1979	2,080	4,583	29,474
1980	1,330	830	11,964
1981	1,338	1,499	4,266
1982	1,528	2,101	5,313
1983	1,255	538	3,593

Source: Employment Gazette.

previously merged with a separate union of women workers. Its membership also includes a large industrial component; recently it has amalgamated with the Water Workers and (in 1982) the Boilermakers. USDAW
is to some extent a third general union: though primarily based among
shopworkers it recruits also in food processing and manufacturing,
particularly in the co-operative sector.

The AUEW is an organization which from craft origins has also
developed into virtually a general union. Amalgamation in 1851 established it as a substantial national union and in 1920 as representative of all
the main higher-skilled occupations in engineering. In the 1920s it opened
its ranks to all male manual workers in the industry, and in 1943 admitted
women. Today its membership extends through the broad complex of
metal-based manufacturing to engineering maintenance workers
throughout industry and the public services; the Engineering Section is also
loosely federated to the Foundry and Constructional Engineering Sections
of the AUEW as well as to TASS, the former Draughtsmen's Association.
The EEPTU has also diversified from a craft background to cover a range
of occupations in electricity supply, electrical installation and maintenance,
and electrical engineering; while its current form and title derive from a
merger with the Plumbers in 1968. UCATT, created through a series of
amalgamations in 1970, is successor to many – but by no means all – of the
traditional craft societies of woodworkers and bricklayers, competes with
the TGWU for many other grades of construction workers, but also has a

significant membership among maintenance and production workers in other industries.

Two of the largest British unions recruit solely among white-collar occupations. NALGO covers the whole range of such occupations – from junior clerks to chief officers – within local government, and also has members in gas, the health service, and universities. ASTMS recruits in a wider range of industries and services but has a narrow occupational base, mainly encompassing technical, supervisory and administrative groups. NUPE organizes primarily in local government and the health service, mainly though not exclusively among manual workers, and often in competition with the general unions (and in the health service, with COHSE). Finally, the NUM is the closest British equivalent to an industrial union, organizing solely among mineworkers and including the great majority of workers among its membership; but it does not enjoy exclusive jurisdiction, for other unions represent supervisory and clerical grades.

It is clear from this brief survey that British trade union structure is extremely complex and reflects a long process of historical evolution.[12] In another respect, however, the pattern is simpler than in most other countries: for all major unions are affiliated to a single central organization, the TUC. By contrast, in such countries as France and Italy there exist rival federations based on different political or religious identities. In West Germany and Scandinavia such divisions do not exist, but most white-collar unionists are not attached to the main central bodies. In the USA, major unions such as the Teamsters and the Auto Workers are outside the AFL-CIO.

Ironically, the comprehensive scope of TUC membership owes as much to government policy as to the efforts of the TUC itself. In 1962 the Macmillan government set up the NEDC with the aim of winning union co-operation in its overall economic objectives, and in particular to obtain some form of acquiescence in wage restraint. As the price of its involvement the TUC gained the right to nominate, directly and exclusively, the six trade union members of NEDC. In consequence, non-TUC unions felt excluded from influence on government economic policy, a serious problem for those representing public sector groups. This encouraged NALGO to join the TUC, to be followed by the main civil service and teaching unions which had previously been outside.

In becoming fully representative of the main British unions, the TUC has inevitably altered significantly. Traditionally its membership was dominated by unions based on manual workers in private industry, or in such industries as mining and railways which were nationalized in the 1940s. The structure of the General Council – which oversees the main activities of the TUC in the period between each annual Congress – reflected the composition of the movement in 1920 when the system of representation by 'trade groups' was introduced. Unions were grouped according to the trade or industry in which they principally recruited, and each group was allocated a number of seats on the General Council roughly proportionate to its aggregate membership. This system has several anomalous consequences. Members of the General Council were elected by the votes of the whole of Congress; but where a trade group contained only one union, or where the various unions could agree amicably on the allocation of their trade group seats, there would be no contest. Where contests did occur there was a behind-the-scenes process of bargaining and trade-off, in which the largest unions could exert considerable patronage. The structure was slow to adapt to the changing composition of trade union – and TUC – membership. The trade groups for 'Public Employees' and 'Non-Manual Workers' – with the subsequent addition of 'Civil Service' and 'Technical Engineering and Scientific' groups – became the residual home of a multiplicity of the fastest-growing TUC affiliates. Conversely, the trade groups of declining sectors of employment retained General Council representation out of proportion to their dwindling membership.

This formed the background to the changes introduced in 1983. Unions with over 100,000 members are automatically represented on the General Council with a total of 35 seats, while the smaller bodies together elect a further 11 members. The number of additional seats for women unionists has been increased to six, elected by Congress as a whole. Debate on these contentious alterations was largely motivated by their expected effect in shifting the political balance of the General Council to the right; and certainly such predictions have been borne out in practice. But it should be noted that, historically, the power of patronage enjoyed by the largest unions under the old system normally buttressed right-wing control; and that the superficial 'left' majority during the 1970s was without practical effect, partly because it failed to reflect the real balance of commitment within the movement.

Trade unions on the defensive

A decade ago, it was largely taken for granted on the Left that trade unionism was both an expression and a vehicle of working class advance. The experience of the Wilson government's attempts to curb trade-union activity, and the more systematic attack on trade unionism by the Heath government, appeared to radicalize the movement. Traditionally, most of the largest unions had acted as bulwarks of the right within the Labour Party; now many were seen as forces for more progressive policies. Strike activity also seemed to demonstrate a rise in the temperature of struggle (see table 5.8). Historically, the pattern of British strikes involved a relatively large number of small stoppages but in addition a regular occurrence of major disputes which registered a high level of striker-days.[13] In the period of inter-war unemployment, the number of strikes fell substantially; and after the defeat of the 1926 General Strike, almost all that did occur were small-scale disputes. From the 1940s, the number of strikes rose again; but disputes remained small. For many years, indeed, the statistics were dominated by minor stoppages in coalmining, typically concerning piece-rates or else working conditions which affected piece-work earnings. But in the 1960s, strikes became more widespread (though socialists might find it surprising how *few* there still were, given the number of workers who still did *not* strike against their exploitation by capital): in 1970 a record figure of almost 4,000 strikes was recorded. Big, protracted strikes also became more common: notably the miners' dispute of 1972, the first national stoppage in the industry since the General Strike. And indeed, the number of striker-days in that year was the highest since 1926. The miners' strike – involving an open confrontation with the Tory government – symbolized the increasingly political character of many disputes, particularly in the public sector.

The period of the Social Contract after 1974 brought significant changes in the level and character of struggle. But trade-union membership continued to increase. More importantly perhaps, the pattern of shop steward organization which for several decades had been a distinctive feature of trade unionism in British engineering spread far more widely, from manufacturing to the public sector, from manual to white-collar workers.

The situation has changed radically in the context of mass unemployment and a rabidly anti-union government. Thatcher's first term of office brought the destruction of a quarter of all jobs in manufacturing, the traditional stronghold of British unionism; while public employment, the more recent growth area, was hit by cuts and cash limits. Hence the decline in union membership, both in absolute terms and as a proportion of the labour force, which is revealed in table 5.1. Some unions have fared particularly badly: the TGWU, for example, which claimed almost 2.1 million members at the end of 1979, lost 28 per cent of these in the following three years. Whatever happens to aggregate employment in the rest of the 1980s – and there are few grounds for optimism, given current economic, political and technological trends – its structural composition will almost inevitably continue to move away from concentrated workforces in the large industrial centres to smaller and more dispersed workplaces and to the private service sector which has traditionally proved resistant to unionism. Even maintaining current levels of membership will therefore involve an uphill struggle. Membership decline has had serious financial consequences, since British unions typically operate on tight budgets with membership dues which are low by overseas standards. Some organizations have been brought close to bankruptcy, a situation which will doubtless encourage further amalgamations.

Employers, themselves often faced by intense economic pressures, have taken predictable advantage of unions' current weakness. Real wages, which rose on average by about 20 per cent during the 1970s, have stagnated and in some cases actually fallen during the 1980s. More serious, however, has been the challenge mounted on the frontier of control over the labour process. Capitalist rationalization has involved major efforts to achieve more flexible use of labour, more intensive working, more elaborate supervision, tighter disciplinary regulations, and hence a systematic assault on established 'custom and practice'. Often integral to this attack has been the imposition of closures and redundancies, particularly in those companies which acquired a diverse range of separate plants during the merger wave of the 1960s and early 1970s. The attempt to reorganize production to enhance management's day-to-day control may be seen as a continuation of a trend widely proclaimed in the 1960s in the name of 'productivity bargaining'. Then, however, the underlying theme of sophisticated employers, government agencies and academic pundits was the need for 'management by agreement': transformation of the labour process had to be negotiated with union representatives in order to win workers' consent. It was this philosophy which encouraged many employers in the early 1970s to give full recognition and extensive facilities to shop stewards, in some cases stimulating their appointment where none had existed before.[14] Today the strategy is often very different: commercial pressures and the changed balance of labour market power have brought the unilateral imposition of reorganization and speed-up, regardless of union (and particularly shop steward) resistance. The threat of closure has itself provided a potent sanction: workers have been offered the stark choice of co-operating with management or losing their jobs.

The altered material environment is reflected in a degree of defeatism and demoralization reminiscent of the inter-war depression. As can be seen from table 5.8, officially recorded strikes averaged 2,600 a year in the 1970s; in no year did the figure fall below 2,000. In the 1980s, the level has virtually halved, with the number in 1983 the lowest since 1941. The number of strikes lasting longer than a single day – indicating sustained resistance rather than token protest – has fallen even faster than the overall total. This seeming erosion of the will to struggle has been effectively exploited by many employers – most notably British Leyland – in appealing over the heads of workplace union representatives to employees as individuals. Fatalism in the face of the employers' offensive is doubtless reinforced by the limited success – or in the case of such groups as the steelworkers, the unqualified defeat – of those trade unionists who *have* proved willing to fight.

'Macho management' characterized by a total repudiation of trade unionism is not yet typical of British employers. Three tendencies are, however, widespread. The first is a far greater strategic sophistication than in the past. Large multi-plant (and often transnational) firms pursue centrally co-ordinated objectives, often in the face of union organization still committed to the autonomy of each workplace; the issues on which to risk or even provoke confrontation are often carefully chosen. Secondly, the area of the negotiable has been sharply restricted; managements increasingly insist on their 'right to manage', merely offering to 'consult' with union representatives over production-related questions. Third, piecemeal encroachments have been made on rights of collective organization: notably, in many companies, a cutback in shop steward facilities. Often this is associated with the cultivation of alternative channels of management-worker relations: various forms of 'joint participation' at workplace level, and in some cases Japanese-style 'quality circles' designed to strengthen workers' commitment to the company's production goals.

To date, most large employers have proved less crudely anti-union than the government (often because their perspectives extend to a possible economic recovery and the prospect that union representatives might again constitute useful adjuncts to personnel management). At the level of the state, recession has exposed the fragile nature of the political status acquired by unions in the 1960s and 1970s.

As has already been indicated, the growing involvement of trade unions since the early 1960s in tripartite machinery of consultation and administration reflected government concern to co-opt them within the overall priorities of national economic strategy. The relatively high incidence of strikes in Britain, the restraints imposed by workplace unionism on management's control of production, and the cumulative effects of fragmented wage militancy were all regarded within government as obstacles to national economic performance and competitiveness. The co-operation of union officialdom was viewed as essential in order to control incomes, increase productivity, and restructure collective bargaining procedures. Integration of union nominees within the elaborate if largely powerless mechanisms of national economic planning, and an extensive system of informal contacts and discussions, were viewed as an important means of encouraging union 'responsibility' and strengthening leadership controls over rank-and-file militancy.[15]

These developments rested, not – as some writers have argued – on a philosophy of 'corporatism', but on the pragmatic need of governments to come to terms with the ability of unions and their members to disrupt (however unintentionally) national economic policy. This disruptive potential has inevitably been much diminished by the unions' current economic weakness. Moreover the process of industrial relations 'reform' in which unions have co-operated since the 1960s – rationalized payment systems, productivity bargaining, formalized disciplinary and grievance procedures – has made labour relations far more predictable and manageable than a decade ago. It is plausible to argue that more bureaucratic procedures of collective bargaining have contributed to a growing alienation of ordinary members from their union representatives, both full-time officials and shop stewards. To the extent that workers' identification with their unions has been eroded, the value of union representatives as mediators between state and capital and the working class has been similarly reduced. Thus Thatcher's anti-union policies have an obvious material basis.

Problems of a socialist strategy

Trade unions are a product of capitalism, and are necessarily conditioned by their relationship with capital. Perry Anderson made this point neatly when he wrote that 'trade unions are dialectically both an opposition to capitalism and a component of it'. He went on to argue that 'as institutions, trade unions do not *challenge* the existence of society based on a division of classes, they merely *express* it. Thus trade unions can never be viable vehicles of advance towards socialism in themselves; by their nature they are tied to capitalism. They can bargain within the society, but not transform it.'[16]

Others would regard this as too mechanical a formulation. 'A trade union', declared Gramsci, 'is not a predetermined phenomenon. It *becomes* a determinate institution, i.e. it takes on a definite historical form, to the extent that the strength and will of the workers who are its members impress a policy and propose an aim that define it.'[17] Three questions immediately suggest themselves. In what circumstances, if any, are workers likely to conceive trade unionism as a vehicle for anti-capitalist class struggle? How far could a membership committed to such a goal impress their aspirations on official union policy? And is it possible for trade unions to challenge capitalism without provoking their own suppression? These questions will be pursued by exploring four familiar sets of antitheses: bureaucracy and democracy; compromise and struggle; class action and sectionalism; socialist politics and economism.

It is customary on the Left to discuss internal relationships in unions in terms of a dichotomy between 'bureaucracy' and 'rank and file'. In their cruder versions, such arguments represent an inadequate analysis and a misleading basis for strategy.[18] The term 'rank and file' is a military metaphor without theoretical content; as employed on the Left it has often involved a romantic and idealized conception of workplace action and shop steward militancy, an assumption that workers are held back from anti-capitalist struggle only by the machinations of a corrupt and reactionary leadership. The notion of 'trade union bureaucracy' – a familiar slogan since the foundation of the Comintern – is itself theoretically flaccid. Where does the rank and file end and the bureaucracy begin? In British trade unions, the vast bulk of administrative and representative functions are performed by 'lay' branch and workplace officers rather than full-time officials; in general, the professional officialdom can exercise whatever influence and control they possess only with the assent and co-operation of large sections of this cadre of voluntary activists.[19]

Of course there are occasions when militant union members are sold out by their leaders. But to make such instances the basis for a general theory of trade unionism is to treat officialdom as scapegoats for contradictions which are inherent in union practice as such. There is indeed a problem of bureaucracy within unions, but the problem is not primarily one of the machinations of a distinctive stratum of personnel; rather, it is a question of a corrosive pattern of *internal social relations*. In this sense, bureaucracy is manifest in a differential distribution of expertise and activism; in a dependence of the mass of union members on the initiative and experience of a relatively small group of leaders – both official *and* 'unofficial'. Such dependence *may* be deliberately fostered by leaders anxious to retain a monopoly of information, experience and negotiating opportunities, and to minimize and control the collective relations among the membership. But it can readily develop even in the absence of such manipulative strategies.

There can be little doubt that this has occurred in British trade unionism, particularly in recent years. It is common for trade union activists to bemoan the 'apathy' of most members. Often this implies a somewhat idealized notion of the traditional, committed trade unionist; more importantly, the notion of apathy makes non-active unionists the scape-goats for unions' own failure to involve their membership. In a capitalist society in which notions, on the one hand of individualism, on the other of the common 'national interest' of employers and workers, form part of the 'common sense' of everyday life, unions cannot rely on a *spontaneous* mass identification with principles of working-class collectivism. 'Making trade unionists' has always required a deliberate effort of ideological struggle. But British unions have of late largely abdicated such an effort. This is partly because many have found it possible to boost membership numbers without winning workers' active commitment. Much union growth in the 1970s reflected the spread of closed shop arrangements, bureaucratically administered by employers deducting subscriptions directly from workers' wages. 'Progressive' companies were happy to operate such 'union membership agreements' as a means of simplifying bargaining structures, preventing inter-union rivalry, and offering union officials the disciplinary sanctions needed to police agreements. Recruitment through such means creates no more than paper trade unionists. And the trend towards largely *passive* union membership has been reinforced by the 'reforms' of collective bargaining which have limited the scope for decentralized control of conditions and have generated more hierarchical shop steward organizations closely involved in high-level relations with senior management.

This helps explain the curious paradox of contemporary British unionism. There is a strong tradition of internal democratic life, of active debate and collective decision-making. Yet most union members regard 'the union' as an alien, bureaucratic and even hostile force. The routines of branch agenda, district committee meetings, conference procedure, of motions, amendments and resolutions, involve a minority distinguished by interest and understanding from the bulk of the membership. Lay activists – who often regard themselves as the authentic voice of the rank and file – may be as far (or even further) removed from the sentiments of their constituents as are full-time officials. Thus union democracy can be reduced to the esoteric pastime of exceptional enthusiasts. It is of course this alienation of the majority which provides the considerable working-class assent to current Tory attacks on trade unionism; in particular it explains support for proposals for compulsory introduction of secret individual ballots, an initiative designed to erode still further the collective basis of members' attachment to their unions.

Compromise and collaboration are often regarded as the special prerogatives of union officials; in Wright Mills's famous expression, 'the labor leader is a manager of discontent.'[20] This may in part reflect the material interests and personal ideologies of officialdom; at the very least, to persuade themselves and others of the significance of their role, officials are likely to stress their individual expertise and competence as professional negotiators acting *on behalf* of the members. This can in turn encourage an exaggeration of the importance of reasoned argument within the institutions of collective bargaining, and a depreciation of mass mobilization and struggle as means of pursuing workers' interests. But compromise and collaboration also reflect the more general contradiction indicated at the outset of this chapter. On the one hand, trade union action can represent a threat to capitalism, an obstacle to the exploitation of workers which profitable production requires. For this reason, most employers in the past and many still today have fiercely resisted unionization, and governments committed to sustaining capitalist production relations have sought to obstruct or suppress trade unionism. But on the other hand, trade union representation can assist employers and the state in containing the unrest which workers are always liable to express. Through collective bargaining, workers' grievances can be channelled and accommodated, can be made more manageable and predictable. Even strikes can often be anticipated, and their conduct is usually subject to such routines and regulations that their disruptive potential is minimized.

Collective bargaining creates what Gramsci called 'an industrial legality'.[21] Usually this involves some material concessions to workers, but against the continuing background of management domination and economic oppression these concessions are relatively marginal. Though this does not mean that they are made willingly by employers; and in a period of crisis even modest demands may be viewed as intolerable. At the same time, the 'rule of law' which collective bargaining institutes helps stabilize and legitimize the employer's control. The unspoken (or sometimes explicit) condition on which employers and governments are willing to recognize trade unions is that unions in turn should recognize the employer's right to exploit workers, and should restrict their demands and actions to those compatible with continuing profitability. Officials who are directly concerned with the institutional and financial security of their unions are particularly likely to favour a cautious approach to policy; and those who are constantly engaged in bargaining relationships with managers or state functionaries are particularly liable to take for granted the 'rules of the game' which such relationships presuppose. But such pressures are by no means peculiar to 'bureaucrats': they are evident to militant workplace activists as well. In essence, they reflect the problem of union survival in a hostile environment. Short of revolution, workers' representatives have to come to terms with the oppressor – or else they will be smashed. Compromise is unavoidable. The danger is that a truce or a pragmatic limitation of hostilities can become transformed into a permanent peace and collaboration.

Collaboration is encouraged by the traditional sectionalism of trade union practice. Where workers' struggles encompass only a narrow constituency of interest, the broader framework of class relations must normally remain unchallenged. The focus of action is what can realistically be conceded by a single employer or within a single industry; conceptions of possibility are bounded by the 'external coercive laws' of capitalist production which at this level confront management and workforce alike. Economic crisis has reinforced this lesson, as even militant sections of trade unionism have faced a stark choice between acquiescence in employer demands or wholesale closures and job loss. The sectional basis of union action is moreover ideologically as well as materially weakening. Given the widespread interdependence of modern capitalist production, and the extensive dependence of social life on 'services' provided by the state or private capital, disputes involving one group of workers typically have a disruptive impact on others as producers or consumers. Where struggles are not explicitly related to broader class demands and interests, workers rarely attract spontaneous support from fellow trade unionists, who are indeed likely to regard themselves as victims. Hence politicians and the media have little difficulty in mobilizing hostility among workers to other workers' strikes.

Sectionalism has other damaging implications for trade unionism. Typically, union officials and activists alike derive disproportionately from relatively advantaged sections of the workforce: male, white, those higher-skilled, higher-paid, in more secure jobs. Holders of 'better' types of job commonly enjoy greater self-confidence, familiarity with official procedures, respect among fellow workers, and identification with work and hence work-related institutions: factors all of which tend to encourage involvement in trade unionism and often pave the way to a 'career' as a union activist. Hence hierarchy within the working class is replicated within trade union organization. In identifying grievances, selecting demands, formulating strategies and determining priorities, the perspectives and interests of the dominant sections almost inevitably exert disproportionate influence. Correspondingly, the concerns of women, immigrants, lower-skilled, lower-paid, less secure workers (not to mention the unemployed and casually employed) are subordinated or excluded altogether in the agenda of union action.[22] This in turn is likely to weaken their identification with 'the union', creating a further disincentive to active involvement.

Such biases can occur 'spontaneously' even in unions formally committed to egalitarian principles. But they may also be deliberately built in to union policy. Historically, *exclusiveness* has often been a dominant theme of collective action. Craft unionism was founded on the preservation of restricted access to a monopolized area of work, resisting encroachments by other workers as much as by employers. In the present century, controlling entry to the job has often seemed the only means of mitigating the disruptive insecurity of the labour market. But as part of such control, the lines of demarcation have often been based upon criteria of sexism (quite openly, until recently at least) or racism (perhaps more usually, covertly). By such means, trade unionism can not only reflect but actually reinforce divisions and antagonisms within the working class.[23]

The tendencies towards bureaucratic practice, collaborative policy and sectional orientation are all associated with a segregation between union strategy and working-class politics. In Russia at the turn of the century, this 'economism' was denounced by Lenin. In the USA, such 'business unionism' is commonly applauded. In Britain, the majority of the larger unions are affiliated to the Labour Party, and professions of socialism are a familiar part of conference rhetoric. But traditionally there has been a sharp demarcation between 'political action' which is the party's responsibility, and 'industrial relations' where the unions concentrate their attention. Within this sphere, 'free collective bargaining' rather than any form of socialist politics provides the guiding principle. The slogan is in one sense absurd: collective bargaining, necessarily, is in large measure the outcome of the more general balance of class forces; and in recent years it has increasingly been conditioned by state intervention (thus dissolving the artificial boundary between 'industrial relations' and 'politics'). But the preoccupation with collective bargaining has tended to exclude any meaningful attention to the possibilities of social transformation; has entailed fundamental commitment to the parochial interests of each discrete 'bargaining unit'; and has increased the dependence of the ordinary membership on those who display the appropriate 'negotiating skills'. The subordination of politics to collective bargaining has meant that even radical trade union strategies are normally essentially *national* in focus (as, for example, in the case of most demands for import controls); the principles of international class solidarity, of common interests in resisting transnational capital, rarely intrude upon the agenda.

What is to be done? The central argument of this chapter is that trade unions operate within an environment of hostile forces which condition and distort their character and dynamics. Bureaucracy, collaboration, sectionalism and economism are all reflections of these potent external forces. Bureaucracy, collaboration, sectionalism and economism are powerful and often overwhelming tendencies; but they are not uncontradictory and irresistible 'iron laws'. The contradictions inherent in trade unionism – as in the experience and consciousness of workers within capitalist society – create space for socialists. The malleability of unions is doubtless limited: many appear rigid and ossified institutions. But in any union there is some scope for members to fight for more democratic patterns of internal relations; for more radical aims and imaginative forms of struggle; for strategies which broaden solidarity among different groups of workers; for policies informed by socialist politics.

Trade unions are *at one and the same time* part of the problem and part of the solution, a form of resistance to capitalism and a form of integration within capitalism. Trade unions can never become fully anti-capitalist organizations, but socialists can help strengthen their anti-capitalist tendencies. They can never be more than one element in a multiplicity of forms of resistance to capitalism, a resistance which must encompass action in every arena of oppression (and not simply the sphere of wage-labour); but they can form an important and indeed essential element in such a wider movement. In recent years, many socialists have rejected the 'workerism' which for so long dominated the British Left: the identification of the working class with a muscular male hewing coal or hammering metal, and the assumption that the trade union militancy associated with such stereotypes was the only valid expression of class struggle. Today it is obvious that we need a broader, more varied conception of the working class; and a far more sensitive appreciation of the range of collective experience and action in which socialist imagination and commitment can be forged. But any credible movement for socialism must still recognize the key importance for analysis and strategy of struggles 'at the point of production'. The collective mobilization inherent in trade unionism remains the most significant example which we have of sustained working-class challenge to the underlying principles of capitalist society; the struggle for socialism must build, though critically, upon this tradition.

6

The Women's Movement: Patterns of Oppression and Resistance

SARAH PERRIGO

When the women's liberation movement emerged in the late 1960s it seemed to many contemporaries to appear like a bolt out of the blue. Since then it has been hailed by some on the Left as the most hopeful sign for social change in the post-war era; others have denigrated it as a divisive bourgeois irrelevance. My aim in this chapter is to outline women's oppression today and to examine the kind of policies the women's movement has developed in order to overcome that oppression.

There are at the outset real difficulties in defining the women's movement; who is to count as part of it and what does it mean to be a feminist? The women's movement in Britain has from its very beginning consciously avoided conventional political organizational forms; there is no formal membership, no committees which may speak for the movement, no constitution or set of principles which all must subscribe to. In a sense all women who meet together to explore their feelings, powerlessness and oppression and who fight to eradicate sexual inequality must be said to be part of the movement whatever their different ideological or theoretical perspectives might be. As Shrew said in 1969: 'our first priority isn't to get over information, but to know what everyone in the room thinks. We believe in getting people to interact, not to listen to experts. We want them to themselves make an analysis of their situation which will lead them to action.'[1]

A defining and enduring feature of the women's movement is its commitment to a radical egalitarianism premised on the view that all women have the ability to be active in the movement without leaders or experts. This view has left individual women free to engage in whatever activity they think is most important for them in their specific situation. In many ways this approach has been very effective in drawing in enormous numbers of women into political activity. Some have begun to argue, however, that this may not be the most effective way to promote and defend women's interests in the present period. The women's movement was born in the heady time of the 1960s when everything seemed possible. The pioneering of a new movement created enormous energy and optimism. Since then the political and economic climate has changed dramatically. The severe economic crisis and governmental policy have combined to threaten and reverse many of the gains won by the movement in the 1970s. In these conditions there are feminists who are urging a more coherent and united political programme with clear objectives and priorities around which women can mobilize.

Situating women in contemporary Britain

The common and specific oppression of women

What is the nature of the oppression that the women's movement has begun to challenge? It is argued by feminists that all women regardless of class and race suffer specific oppressions. All women are subjected to an ideology which stresses gender difference; such difference being inscribed in all the institutions and practices of society. Whatever else institutions and practices 'are', they are patriarchal in the sense that they differentiate between men and women and assign to women inferior and dependent positions *vis-à-vis* men. Thus for example all women in western capitalist societies are expected to be sexually attractive to men, to be passive, pliant and pleasing. The major social function assigned to women is that of wife and mother located firmly within a privatized family household system. All other functions whether in paid work or more generally in public life are held to be of secondary importance. Women are therefore conspicuous by their absence in positions of power and authority, and in paid work generally women have lower-paid and less secure jobs. Though all facets of life are permeated by sexist attitudes and assumptions, women's oppression is most firmly located in central institutions and practices which have to a large degree determined the women's movement's focus for struggle and change.[2]

The family

For many feminists women's oppression is most firmly located within the family understood both as an historically specific and an economic institution and ideology – that is, as an ideal representation of what families are assumed to be. The dominant contemporary 'idea' of the family is of a man and a woman united by marriage living as a single household with their children. Within this household there is a strict division of function determined by gender. The man/husband/father is head of the household; he is presumed to be the breadwinner and has obligations to provide materially for his wife and children. The wife/mother on the other hand is presumed to be dependent economically upon her husband. She is expected to service her husband and children through the performance of unpaid domestic labour and childcare. This idealized family is represented as natural and timeless as well as essential to the stability and well-being of society as a whole.

In fact of course few families conform to the ideal representation. Increasing numbers of married women perform paid work outside the family. Households themselves are extremely varied; many, especially the elderly, live alone; there are couples without children; there are a growing number of single parent households.

This reality of a diversity of family forms does not, however, appear to weaken the effects of the ideal assumptions. Though vast numbers of married women are in paid employment they still take responsibility for the bulk of domestic work and childcare. Their responsibilities as wives and mothers determine the kind of paid work they can perform and the wages they receive. Most married women remain economically dependent whether or not they are in employment. Further, as we shall see, such assumptions regarding women's role underline those policies of the state in relation to women which seek to reinforce women's dependence economically and emotionally. The family is clearly an emotive subject. It is often portrayed as a centre of warmth and affection, a refuge from the outside world where social relations are predominantly instrumental and impersonal. Clearly there is an element of truth in this, which might explain why many women as well as men react so fiercely when the 'family' is criticized. However, behind the myth of domestic harmony exists another side of family life where women (and children) are subjected to physical and mental cruelty and abuse. Domestic violence, the dependence of women on men, economically and psychologically, and the sexual division of labour in the home, have all been part of feminist critiques of familial ideology and practice.

Women and waged labour

As we have seen women's position in the labour market is structured to a large degree by their position within the family. Familial ideology is reflected in the attitudes and behaviour of employers, the state and most male trade unionists. Women have steadily increased their percentage in the workforce over the century, now constituting around 42 per cent; 62 per cent of working women are married and half of all married women work. Despite this, women workers are viewed as marginal and secondary.

Women's work is characterized by its high concentration and by its low pay and social status. In terms of concentration over 75 per cent of all women workers are in the service sector, working for example as cooks, cleaners, caterers, nurses, secretaries and hairdressers. In manufacturing, too, women are found in a narrow range of industries. Over half of all women employed in the manufacturing sector are in just four areas: food and drink, clothing and footwear, textiles and electrical engineering. Only 13.5 per cent of women in 1971 were classified as skilled manual workers. In the professions a similar concentration is found: women are the primary school teachers, the social workers and the nurses. Very few are lawyers, architects, bankers, scientists or engineers.

Women's work tends to have low social status. Because of assumptions about gender appropriateness much of the work women perform is seen as 'women's work' in that it so closely resembles the domestic work they perform in the family. Women's work tends also to be low-paid. This is partly due to the social status associated with women's work. It is compounded by the fact that many women work part-time (around 23 per cent in 1975) and that men are more likely to increase their earnings by overtime payments. Despite the Equal Pay Act in 1983 women's hourly earnings (excluding overtime) constitute 73 per cent of that of men. When overtime was included women's gross weekly earnings were merely 63.6 per cent of that of men.

The state

The state plays a crucial part in the oppression of women. Increasingly in the twentieth century the state has intervened actively to construct and maintain the particular family form described earlier. Welfare provision with its system of incentives and disincentives acts as a way of conserving men as breadwinners and women as dependants with primary responsibility for childcare and domestic work. Though there have been some changes in recent years due to feminist pressure, taxation, supplementary benefits and National Insurance are still determined by marital status and assumptions of female dependency. State policy acts as a major disincentive to women combining paid work with family responsibilities, because of its failure to provide adequate nursery provision and other necessary support services. Only in 1975 with the Employment Protection Act did most women obtain adequate maternity leave and even this is under threat by the present Tory government. Other social provision, or its lack, has an important effect upon women's lives; care for the elderly, the sick and the disabled clearly falls upon women when state provision is inadequate and under-resourced as is increasingly the case at the present time. Elizabeth Wilson has summed up the social welfare policies of the state as amounting to no less than the state organization of domestic life.[3] Through its control of abortion and birth-control facilities the state even plays an important role in controlling women's reproductive life.

It is not only state intervention, however, which plays a part in reproducing and maintaining women's oppression. The state clearly intervenes in the family and personal life; yet in many instances the state, using as its justification the idea of the family and personal life as a purely private and non-political sphere, refuses to intervene. This is particularly the case in incidents of domestic violence where the refusal to act to protect women leaves the system of domination and subordination unchanged. This refusal to interfere serves to mystify the real power the state has to determine the behaviour and expectations of both men and women. It can be seen to construct divisions between public and private, and between the state and civil society, which have the effect of 'depoliticizing' economic decision-making and the allocation of scarce resources, and of preserving the existing power relations between men and women.

Culture and the construction of sexuality

I have attempted to show how familial and sexist assumptions pervade the practices of the family, the labour market and the state. They do not stop there, however, but are present in our culture in a pervasive and insidious manner. Education, the media, films and advertisements are replete with images of women which serve to demean, devalue and restrict the scope for the development of a positive self-image for the majority of women, and thus determine the kinds of personal and sexual relations they will enter into. A cultural representation of masculinity and femininity (which is constantly identified with biological men and women) generally assigns to men most of the socially desirable characteristics (or at least the ones which are most rewarded) such as assertiveness, confidence and independence. To women it assigns dependence, passivity and conformism. Nowhere is this more clearly demonstrated than in the area of sexuality. Despite the so-called 'liberalization' of attitudes towards sexuality and sexual practice in the 1960s women's sexuality remains firmly constructed as vicarious; defined in relationship to men and their wishes and desires. Ideas of female sexuality reinforce and reproduce women's dependence upon men in an extremely powerful way. Both male and female sexuality is constructed on the assumption of heterosexual normality. Male sexuality is held to be virile, powerful, aggressive and uncontrollable; it is penetrating, forceful and dominant. Female sexuality on the other hand is held to be receptive, passive and submissive. The object of male sexuality is the attractive female; hence women must appeal – must become sex objects for the satisfaction of male sexual needs. The contradictions surrounding female sexuality are abundant. Though less obvious than in the past the double standard for judging sexual behaviour still continues to be a dominant theme of conventional morality. Good women are expected to be chaste or at least sexually constrained before marriage and after to be monogamous and faithful. Sexual promiscuity which is considered as normal for males is identified with deviancy or prostitution in females.

Strands and perspectives in the movement

Attitudes towards women's oppression vary widely among feminists. It has already been stated that the women's movement is not some monolithic organization with a unified view of the causes and remedies for women's oppression. Though positions are shifting and overlapping, there are, at the cost of over-simplifying, perhaps three dominant approaches to women's liberation within the movement.

Liberal feminism

The liberal feminist position with its stress on equal rights, though dominant in the first wave of feminism, is relatively weak within the contemporary British movement. In other countries, particularly the USA and Scandinavia, it is much stronger and more influential. Whilst accepting that women are oppressed and discriminated against at the present time the liberal feminist position argues that progressive reforms in the field of legislation and education can bring about equality without the necessity of radical or revolutionary social change. The focus of their activity is on the opening up of positions of power and authority to women so that they can begin to compete with men on equal terms. The American National Organization of Women (NOW) document of aims illustrates this position quite succinctly. 'To take action to bring women into the mainstream of American society now, expressing all the privileges and responsibilities thereof in a truly equal partnership with men.' NOW sought therefore through a package of reform proposals to 'remove the legal and economic barriers to women's progress in a competitive world'. In terms of specific proposals the Bill of Rights formulated by NOW in 1967 is not that unlike many of the demands formulated by the British movement between 1970–5. They both include demands for childcare provision, equal opportunities in education, and the right to control reproduction. However the British movement has been far more pessimistic about the possibility of incremental reforms of this nature achieving real emancipation from oppressive conditions for many women. Many argue that such reforms will only really benefit those professional and educated women who are already privileged *vis-à-vis* others of their sex. This is not to say that many British feminists, especially socialist feminists, have not become involved in pressing for positive action of this kind, only that they have not seen it as an end in itself but as a part of a wider struggle for more fundamental social and political change. They would argue that for equal opportunities to be really effective it would mean women being represented in all positions in accordance with their numbers in the population; that is 52 per cent of judges, politicians, scientists, plumbers and electricians. Such a state of affairs it is argued is not possible without a radical reconstruction of time, work, home and family life, in short a political and social revolution.

Further it is argued that the kind of equality suggested by equal rights feminists is undesirable and male-defined. Its aim is for women to be equal to compete with men on their terms. Many feminists have a totally different object, which is the wholesale transformation of masculinity and femininity, and of the sexual division of labour, which involves a radically different view of equality.

Radical revolutionary feminism

For radical feminists the causes of women's oppression are clear. They lie in the patriarchal structure of society whereby women are systematically controlled and exploited by men for their benefit. The strategy for women must be the destruction of this male power through the development of a sexual politics which focuses directly upon the ways in which men dominate women. In practice this means that the focal points of attack are the institution of marriage, the family, and sexuality, and the control of reproduction. Radical feminists believe that women are controlled by men in a multitude of ways. At one end of the spectrum they have emphasized the part violence or its threat plays in keeping women 'in their place'. Their exposure and analysis of domestic violence and rape have demonstrated the ways violence and its threat controls and intimidates all women. But violence is not only the most blatant and obvious manifestation of male power. They have pointed to the more subtle ways in which male power is exercised and through which women have 'consented' to their own domination, thereby thwarting their potential for autonomy and liberation. For this reason the monogamous family as a major institution of patriarchal power is the prime target for attack. Conceptions of love, sex, marriage and domestic bliss must be exposed for what they are: mechanisms for binding women to their oppressors in the most intimate way. In the search for love and romance, intimacy and human companionship women are forced to collude in their own subjection. As Sally Alexander and Barbara Taylor have said, 'In learning to love men we learn also to subordinate ourselves to them. The ropes which bind women are the hardest to cut because they are woven with too many of our own desires.'[4]

If the aim of the women's movement is the destruction of male power women must struggle to liberate themselves from male-female relationships as presently constituted. They must learn to develop their own power within and between themselves. Hence the bedrock insistence on the part of radical feminists on the autonomy of the women's movement from all others. Sisterhood is the potent symbol of this process whereby women strive to rid themselves of their dependence upon men both physically and emotionally in order to destroy once and for all the 'father' in the head. Many radical feminists are profoundly sceptical of women's ability to liberate themselves without withdrawing from personal relations with men at least in the short term. Thus a main part of a radical feminist strategy is the building of an alternative culture – a counter hegemony to the dominant male-defined culture, and an alternative living situation to the present family system where women can support each other, bring up children if they wish, and learn to love and respect each other free from male intrusions.

Although the original impetus in developing an all-female environment was to allow women to define themselves, 'free' from male-defined definitions, for some feminists it has led to a celebration of femininity as conventionally understood and to the view that feminine *values* are *ipso facto* superior to masculine ones and that men as 'bearers' of masculinity should be blamed for all the evils of the world. Aspects of this are to be found in the women's peace movement as well as in the slogan that all men are potential rapists/wife batterers, etc. Other feminists have been alarmed by this position. First, it comes dangerously close to the biological argument that men and women are by nature fundamentally different, an argument more usually employed by male supremacists.[5] Second, if women are different by nature it is unclear what kind of world such feminists would envisage in the future other than a kind of matriarchy: a mirror image of patriarchy with all the aspects of subjection and domination merely reversed.

Socialist feminism

Socialist feminists share many of the concerns of radical feminists but they insist that women's oppression cannot be explained simply as a result of male power. Women's oppression must be located in a complex interplay of both capitalist and patriarchal imperatives. In practice, as Michelle Barratt and others have pointed out, it is often impossible to separate out the influence of capitalism and men in the reproduction of women's oppressive conditions; in many cases their interests coincide. For example capital may have an interest in the reproduction of an efficient and reasonably healthy labour force provided through a particular family form;

the family form may further act as a conservative force transmitting social values desirable for maintaining that particular system. At the same time it not only serves male interests through the provision of the domestic labour and servicing that women provide free, but also helps to maintain men's economic dominance over women. Similarly in production: capital may well demand that a sector of the population be available as a reserve army of labour, cheap and expendable. That women largely constitute the reserve army also satisfies male interests in the perpetuation of its monopoly of skill and pay within the labour market. Several socialist feminists have pointed to the ways in which conflicts between capital and labour are frequently solved at the expense of women.

The object of socialist feminism is to develop a strategy that will simultaneously attack both male power and capitalism; which will abolish class exploitation whilst at the same time radically restructuring male and female relationships. In practice this means that socialist feminists are not only active in the development of sexual politics but in the incorporation of this into the male-dominated left of the labour and socialist movement through their work in trade unions, the Labour Party and other left-wing groups. Working within the socialist and labour movement reflects a real concern that the women's movement in Britain remains dominated by white, middle-class and highly-educated feminists. Though all women may suffer the effects of patriarchal oppression, the context of that oppression varies significantly by class and ethnic origin. The ideal of 'sisterhood' is not unproblematic and often masks real, material differences between women. For women whose daily experience is of grinding poverty, bad housing, unemployment and racialism, feminist demands often appear irrelevant to their needs, particularly if they are not part of a wider strategy which challenges the structure of class and racial inequality. Prioritizing issues such as low pay, bad working conditions, part-time work and the lack of resources allocated to women is seen by socialist feminists as an important step in building a strategy for women's liberation within this wider context.

The politics of the women's movement

Given the insidious and diffused nature of women's oppression and the various explanations of that oppression that exist one should not be surprised to find feminists involved in a wide variety of different forms of activity. In what follows I will attempt to give an overview of the sorts of political activity that the women's movement has generated.

The small group

The women's movement in a sense was born when groups of women in different parts of the country began to meet with each other in order to explore their experiences of being female in our society. These informal groups provided the early nucleus of the movement. Many of the groups began initially as consciousness-raising groups, where in an atmosphere of trust and support women could share their feelings of powerlessness, frustration and anger and could begin to develop a sense of solidarity and sisterhood with other women. The idea was that such CR groups would generate action as women began to realize the structural and political nature of their experiences. Clearly in the early days of the movement this worked effectively. Out of discussion and the sharing of experience came theoretical understanding and the will to act. The kinds of activity varied from place to place. Many initiatives were local and community based in order to involve as many women as possible. Campaigns over issues such as nurseries and women's health spread rapidly from place to place, as did the idea of setting up local women's centres. The importance of community-based activity clearly fits with the movement's stress on egalitarian and democratic forms of political struggle. It also provided an appropriate setting for involving women not normally active politically. Women's lives on the whole are more rooted in the neighbourhood where they live than are men's. In many ways this strategy proved enormously successful and transformed the lives of many who had never previously been engaged in political struggle at all. However on many issues there was a perceived need to co-ordinate campaigns on a national scale if certain objectives were to be realized.

The national campaigns

A variety of feminist campaigns emerged throughout the 1970s. Between 1970 and 1976 the women's movement held national conferences which formulated a series of demands. Many of these specific demands provided the basis for nationally co-ordinated campaigns of action. Many of the campaigns described here are part of a strategy for constructing a sexual politics, focusing as they do on sexuality, reproductive control and the issue of male violence. Others are more related to the promotion of equal rights and the eradication of legal discrimination against women and the development of a policy of positive action.

The campaign for the control of reproduction –
NAC and the Women's Reproductive Rights Campaign

The right to choose if and when to bear children is seen by almost all feminists as crucial for women's self-determination and is part of a woman's right to control her own body and define her own sexuality. The third demand of the Oxford Conference of 1970 read 'free contraception and abortion on demand'. From the 1920s feminists and social reformers had been pressing for both the availability of birth-control and for the liberalization of the laws regulating abortions. It was not until the early 1960s that contraception became freely available on the National Health Service and not until 1967 that the laws on abortion were relaxed with the passing of David Steel's Abortion Act. The 1967 Bill legalized abortion up to 28 weeks of pregnancy provided two registered doctors agreed that otherwise the life or health of the mother or of the children would be at risk, or that the baby was likely to be handicapped. The Act was passed in the liberal climate of the 1960s, helped by a sympathetic Labour government and the thalidomide scandal. For many feminists the Act is flawed in that it was clearly designed to help 'abnormal' or 'inadequate' women rather than to establish abortion as a right which women as bearers of children have. However, for most of its life the women's movement has been actively involved in defending the Act from repeated attempts to amend or restrict its scope. Immediately after the Act was passed the counter-abortion lobby began to organize. The National Abortion Campaign (NAC) came into existence in 1972 explicitly to counter this offensive. The NAC campaigns have frequently been cited as a very successful instance of women's movement politics. Certainly to date NAC has successfully defeated the anti-abortion lobby. In July 1975, in response to James White's Bill it mobilized around 20,000 supporters to demonstrate in defence of a woman's right to choose. It has not been shy of collaborating with other sections of the pro-abortion lobby such as Abortion Law Reform Association (ALRA) and has provided information for Labour Party women who spearheaded the campaign in parliament to defend the 1967 Act. NAC members have been active in the unions and have succeeded in gaining TUC support for the pro-abortion lobby.

NAC has at the same time come in for criticism by some feminists. Some have resented the fact that men have been involved in the campaign. Some members of NAC have campaigned for the organization to widen its sphere of activity to cover other aspects of women's rights to control their own fertility to include such issues as contraception, sterilization and the development of reproductive technology. At the NAC National Conference in September 1983 it was clear that there was a wide split in NAC on this issue. This led to the formation of the Women's Reproductive Rights Group whose aim is to campaign on this broader front. It is too early to state how successful this campaign will be. It has already begun to campaign vigorously against the attempts to deny contraceptive advice to girls under 16 without their parents' consent. It may offer a way forward for linking the various aspects of women's reproductive rights in a coherent programme rather than remaining a single issue campaign defending a less than perfect abortion provision. It may also draw new women into the movement, particularly black women for whom the problem is not lack of abortion facilities but attempts by the state to control their reproduction through forced sterilization and the use of inadequately tested contraceptive drugs.

Campaigns against male violence

In 1976 an international tribunal on crimes against women was held in Brussels which produced evidence from all over the world on the violent abuse of women, from genital mutilation to wife battering and rape. Before the rise of the women's movement these issues had hardly appeared on the agenda of any political group. Rape and wife abuse were thought of as isolated, sporadic and abnormal if regrettable occurrences of male violence. For many feminists such violence was seen as a major manifestation of male power. Campaigns over male violence have, however, led to deep controversy within the women's movement. Though all feminists are obviously outraged by the levels of violence against women they have vehemently disagreed over the question of who is to blame: whether it is men *per se*, or the structure of patriarchy with its social construction of masculinity and femininity. Some feminists have felt that a wholesale attack on men as individuals through such slogans as 'all men are potential rapists' is not only misleading but serves to drive many otherwise sympathetic women away from such campaigns.

The first campaigns centred around the plight of battered women and served to highlight the gross neglect of this issue by politicians; they pointed to the lack of social provision for women in such circumstances. The first Women's Aid refuge was founded in Chiswick in 1970 and by the mid-1970s there were over a hundred such refuges all run on participatory, democratic lines, offering support, temporary accommodation and legal advice to victims of domestic violence. A National Women's Aid Federation was established which forced the politicians and the public to take the issue seriously and led to a series of legislative reforms which gave improved protection to women against their violent cohabitees and imposed certain obligations on local authorities to rehouse women. The Federation has also campaigned for law enforcement agencies, particularly the police, to treat such violence seriously rather than to trivialize it as a domestic and private issue between husbands and wives in which they should not become involved.

Rape, too, became a major focus of concern in the 1970s. Feminist analyses of the widespread, almost universal, crime of rape seemed to many a major manifestation of patriarchal power rather than the act of abnormal over-sexed men egged on by sexually provocative women. The first Rape Crisis Centre was opened in London in the 1970s and was soon followed by others up and down the country. These centres offer counselling and advice and support to rape victims and help such victims deal with the gruelling experience of having to deal with the police and the medical authorities if and when they report incidences of rape. The campaigning group Women Against Rape was formed in 1976. It has campaigned to change public attitudes and understanding of rape and to change the law so that women victims of rape are not seen as culpable victims 'who asked for it'. The group has argued persuasively that a woman's previous sexual activities are irrelevant to the issue of whether she was raped or not. This led to some success with the passing of the Sexual Offences Act of 1976. The group also campaigned to extend the crime of rape to husbands, arguing that marriage does not give men unconditional rights of access to their wives' body without their consent. Its concern with the ways in which rape is presented in the media, generally reflecting as it does patriarchal notions of male and female sexuality with its implied message that women enjoy being raped, has meant that campaigns over rape have been closely connected with campaigns over sexuality, pornography, attitudes towards prostitution and generally to the cultural productions of gender.

In the late 1970s, after a particularly brutal spate of murders in Leeds, more general campaigns on the whole issue of male violence developed. The 'Reclaim the Night' marches attracted thousands of women who marched at night for the right to walk the streets in safety without fear of attack from men. The group 'Women against Violence against Women' which began in 1980 has extended this concern to an attack on pornography and sex shops as purveyors of violent and sadistic images of male and female sexuality which, it is argued, not only insult and degrade all women but which foster and encourage rape and other forms of female sexual abuse.

Sexuality

Campaigns over male violence have been closely connected with a general feminist attack on male-defined sexuality. One of the earliest feminist actions was the attack on the Miss World competition which seemed to many to symbolize the objectification of women's bodies and the consequent degradation and contempt with which women are treated. Groups of women such as the Women in Media group and Women's Report have led a concerted campaign against the media and advertising, attacking the various ways in which women are stereotyped, trivialized and demeaned. It is difficult to gauge the success of these campaigns. Officially for example, the National Union of Journalists has taken the issue seriously, producing guidelines for promoting equality through journalism. Clause 10 of the NUJ's code of conduct states 'a journalist shall not originate material which encourages discrimination on the grounds of race, creed, gender or sexual orientation'; and officially members who break the code can be punished. However the guidelines have been widely ignored and the NUJ has failed to enforce its code of conduct. In advertising the Advertising Standards Authority (ASA), though it has come under pressure from the women's movement, has refused to take action to bar sexist advertisements and women's bodies continue to be used to sell everything from motor bikes to spare parts. It is extraordinarily difficult to sum up the activities women have engaged in in this area, or to assess their success. Campaigns over sexual harassment at work have highlighted the seriousness of a type of sexual abuse which leads to misery, victimization and intimidation of women at work. Campaigns by prostitutes against police harassment have highlighted the sexual double standard, particularly of the police who harass and intimidate prostitutes while ignoring the curb crawlers, pimps and organized crime that lies behind much prostitution. Finally, and for many feminists most importantly, there have been vigorous campaigns over the rights of women to determine their own sexual orientation, and these have organized action against the discrimination of lesbians in employment and as mothers.

These campaigns have stimulated a public debate over issues that previously had lain silent and unacknowledged and have led to some real questioning of stereotypical attitudes and forms of behaviour. At the same time conventional images of masculinity and femininity have remained firmly inbedded within our culture and they will persist unless there is some radical restructuring of the relationships of power between men and women.

The Equal Pay Act and the Sex Discrimination Act considered

For reasons outlined earlier many feminists in Britain have been sceptical of the power of equal rights campaigns to alter radically the balance of power between men and women. The passing of the Equal Pay Act in 1970 and to some extent the Sex Discrimination Act in 1975 owes more to sections of the trade-union movement and the Labour Party (as well as the need to conform to EEC regulations) than it does to pressure by the Women's Movement. However when these Acts came into force organizations such as the Rights of Women Unit of the National Council of Civil Liberties (NCCL) and the Campaign for the Legal and Financial Independence of Women came into existence to defend and strengthen equal rights provision and to rectify discriminatory practices in areas excluded from the Act.

The demand for equal pay legislation has been TUC policy since the 1880s, though little was achieved in this direction until the post-war period when teachers and civil servants secured equal pay. In 1964 the Labour government published its commitment to equal pay in its manifesto and in 1970 the Equal Pay Act was passed. The Act stipulated that women should receive equal pay with men doing the same or equivalent jobs. Machinery for complaints was to be the same as for other industrial disputes: ACAS, industrial tribunals and in the last resort employment appeals tribunal. The Sex Discrimination Act was intended to supplement and reinforce the Equal Pay Act. It aimed to eliminate sex discrimination in employment, education, housing and the provision of other facilities and services. Significantly the Act excluded certain areas such as Social Security, pensions, taxation, immigration and nationality law and birth-control provision. The results of the Acts have proved disappointing. Sadie Robart writing for the NCCL in 1981 wrote 'there are no notable signs that deeply entrenched patterns of discrimination which serve to perpetuate job segregation and unequal pay have been disturbed by the new laws.[6]

The Equal Pay Act had some initial impact in narrowing wage differentials but by 1980 they had begun to widen again. The major problem with the Equal Pay Act is that it only applies to men and women doing very similar work. Given the extraordinarily sex-segregated nature of the labour market few women are actually covered by the Act. Employers are seen to have evaded the Act, for example by regrading men's and women's jobs so that they do not come under its umbrella. For some time feminists have been demanding that equal pay be extended to include work of equal value which would allow women to compare themselves to some notional man doing the same work. Their demand has been strengthened by a recent EEC court ruling that British legislation on equal pay falls short of the EEC regulations. To date the government has refused to act to deal with this issue satisfactorily. In December 1983 Jo Richardson introduced a private member's Sex Equality Bill which, along with other proposals, would have extended the scope of the Equal Pay Act to the benefit of many women, including the large numbers of women part-time workers. The Bill was defeated by the Tory House of Commons but given the pressure from women within and outside the Labour Party it is likely that similar legislation will be introduced if a Labour government is returned to parliament at the next election.

The Sex Discrimination Act is similarly full of loopholes. It is often extraordinarily difficult to prove discrimination under the Act. The Equal Opportunities Commission which was established with the Act to monitor its workings, to issue non-discriminatory orders when necessary, and to investigate and recommend policy changes in equal opportunity policy, has, despite some notable successes, acted very cautiously. Campbell and Coote conclude that its record to date has in fact been abysmal in that it lacks both the political will and the expertise to act decisively.[7] Moreover, although the Sex Discrimination Act has made some provision for positive discrimination for women in areas of training and employment, in those areas traditionally seen as male preserves unions and employers on the whole have been tardy in promoting such policies.

A major problem with both the Acts is that women on the whole are not aware of their rights under the Acts and even if they are aware are fearful of taking action for fear of victimization and intimidation. Many women, especially from the working class and women in ethnic minorities, are caught in a vicious circle. Entrapped within dominant views regarding male and female appropriate behaviour they lack the confidence and the knowledge to use the law. Without that the law remains an inadequate vehicle for the advancement of sexual equality.

The Campaign for Financial and Legal Independence for Women

Founded in 1975 the Campaign for Financial and Legal Independence for Women set itself up specifically to campaign against the idea that husband, wife or cohabitee form a single economic unit. Their target has been those areas specifically excluded from the Sex Discrimination Act such as pensions, Social Security and taxation. They have demanded that each individual should be treated separately and have argued vehemently that equal pay, for example, will only become a reality when the myth of the male breadwinner which is supported by state policy has been completely abolished. Amongst a variety of activities which centre around the financial and legal independence of women they have produced pamphlets, given evidence to parliamentary committees on pensions and the cohabitaton rule and have also played an important part in the 1977 'Why Be a Wife' campaign. This publicized the ways in which marriage and cohabitation transform women as persons in the eyes of the state and the legal system to dependants with inferior claims on resources. The campaigns have had some limited effects. The 1975 Social Security Pensions Act and the Social Security Benefits Act of the same year have modified the principle of a wife's dependence on her husband to some extent. Many anomalies, however, still remain. Particularly resented is the Supplementary Benefit scheme which is non-insured and means-tested. Benefit here is assessed on the principle that where a husband and wife are members of the same household the requirements and resources shall be aggregated and shall be treated as the husband's. This rule applies similarly to cohabiting couples.

Feminist action and local authority equal opportunities programmes. The development of women's committees

The 1980s have seen the involvement of feminists in the development of local authority equal opportunities programmes. Given the inhospitable climate for progress at national level local authorities controlled by progressive Labour councils have appeared to offer a rather more favourable terrain for feminists' initiatives. Initial pressure for action on equal opportunities came through public concern with race issues in the

wake of the inner-city riots. Several local authorities declared themselves
to be equal opportunity employers at which point political activists in and
outside the Labour Party began to push for positive action to ensure that
the expressions of commitment to equality of opportunity meant
something in reality. The impetus to set up equal opportunities for women
units came from a variety of sources. In London it came mainly from
feminists active in the Labour Party as councillors or as constituency
activists. In Sheffield the pressure was exerted initially by local government
officers in the Department of Employment; and in Leeds it came from
outside both the council and the Labour Party, from feminists in the area.

In some areas the setting up of equal opportunities units has been
accompanied by the development of women's committees. The GLC was
the first to set up a women's committee in 1982. Since then many of the
London boroughs and cities such as Leeds have followed a similar path.
Such committees have clearly developed out of feminist concerns to widen
the democratic process of policy and decision-making with the aim of
making local authorities more responsive to the needs of women both in
terms of employment practices and in the provision of services in areas
such as housing, transport, education and nurseries. Many of the
committees include not just councillors but representatives of women's
organizations in the community. In Leeds for example its representatives
were elected at a conference widely advertised locally. Many women's
committees have open meetings which are also widely advertised to
encourage the attendance of women to discuss policy and resource
provision. Working groups have been set up to discuss policies in particular
areas and to provide information to the formally elected women's
committees. In London much of the work of the working groups has now
been put together in a draft programme 'Action for Women in London'.

It is too early to say how effective these new initiatives will be. The GLC
Women's Committee, which is one of the few with a large budget and
therefore powerful resources, will disappear if the government is successful
in its intentions to abolish the GLC and the metropolitan councils. In other
local authorities, central government control of finances is such that the
resources available for equal opportunities programmes and women's committees are extremely limited. Beyond the merely financial constraints,
equal opportunity offices of women's committees are often faced with local
government bureaucrats who have little sympathy or understanding of the
women's movement. Further the fear of incorporation and the danger of
what some have called a 'femocracy' has left many feminists uneasy about
these kinds of initiatives. At the same time feminists feel that a willingness
to confront Labour bureaucracies and to construct alliances with sympathetic local politicians, trade unionists and local authority workers may
prove effective in defending some of the rights women have won in the past

decade and may provide a basis for a more coherent feminist politics in the future.

Women in the labour movement – the trade unions and the Labour Party

From the beginning of the movement there have been women who have defined themselves as both socialist and feminist. Indeed some of the earliest debates within feminism were over the relationship of the movement to the Left, between those who were committed to the autonomy of the movement and totally refused to work with men at all and those who believed it important to struggle for the acceptance of feminist ideas in the male-dominated organized Left if their ideas were to have any real influence on the lives of most women.

The trade unions

With the massive post-war increase in women's paid employment there was a dramatic increase in women's membership of trade unions. In 1983 there were over 3.5 million women in trade unions. Yet unions still remain bastions of male power and privilege. Few union leaders are women and the policy of the unions and the TUC still reflect the interests and outlook of male experience. The struggle to change the situation has been slow and painful though there are signs that some of the unions have begun to take the issue of sexual inequality more seriously. By 1975 feminists had succeeded in pushing the TUC to adopt most of the demands which the feminist campaign around the working women's charter had demanded, which included for instance the demand for a national minimum wage. On childcare, too, feminist pressure led to the TUC charter for the under-fives calling for a comprehensive and universal service of care and education for the under-fives with flexible hours to meet the needs of working parents. A further significant breakthrough for feminists came in 1979 with the TUC's official demonstration against John Corrie's restrictive Abortion Bill which resulted in over 80,000 women and men demonstrating on an issue that had been traditionally seen as completely outside the scope of the labour movement.

The influx of feminists into the trade unions has revitalized the women's trade union conference which has become not only a meeting place for feminists and other women trade unionists but also a springboard for pressure on the TUC generally on a range of issues from low pay to domestic labour. By 1980 the TUC had accepted the necessity of positive action if the underlying causes of women's oppression were to be effectively challenged. The kinds of positive action envisaged included

special TUC courses for women, childcare arrangements for union conferences, and training sessions and reserved seats for women on national
and local bodies in those unions where women were grossly under-
represented. Many of the positive action initiatives were concerned to
increase the active participation of women in the union movement which
remains pitifully weak. There is evidence that women only courses and
training sessions have a very positive effect upon the women concerned,
leading to increased confidence. However, only relatively few women had
the chance to participate in such programmes up to the present time. One
of the major problems for trade unions is that their bureaucratic
organization results in poor communication. Official policy may look very
good but many women and men remain ignorant of their union's official
policy and attitudes towards women members. Many women trade
unionists still feel that the union is not 'theirs'; that they are only of
marginal concern to their union officials. This is particularly true of part-
time workers who often see little positive benefit accruing to them as trade
unionists. Male trade unionists remain insensitive to gender issues. They
are firmly committed to the defence of customs and practices such as closed
shop agreements and apprenticeships systems which all too often serve to
maintain the sex-segregated labour market. Most, too, remain firmly
wedded to a familial ideology which proclaims that men deserve more than
women because of their supposed position as breadwinners within the
family.

Women in the Labour Party

The problems faced by women in the Labour Party are similar to those in
the trade unions: an entrenched male bureaucracy, an almost entirely male
leadership and a conception of politics and socialism which reflects male
interests and experience. The few women with positions of power in the
party rarely reflect the interest and aspirations of women or feminists.
Nevertheless over the past few years feminists have begun to have an
impact as women have entered the party in significant numbers. In the
view of Joyce Gould, national women's organizer, the National Women's
Labour Party conferences have been transformed. Rather than being
rubber-stamping exercises for national Labour Party policy they have
become the focus of high-level critical political debate where a vigorous
socialist feminist politics has begun to be articulated. Though there are
many Labour Party women (particularly those who are supporters of the
Militant Tendency) who vehemently resist the idea that women's situation
has anything to do with men as such, there is a growing acceptance that not
only has capital to be resisted but that male power both generally and
within the party is an issue that has to be tackled head-on. Though a

significant number of Labour Party members are women they are grossly under-represented in all the decision-making bodies. At present there are only nine Labour Party women MPs and the situation is little better in the local authorities. One of the real problems faced by feminists is how to increase the visibility and influence of women in the party. At present there are five places reserved on the NEC for women. These women are elected at national conference and are in consequence not elected by women but by men and mainly trade-union men at that. Even on the constituency section of the NEC women who do get elected usually only scrape in at the bottom end in terms of votes.

The Labour Party has made some moves to improve the situation. A national women's charter was drawn up by the NEC in 1982 which calls upon all constituencies to take action to increase women's representation at all levels in the Party and to provide services for women attending courses and meetings. In addition Neil Kinnock has appointed Jo Richardson as women's spokesperson with responsibility for women's issues in the House of Commons. The women's sub-committee of the NEC has been formed to formulate policy in relationship to women and to advise the NEC generally on such issues. Its members are also members of the National Women's Committee which is elected by women at regional conferences throughout the country, thus providing a direct link between the NEC and the women's organization. Many feminists are arguing however that this is not enough. There were recent demands at the women's conference for a policy of positive action in relation to the representation of women. Such demands include the right to send five resolutions as of right from the women's conference to the national conference, and the right to elect the women members of the NEC directly. So far such proposals have been strongly resisted by the Labour Party establishment. Some quite clearly approach this issue on principle. For others there is resistance to constitutional change at the present time in view of the strife caused by the campaign to democratize the party in the recent past which led to changes in voting for the leadership and to the right of constituencies to reselect their candidates.

Success in terms of the reorientation of policy and priority is as yet quite marginal. Audrey Wise has said that the aim of socialist feminists in the Labour Party is simultaneously to feminize general issues of policy and to generalize issues that are currently defined as women's issues. On this criterion feminists clearly have a long way to go. It is true that the party is committed to defending abortion rights and contraception and that issues such as rape and wife battering are issues which now get debated in the party. Nevertheless such issues are clearly seen as marginal to the major concerns of the Labour Party. In the last general election the Labour Party manifesto contained very progressive statements about women's rights but that section of the manifesto was hardly even mentioned in the general election campaign and few women in the party, let alone in society generally, ever knew of its existence. There still remains a tendency for Labour MPs in particular to see so-called women's issues as non-political or ethical questions over which members should be free to make up their own minds rather than be subjected to party discipline. Major policy statements, for example, on the alternative economic strategy have remained blind to gender divisions in the working class. They have been vehemently criticized by socialist feminists for their failure to tackle the unequal distribution of resources between men and women, and for their tendency to relegate women's issues to some future date when the economy has been reflated and economic growth secured.

Conclusion

In little more than a decade the women's movement has made enormous strides forward. Feminists have generated a vast amount of knowledge about women's lives and the mechanisms by which women are oppressed and discriminated against. The process of struggle itself has transformed countless women's lives and opened up new opportunities. A 'woman's voice' is increasingly heard on all kinds of issues, from transport to peace and security. Important inroads have been made against familial and patriarchal state practices. There has been a definite shift in the climate of opinion on various issues related to sexual politics, notably on rape and domestic violence. Nevertheless, traditional concepts of masculinity and femininity, and familial ideas of male/female responsibilities, continue to exert a real hold over both men and women. In the present economic and political climate gains won remain precarious. When unemployment appears endemic, and when social services are being drastically reduced, 'common-sense' definitions of male/female relationships reassert themselves very strongly. In this situation the women's movement definitely requires sympathetic allies if women's rights to jobs and resources are to be defended.

The problem remains what kind of alliance can be constructed? On the one hand it is quite clear that the women's movement must remain autonomous from other social movements. The history of the socialist and labour movement, for example, demonstrates quite vividly the invisibility of women and their aspirations unless there is a vigorous independent feminist movement. Yet at the same time feminist campaigns around women's issues remain fragmented and disjointed. Many women remain untouched by feminist ideas and for others such demands appear far removed from their daily lives. Many women's experiences remain far more rooted in class and racial oppression than in sexual politics as such.

It does seem to me that there are some encouraging signs that a more structured and coherent feminist politics is beginning to emerge. Increasingly, links are being formed between feminist campaign groups and the trade unions, the Labour Party and local authorities. Campaign groups have themselves widened their areas of activity from single issue campaigns to broader areas of sexual politics. As more and more feminists become involved in 'mainstream' Left politics it becomes more difficult for women's experience to be ignored or trivialized. There are obvious dangers attached to collaboration with the bureaucratic and male dominated organizations of the labour movement. Feminist fears of incorporation and marginalization are real. However recent initiatives, particularly around local authority equal opportunities programmes, suggest that it may be possible for feminists to work closely with trade unions and Labour Party officials without compromising either their views or ways of working.

In the last analysis the provision of services for women, such as adequate childcare, and the right to work with decent pay and conditions, are fundamental pre-conditions for women's liberation, without which women cannot hope to change the balance of power between men and women. Until now feminists have been reluctant to involve themselves in the struggle for power within the state, either nationally or locally. Yet without feminist involvement in this struggle it is difficult to see how these pre-conditions can be met, or more generally how the movement can survive and advance.

7

Racism and Resistance in Britain

KUM KUM AND REENA BHAVNANI

If you want to understand British racism – and without understanding no improvement is possible – it is impossible to even begin to grasp the nature of the beast unless you accept its historical roots; unless you see that 400 years of conquest and looting, centuries of being told you are superior to the fuzzy-wuzzies and the wogs, leave their stain on you all; that such a stain seeps into every part of your culture, your language, your daily life and nothing much has been done to wash it out.

The worst, most insidious stereotype however, is the characterisation of black people as a Problem. You talk about the Race Problem, the Immigration Problem, all sorts of problems. If you are liberal, you say that black people have problems. If you are not, you say they are the problem. But the members of the new colony have only one real problem. That problem is white people. Racism of course is not our problem. It is yours. We simply suffer the effects of your problem.

Salman Rushdie, 1982[1]

We should like to begin with a discussion of terms. There are currently two in common use: 'racism' and 'racialism'.[2] A more careful definition helps to understand how they are linked and the processes behind them. We shall use 'racism' to refer to the institutionalized practices and patterns which have the overall effect of developing the system which places black people at a disadvantage.[3] We recognize, of course, that other non-black groups experience racial disadvantages in Britain: Jewish people, Cypriot people, Irish people and so on. But we want to limit this discussion to the relationship between black and white people. 'Institutions' can mean both the more general ways in which a society is organized (and through which its values are enshrined, such as the law, and the education system) and it can mean more concrete aspects of those (such as the courts, the police force, schools and hospitals). We will use 'racialism' to refer to individual acts of discrimination that many white people carry out in an attempt to 'put down' and harass and humiliate black people. Some of these white people may be the agents of institutions such as police officers, magistrates, teachers, doctors, housing officials, prison officers, so it may mean the refusal of housing, services, goods or 'justice' to black people, with acts of harassment and aggression towards them. Racialist acts are also carried out by so-called 'ordinary' white people who are not directly agents of the state. They vary from explicitly racialist statements referring to 'jungles', 'smells' and so on, to more 'kindly' meant remarks by people who speak slowly, and say, 'I don't know how much you and your people know of our [*sic*] education system/parliament/NHS, but you really should find out more about it so that you can get your rights.'

Obviously there is a link between racism and racialism. But racialism is made both respectable and legal by making such attitudes concrete within all the major social and political institutions. The Nationality Act of 1981 is a clear case in point. It is a racist law (institution) enshrining racialist values. It reassures white people that it is perfectly reasonable to hold the view that black people in this country are fundamentally aliens, who should therefore be defined as second class citizens.

We cannot eradicate racialist attitudes and acts without understanding and demolishing racism in its institututional manifestations. Many white women and men on the Left in Britain have not grasped this fundamental point in the fight against racism. Much anti-racist work in Britain has been strongly influenced by the 'tolerance' and 'rejoice in differences' approach. But this form of multiculturalism is not anti-racism. In fact, it can sometimes lead to the reinforcement of racism by stressing notions of tolerance rather than respect; and by stressing the differences due to culture (implying that there is only one culture not divided by class etc. in Britain) rather than by examining inequalities of power. Yet because Britain is a society which is divided along race, class, gender *and* age lines it is necessary – if we are to understand racism – to analyse social set-ups within class terms, and to be explicit about integrating other power inequalities within such analyses. We have not, in this short chapter, been able to analyse the specific of black women's oppression and resistance, but this has been explored in depth in a recent issue of *Feminist Review* – an issue produced by black women in Britain.[4]

The need to integrate analyses can be demonstrated through the apparent contradictions that are to be found within certain political demands. The issue of import controls is one example of such a demand. It is a demand which takes no account of power and wealth inequalities arising out of imperialism and is perpetuated both by modern capitalism and by racist and nationalistic ideologies. It is a demand which sets up competition between the international labour movement and the labour movement in Britain on the basis of a protectionist approach to the indigenous labour movement at the expense of an international labour movement. This notion can also be seen in the 'ring-fence' agreements often negotiated by trade unions at particular workplaces. Clearly this practice has arisen for a number of highly specific and obvious reasons. But in the present-day context of Britain such practices can prevent black people and white women entering particular occupations and workplaces. Thus, any analysis of power inequalities, or any political campaign necessitates an *integration* of race, class and gender analyses and a rejection of crude and simplistic approaches to the issues involved.

In addition, racism operates in such a way that many white people are not prepared to believe the experiences of black people. There is a denial of the present-day reality described by black people. Historically, racialist practices were legitimated by racist social systems in countries colonized and conquered by Britain. The ideological basis for racism is very powerful, and helps to provide an explanation and legitimation of racist acts. So, the occupational segregation of black workers, the operation of the 'colour bar', and the passing of a series of repressive immigration laws, all serve to entrench racist ideologies and practices. Racism is about the development of an unequal system where white people have greater access to power than black people. Part of the basis of retaining this power is through systematic discrimination against black people. So, multi-culturalism and a 'tolerance' approach are felt by many black people to be patronising and offensive. It is also felt that such approaches do not confront the basic power relationships which perpetuate racism: racism in economic, social, and political institutions. Such approaches usually ignore the fact that revolutionary change is also necessary to eliminate racism. An example is multicultural/ethnic/racial education. The attitude behind much of this work in schools is that if there are maps of Jamaica on the wall, or pictures of Bangla Desh, with photos of yams or mangoes and projects in progress on saris, all will be well. This type of work is often referred to as the 'steelbands, saris and samosas' approach. The racist education system, the racialism of schoolteachers and white students can be safely ignored within such an approach.

Another related approach expresses the need for more facts and figures about black people in order to decide 'where resources should be chan-nelled'. This happened over the discussion of whether or not to include a question on race in the 1981 census. Many black people refused to participate in the pilot which contained such a question, and many groups, including black women's groups, campaigned widely against it. Since there is already a great deal of information about race from previous inquiries that has not yet been used to the advantage of black people, it was clearly felt that additional collection of data would mean additional means of control – a central register of all black people in Britain.

The roots of racism

There have been black people in Britain for many centuries, a fact which is generally omitted from historical studies of Britain. In fact, the first official 'swamping' speech was made by Elizabeth I in a proclamation of 1601, after an order had been made in 1596 to send all black people abroad. This proclamation was unsuccessful. For the next century or so, continual efforts were made to send black people to Sierra Leone on the West Coast of Africa. This was to be funded by the government for any 'volunteers' who wanted to go; however because black people were not willing to go, the government then refused aid to poor black people, trying to place them forcibly on ships. No less than 441 women, children and men were 'repatriated' to West Africa in this way. In the nineteenth century Irish, Jewish and Ukrainian immigrants came to Britain. Racialist opposition mounted, and the government brought in the 1905 Aliens Act which set the basis for modern racist legislation. There was a control of immigrant workers and a restriction on their rights, in a way which is seen today. The massive unemployment that followed the First World War meant that the black and white men returning from the Front found there was no longer any work for them. In areas where there were considerable settlements of black communities, docks and seaports such as Liverpool and Cardiff, and Canning Town in London, all places where many black seamen and dockers were settled, serious 'race' riots broke out. An Irish man and a black man were killed in Cardiff, both victims of racialist attacks. In Liverpool, Charles Wootton, a black man, was chased by a white mob and died by drowning in the river. Violent rioting broke out in various parts of London.

The hysteria of the white unemployed who felt that they should have 'their' seaport jobs 'back' caused the government to bring in the Special Restrictions (Coloured Alien Seamen) Order in 1925. Most black workers were openly discriminated against, and the League of Coloured People began a long campaign to expose this discrimination and to expose the National Union of Seamen's unwillingness to support its black members.

After the Second World War (in which thousands of black men were recruited to fight for Britain), the state needed labour to keep the wheels of industry moving. It did this by encouraging people from the colonies to come to Britain to fulfil the needs of the labour market. These workers (women and men) were pushed into the dirty, low-paid, shift work jobs which white workers did not want. The employment of black workers was concentrated in London Transport, the NHS, factories, textiles and foundries. The widespread labour struggles in the Caribbean and West Africa in the 1930s and the liberation struggles in both the Indian sub-

F

continent and other areas, meant that black arrivals to Britain were already experienced in resistance – both as workers and as colonized peoples.

It was clear that the colonial relationship betwen Britain and the areas from which the workers came had been one of Britain stripping those areas of resources over a very long period of time, and using them to increase Britain's own wealth – a process that has benefited the white working class in a range of ways, including the funding of the welfare state. Consequently, by the time black workers were recruited many of them *needed* to come to Britain in order that they, and the relatives they often had to leave behind, need not go hungry.

From the late 1950s to the mid-1960s a range of racialist anti-immigration activity developed: for example, in Notting Hill and Notting-ham. In Ealing, in West London, white parents demanded that schools restrict the intake of black students. In response, the local authority introduced 'bussing' – taking black students out of their home area to attend schools elsewhere – thus disrupting the community and making parent-teacher contact almost impossible. The criterion was established, and propounded in government circles, that more than one-third black students in a school was 'undesirable'. Bussing is not supposed to happen today. In effect, it often still does, under the guise of special language centres, and the disproportionate sectioning off of young people into ESN (educationally sub-normal) schools, and into schools for the maladjusted.

Other kinds of anti-immigration racialist activity took the form of a vast proliferation of pressure groups who had opposition to black immigration as their only reason to exist. Two of the most virulent were the British Immigration Control Association in Birmingham, and the Southall Residents' Association. Such groups often started off by organizing opposition to a black family moving into a particular street – but often extended their activities to propagandizing that a black presence in Britain was in itself a massive threat. During this period, Enoch Powell, then a Conservative MP, made many racialist speeches, making racism and racialism respectable among those who saw the Tory party as the epitome of conformist respectability. In fact, in the early 1960s, both major political parties seemed to be competing with each other as to who could be the most racist. Each was boasting that its policies on immigration were or would be the toughest. By 1964, the Tories had been in office for 13 years, and intended to stay there partly through promising stronger anti-black immigration legislation. In Smethwick, traditionally a safe Labour seat even in times of crisis, the Tory candidate was supported by the slogan 'If you want a nigger for a neighbour, vote Labour.' Under the circumstances, Patrick Gordon Walker, not particularly known for his anti-racist work or sentiments, lost his Labour seat, even though there was a victory for Labour nationally.

So the demands for cheap labour had been met, and one could see the beginning of a series of immigration laws, culminating in the 1981 Nationality Act, which builds on and contains the main concepts enshrined in the earlier immigration Acts. The Tories passed the first post-war Immigration Act in 1962, restricting entry of black Commonwealth people by introducing an employment voucher scheme in addition to the category of those who could enter on a 'first come first served' basis. The employment vouchers meant that entry could only be obtained if someone was coming in for a specific job, or to offer a specific skill. Wives and children under 16 years were to be allowed in, but this was to lead to the kinds of tests to prove eligibility introduced by the immigration authorities, such as internal examinations for prospective wives and bone X-ray tests for children under 16.

The Labour Party came to power in 1964 in a climate which called for even more stringent controls against black immigration. The Tories had already begun to put forward proposals to limit immigration to those with parents or grandparents born in Britain.[5] Shortly after Wilson came to power, his government produced the 1965 White Paper on Immigration, as a result of great pressure and general anti-black hysteria. It abolished the 'first come first served' category in the 1962 Immigration Act, and cut down severely on numbers within other categories. It also introduced the possibility of deportation, at the Home Secretary's discretion, without a court ruling, of any immigrant of less than five years' standing who was considered to have flouted immigration legislation. Now numbers became the central point at issue. Black people were openly cited as the cause of many social problems, which, according to the racialist argument, would disappear if Britain could make sure only a few were here. By now, the ideas on the right of the Conservative Party, and even those to the right of *them*, were almost completely legislated for. What had once been extremism was now common sense, and to discuss the matter in any other terms was said to be unrealistic, in a 'small, crowded island'. It is also worth remembering that the Communist Party also implicitly accepted numbers as the point at issue by not making repeal of immigration legislation a central plank of its struggle against racism.

The pretence of the non-racial nature of immigration legislation vanished quickly with the passing of the 1968 Commonwealth Immigrants Act, which was specifically designed to keep out of Britain black people from Kenya who had full British citizenship. Passed in a record two days under the then Home Secretary James Callaghan, and commonly known as the 'Kenyan Asians' Act, this legislation was internationally condemned. It is worth noting that it was in the same year that Enoch Powell made his notorious speech about 'rivers of blood', predicting 'racial violence' unless numbers were restricted and repatriation brought in, which motivated East

London dockers to march in support of his statements. 1968, the year of radical student-worker rebellions in many countries, was also the year of the further consolidation of racism in Britain.

It took one more Act finally to establish all these conditions. The 1971 Immigration Act introduced by the Conservatives legally embodied the concept of patriality, a notion set up through the 1968 Act. The proposals to limit immigration were based on the qualifications of those with parents or grandparents born in Britain. Non-patrial Commonwealth citizens have no right to settle in Britain, and are kept at the level of completely controlled migrant workers who (as in many other countries in Western Europe, like France and West Germany) can be expelled when their work permit is no longer renewed. The 1971 Act extended the power of deportation, set the conditions for police to be involved even more in tracking so-called 'illegal' immigrants, and therefore strengthened the power of immigration and police officers and legitimized their racialist harassment. The logical development of patriality in the 1971 Immigration Act laid the basis for the 1981 Nationality Act which established three tiers of citizenship and set a tone for strengthening immigration rules which made it increasingly impossible for families to be united, and for women and men to marry whom they pleased without affecting their right to live in Britain. It established a climate for internal controls which operate in such a way as to lay doubt on the claims of any black person in Britain for access to the services of the welfare state. The recent campaigns around Anwar Ditta, Bangladesh Divided Families, Josephine Thomas, and Mohammed Idrish all show up the racist and sexist nature of the immigration laws.

A secret immigration guide 'biased to refuse entry', concerning the rights of 'foreign' men to enter this country to live with British wives, was issued in February 1984.[6] In February 1984, the government changed the immigration rules to exclude foreign husbands and fiancés unless they could prove that the primary purpose of the marriage was not to gain entry to Britain. This specific rule, which has been introduced in order to appease demands from the Tory right wing, is ostensibly against the arranged marriage system. This raises the question of what is an 'arranged' marriage, and whether it is for the state to determine who should marry whom on the basis of place of birth. In addition, the Home Office is not saying what is meant by 'primary purpose'. Consequently, individuals are being refused entry into Britain on the grounds of the 'primary purpose' phrase, which means that there is no clear indication as to why they are being refused entry. This apparent condemnation of the practices of a group of people from the Indian sub-continent brings into sharp focus the hypocrisy of the government's attempt to strengthen family values and ties. What we have seen over the years, particularly in the immigration laws and rules of the last two decades, has been a process by which black people in Britain have had their status redefined.

The 1965, the 1968, and the 1976 Race Relations Acts are on the statute-book. But the introduction of this series of legislation has been encompassed within a framework designed, apparently, to cushion the sharpness of the immigration laws. The 1976 Act includes a clause on 'indirect discrimination' – which makes it illegal to promote policies which may unintentionally discriminate against groups of people because of skin colour or ethnic origin. But there is also an exclusion clause which disallows any challenge to central government's legislation on this basis. This means, for example, that students from overseas are charged much higher fees in tertiary education than those who are termed 'home based'. It is also this sort of racism which allows and legitimates the DHSS memos on hospital treatment for 'foreigners', enables a headteacher in Newham to demand to see the passports of children of South Asian origin before enrolling them, and allows the police and immigration officers to harass and intimidate black people without legal redress under this Act. The veneer of liberalness of this Act begins to vanish in the light of such instances. Moreover, whilst the national interest and good race relations are presented as reasons for the legislation, the democratic rights associated with parliamentary democracy are quietly redefined. The Commission for Racial Equality was set up under the 1976 Act and replaced the Race Relations Board, set up under the previous Acts. It is funded by the state through the Home Office – and is therefore in the invidious position of having to investigate malpractices such as the notorious virginity tests carried out by other Home Office employees. In fact, such an investigation was launched by the CRE, and squashed by the Home Office.

Less well-known than the internal examinations of black women but still widespread and serious, have been the raids on workplaces – another racist practice exempt under the 1976 Race Relations Act. On 13 May 1980, police and immigration officials went to Bestway Cash and Carry Warehouse and shops in Harlesden, London, and arrested 37 people for alleged breaches of immigration law. On 22 May 1980, the Hilton Hotel was also raided – 100 workers were interrogated and 35 arrested on alleged breaches of immigration law. On 20 June 1980, 79 police officers and 22 immigration officials raided the Main Gas factory in Edmonton, North London, and arrested 31 people from 47 who were interrogated. Many of those who were arrested were subsequently released – some after seven hours. One employee of Bestways was arrested despite being able to quote the number of his British citizenship certificate of registration.

On 3 July 1980, Timothy Raison, Secretary of State for the Home Office, said in the House of Commons 'May I make it clear that no blanket raids have been carried out . . .', when answering questions on this issue. Yet 'fishnet' raids began fairly soon after the 1971 Immigration Act came into effect in 1973. They have been a periodic and area-wide occurrence both under Labour and Conservative Home Secretaries. One of the largest, until the Bestways raid, was in Newcastle in December 1977: 11 Bangla Deshi restaurants were raided, 60 people interrogated, 24 detained – of whom 18 were subsequently released. Raids like this indicate how immigration legislation (and the Nationality Act) make such actions legal (even though they would be illegal under the 1976 Race Relations Act if the exemption clause had not been written in). In fact, immigration/ nationality legislation actually *requires* agents of the state to carry out such acts. In addition, the racialism of such police and immigration employees can be given full vent under the guise of 'doing their job'.

Racism and the white Left

The issue of workplace raids also raises the issue of the response of the trade-union organizations. Both the General and Municipal Workers Union and the Transport and General Workers Union paid lip-service to fighting racism by officially condemning the raids. But the British trade unions have not been in the forefront of the fight against racism in Britain, in spite of the fact that most black people in Britain are working class. For example, the TUC's Hotel and Catering Industry Committee has pressed for action against illegal workers, despite the fact that the TUC eventually opposed a directive from the European Economic Community aimed at trying to make workplace raids an EEC requirement. The official record of the trade unions in supporting black workers is appalling. There is a long list of disputes where racialism of white members and officials is much in evidence, including the lack of strong official (central) support despite local demands: the disputes of the black workers of Red Scar Mills in Preston, at the Woolf Rubber Company in Southall, at Mansfield Hosiery in Loughborough and two London companies – Stanmore Engineering and Standard Telephone Cables — are all cases in point.

The strike in 1974 in Leicester of black women workers at Imperial Typewriters is one of the sharpest examples of a workplace dispute around racism and racialism, and black resistance to them. Imperial Typewriters had a workforce of 1,600, 1,100 of whom were black. The workers came out on the issue of how bonuses were calculated on different bases for black and white workers. Other forms of racialism were also clearly described. The black workers were opposed by management, white workers and their union, the Transport and General Workers Union, which never made the strike official, despite considerable criticism of the TGWU convener. The 50 strikers received much of their support and solidarity from black organizations, both local and national. In addition, a women's conference in Edinburgh, and the European Workers' Action Committee, gave the strikers at Imperial Typewriters their support.

It is no coincidence that when the strike began, 27 women and 12 men came out. The exploitation and profit motive on which capitalism rests ensures that black women will get extremely low wages. This was also the point at issue in the strike at Grunwicks. Racialism and the low wages associated with 'women's work' were central to the strike, but union recognition was usually presented as the main issue. The other dimensions disappeared as the official support of the trade unions grew.

Trade-union bureaucracies do not support black members fighting for basic union rights when that dispute is permeated by and is a result of racist practices. Where they *do* support black workers over basic union questions, as in the case of Grunwicks, they ignore the dimension of fighting racism, and do not place it on the agenda or struggle over it. As a result, black struggles get lost as part of the overall class struggle. Rather than bringing the issue of racism to the front, it is lost beneath patronizing statements from officials – and at worst black people are told that they have 'chips on their shoulders' and are subjected to racialist abuse.

The TUC has a Charter for Equal Opportunity for Black Workers. This makes modest suggestions for examining union structures for racialism. However, since there is little discussion and no action (at a wider level) against state practices which may inhibit the active participation of many black workers in their unions – such as immigration legislation – the tone of the Charter becomes moralistic and implicitly views black people as 'passive victims'. This is despite the struggles in the last ten years or so. The part played by black resistance is either ignored, or the racial aspect of it systematically played down.

If resistance to racism is to gain strength, all campaigns, in the workplace or outside, need to develop a perspective that looks into and opposes racism and imperialism. And this must be done whether or not black people are involved in the campaigns as such. That is, the politics of the campaigns must reflect such a perspective. The struggles of black women in white feminist campaigns have forced some of the groups to begin to reflect black women's oppression and exploitation. For example, the National Abortion Campaign has had to adapt and adjust positions and slogans in order to take into account that *black* women sometimes find it only too easy to be sterilized or given abortions. White-dominated women's health groups are only now beginning to take on the issue of contraceptives such as Depo Provera which are tested on black women in South America, and on black women in this country. The discussion amongst the Left and in the women's movement that the family is an oppressive institution for women ignores the particular experiences of black women affected by the immigration and nationality legislation and rules so that they are unable to be united with their families – on whose support they must rely heavily within such a racist society.

In groups which campaign against violence against women, the issue of violence against black women by, for example, state representatives (police and immigration officials) is not included. In addition, when black people are subjected to violence within the home, in cases of rape for instance, it is necessary to acknowledge that the racialism of the police and of neighbours is yet one more thing that has to be dealt with at a time of great stress. As Angela Davis points out, anti-rape campaigns need to be aware that part of racist ideology depends on the racist notion that all *black* men are potential rapists. So simple demands for stiffer penalties, or ones which do not take into account the need to 'prove' rape has occurred, can operate to put black men accused of rape in a position where the racialist state agents and laws are used to 'protect' white women at the expense of black men. Similarly, the 'race' dimension of rapes of black women by white men is often left out of many analyses.

The setting up of refuges for women who wish to leave their domestic situation can also be seen often to work in such a way that racialism is 'swept under the carpet'. Many of these Women's Aid refuges operate as if all the potential users are white, and take no account of differences between women such as different perceptions of marriage, divorce, separation, and family. In addition, a clear position needs to be taken by workers in such refuges on any racialist abuse which may occur between users. It is also necessary to examine the Police and Criminal Evidence Bill to see how it will be used against both black women and men. The assumption that 'All the blacks are men, all the women are white' must be constantly challenged.

Black resistance

Black people are constantly doing this. The setting up of refuges and resource centres for and by black women is one example of black resistance. Similarly, the monitoring campaigns which are now developing to monitor racialist and racist attacks are another instance of black resistance in Britain in the 1980s. Black school students are resisting their treatment in schools both by challenging the attitudes and perceptions of white teachers and by encouraging their parents to raise these issues within the schools. The urban uprisings of 1981 can also be viewed as a challenge and resistance to racism and police action among other issues. The defence campaigns of the Newham Eight and the Bradford 12 could also be cited, alongside the black people's Day of Action following the New Cross massacre, as examples of the black-led and black-defined resistance developing in the current British context. Many of these activities involve women and men and necessitate both community and trade-union support integrated together – a different concept to some of the more traditional white-dominated political activities, which are often *either* community *or* trade-union oriented.

For example, some of the anti-deportation campaigns throw up questions not only centred around immigration and nationality legislation, but also about workplace organizations, enrolment for school children, anti-racist activity within schools and so on. The point we are trying to make is that black-led campaigns most often necessitate social and political and economic resistance simultaneously. For white anti-racists, this is often a comparatively new idea and requires systematic discussions with black groups in order to realize and work within the contours of black-defined campaigns.

Issues such as the development of anti-racist education policies within unions can be usefully taken up by those active in labour movement political work. If activists are discussing the rundown of the National Health Service, this may be contextualized by reference to the low pay of the black workers in the NHS, of both men and women, at whichever level they are employed, whether as cleaners, nurses (who may not get registra-tion and promotion as easily as white nurses) or as doctors who are employed in those sections of medicine which have low status. In discussions on the rundown of the educational services, issues such as the disproportionate placement of black children into special schools, and disruptive units can be integrated within the campaigns. Similarly, the need to employ black people as teachers within schools and colleges, and in higher education, are not matters commonly raised by white-dominated campaigns.

The issue of white-dominated campaigns making links with black organ-izations in their areas is also something which should be borne in mind. Such campaigns and organizations should consult with black organizations both locally and nationally to develop links. Tackling racism and racialism should involve questioning issues such as mental health, the penal system, the role of political parties, trade unions and left-wing groups. Feminist campaigns may also need to examine whether their approaches and slogans address the needs of black women. All this necessitates challenging the use of certain words, or the making of 'jokes'. When racism is discussed in meetings, is it ever discussed thoroughly? Is it often left to the end of a meeting, or reduced to one sentence in the minutes? Is it only raised through such issues as language classes for black people? Is it always tucked away, or put into the end pages of political publications? If it is tackled, is it done via isolated articles rather than a clear anti-imperialist anti-racist policy permeating *all* the features in the publication?

Racism is a *white* problem and so it is essential that white people are involved in anti-racist work, which includes developing anti-racist pers-pectives in all campaigns and workplaces. How this occurs, and its political basis, clearly needs much more discussion. An international approach is crucial, as are links with black groups. Black resistance – and the forms it takes – is growing. And yet most white women and men still need to acknowledge that it exists.

BRIGHTON POLYTECHNIC
LEARNING RESOURCES

Black people, both individually and in groups, are constantly involved in challenging racialism and racism. This occurs both in personal encounters with white people and through immigration campaigns, black trade-unionists' groupings, and black women's groups, as well as through the setting up of resources and libraries which set the record straight about the history of racism and black resistance. There are many ways in which black, or predominantly black, groupings organize. Below are some examples of this type of activity, which is often community-based.

The anti-deportation campaigns, or campaigns for individuals settled in Britain to have their dependants come and live with them, are a significant example of community-based activities which are usually led by black people, although sometimes some white anti-racists are involved. Campaigns centred around, for example, Anwar Ditta and Cynthia Gordon are well-known. The campaign for Mohammed Idrish was the first of such campaigns to gain the support of a trade union nationally, NALGO. It provides an indication of how labour movement organizations can support black struggles in an anti-racist manner.

Since the beginning of 1983, a number of monitoring groups have been set up which try to support the victims of racialist attacks. In addition, these monitoring groups try to keep records of the levels and incidence of such attacks in a locality. At the time of writing, these monitoring groups are based mainly in different parts of London.

There are also many black women's groups across Britain which may be, and often are involved in the anti-deportation work. The Brixton Black Women's Group and the Sari Squad are two examples of such groups. In addition, the groups have supported black women workers out on strike such as those at Chix in Slough, and Futters in Harlesden. These groups may also campaign for particular resources for black women and for black men in a locality. Such resources could be, for example, a refuge for black women, a resource centre for black women and so on. In addition, black women's groups were active after the uprisings in Britain, in presenting black responses to the Scarman Committee's Report, and in organizing community responses to the police actions.

There are also ethnically organized groups whose focus can be on a range of issues affecting a community. The Indian Workers' Association is an example of this. There are also some black Labour Party members who are arguing for the need for black caucuses to be set up within the Labour Party, in a similar way to the women's section within the Labour Party. We do not as yet know whether they will succeed in this, as there has been opposition voiced by some of the leading white members of the party to such a section being established. The Race Today Collective is a collective of black people which produces *Race Today*. The Institute of Race Relations, based in London, is an organization which produces the journal *Race and Class*. Its history is important, as it brings out a number oif issues relating to the struggles around racism and racialism. It is acknowledged to have one of the best libraries of material pertinent to race and is a useful place to find out of print, as well as current, material on race. Both *Race Today* and *Race and Class,* in their different ways, provide important material which often presents issues from an international perspective. The Runnymede Trust is a London-based charity which produces a Bulletin. This is a very good source of regular information which can often be of use in campaign work.

Finally, there are a number of campaigns against racism and fascism (CARF) in different areas. *Searchlight* is also an extremely good anti-racist magazine. Many white anti-racists are involved in these groups.

8

Green Politics and the Peace Movement

RICHARD TAYLOR

The Green Movement is an international phenomenon of considerable political importance in the 1970s and 1980s. In North America and West Germany in particular the Movement and its ideas have made a major impact. In electoral terms the Greens made their first breakthrough in Belgium where, in 1981, they won four seats in the Lower House and five in the Senate. But it was in the German election of March 1983 that the Greens became 'established. . . as a serious alternative to traditional ideologies, and inspired "green growth" everywhere'.[1] With 5.6 per cent of the popular vote, the Greens won 27 seats in the Bundestag, and gained not only media exposure but political credibility.

The importance of the Greens goes far beyond orthodox politics. The awareness of the inter-relationship between the resources crisis, the arms race and threat of nuclear holocaust, the dire effects of the North/South division, and the political structures which dominate the world, has awakened a wide-ranging movement, with social, cultural and psychological, as well as political ramifications. Central to the definition of the Green Movement is a concern both with the protection of the natural environment, and with a radical re-ordering of values, relationships and political structures. As 'Green CND' has put it in a recent pamphlet:[2]

> . . . green people are united by their love of nature, their respect for the Earth's resources, and their commitment to the ideal of harmony between people of every race, colour and creed. These fundamental beliefs imply other values: respect for the gentler side of human nature; a dislike of materialism; a willingness to share the world's wealth amongst all its people; a desire for decisions to be open to all concerned; and the search for personal truth.

The Greens thus have both a very broad range of concerns, and a series of fundamental objectives, neither of which fall within any particular ideological tradition. They are certainly 'radical' (although even here the continuum shades into conservationist and traditionalist pressure groups, some of which, such as the National Trust and the Council for the Protection of Rural England, exercise considerable influence). But they are not 'socialist' in any orthodox sense, nor are they 'anarchist': though they have strong tendencies towards certain socialist and libertarian viewpoints. David Bellamy has articulated the predominating mood succinctly:[3]

> It took 3.6 billion years for the earth to be covered in a mantle of living green. Yet now a third of the world's population suffer malnutrition, and 28 children die every minute of every day and night from conditions resulting from malnutritition . . . our only hope [lies] in the genetic diversity of the plant and animal kingdom . . . Yet we are losing one species every day, and by the end of the century it could be one an hour . . . As ideology fights ideology for control of the world's diminishing resources, human hands and minds hold within their grasp the power to create a hell-hole or a garden of Eden . . .

The result of industrial civilization for the Greens has been the stark immorality of resource misallocation, so that, for example, 'what is spent in just *two* weeks (on armaments) could house, clothe and feed *everyone* in need for a year.'[4] What is stressed by the Greens, therefore, is the need for a radical change, both in patterns of consumption (and an end to the growth-oriented economy), and in attitudes, individually and socially. The Greens concentrate, therefore, on neither class nor gender issues; nor are their central concerns related to imperialism. Their environmental and moral perspective leads them in practical policy terms to focus upon ecological and defence issues.

This is an international movement. In Britain, however, although advances have been made since the early 1970s, the Greens are less influential than elsewhere. Whilst it may be true that 'there are more environmental organizations per head of population in the UK than in any other country',[5] none has been a major political force; and, equally important, several of the largest and most influential do not fall within even the broadest definition of a radical Green movement (e.g. The National Trust et al.). Thus, the Ecology Party – the only major Green organization to contest general elections in Britain in recent years – has performed mcdestly. In 1983, for examply, over 90 Ecology Party candidates stood at the June election and secured only 1.1 per cent of the popular vote. In no constituency did the Party come anywhere near victory, and indeed in all cases the deposit was forfeited. The highest percentage secured was 2.9 per cent at Ogmore (Jonathan Porritt, one of the most prominent of Ecology Party activists secured only 2.1 per cent in Kensington). Of course, this reflects in part the notoriously discriminatory nature of the British electoral system as far as minority parties are concerned. (The far left parties, and the National Front, fared less well than the Ecologists: the National Front secured an average of only 1 per cent of the vote in each seat contested, and the Communist Party only 0.8 per cent). Even so, the Ecology Party's performance is hardly indicative of mass popular support for the Greens.

The continuum which makes up the Green Movement in Britain has a wide span. One of the most crucial divisions lies in the nature of the political methods advocated. A major contribution of the whole Movement has been to offer a third alternative on the Left to the long-established dichotomy between social democratic reformism and Marxist-Leninist revolutionism. Peter Cadogan has put the point clearly. The Green Movement is divided, in Cadogan's view, into two sections:[6]

(1) the old-fashioned who still believe in political parties, Parliament etc.
(2) the anarcho-Greens who go for war – rejection, non-violence, decentralization, direct democracy and the whole alternative scene – feminism, ecology, scale, peace, life-style.

Both of the major Green organizations in Britain – the Ecology Party and the Friends of the Earth – include both types of activist perspective, and both are thus fundamentally ambivalent over crucial aspects of ideology and political strategy. The Ecology Party was the only Green Movement organization to contest the 1983 General Election and, as has already been noted, it was markedly unsuccessful. The Party was founded in 1973. It has approximately 6,000 members and is affiliated to CND and to the National Council for Civil Liberties. Its stated objectives are uncompromisingly political, concentrating upon *electoral* politics. Its central aim, it claimed in 1982, was 'to influence the electorate and form a Government'.[7]

Its 1983 Election Manifesto is indicative of the Greens' preoccupations. Summarizing the Ecologists' policies, the Manifesto argues that:[8]

This is what we mean by Green Politics:
PEACE – through unilateral nuclear disarmament, complete withdrawal from the arms trade, a reduction in international tension through re-source conservation, and a secure and credible alternative defence strategy.
WORK – guaranteeing basic material security and good work for all, based on renewable resources, human-scale technology and the sustainable economics of self-reliance, recycling. rehabilitation and repair.
LAND – with a deep reverence for the Earth, and for all its creatures, leading to radical land reform, changes in farming practice, and comprehensive measures to control all forms of pollution.
PEOPLE AND SOCIETY – living in decentralized communities, with a proper balance between feminine and masculine values, protected by a Bill of Rights, working nearer home, leading healthier lives and ensuring that our children get a creative, constructive education.

THE WORLD – working for one world by helping the Third World, stabilising world population through genuine redistribution of wealth, eliminating our wasteful resource and energy depletion and protecting the global environment.

THE SPIRIT – responding to people's hunger for meaning, placing less emphasis on material values, and more on personal growth and spiritual development – the life and soul of Green Politics.

We believe that a programme like this is both radical and realistic.

This is not Utopian dreaming, it is already happening in Germany, Belgium, Italy and other countries. Green Politics is the single most significant international movement since the birth of Socialism at the end of the nineteenth century.

No Cruise. No Trident. No Polaris. No nuclear weapons of any description. No chemical or biological weapons. No American bases. No involvement in NATO. This makes the Ecology Party the only uncompromisingly unilateralist Party in this election.

Phase in a National Income Scheme to remove the poverty trap.

Animal Rights Charter: introduce mandatory production for endangered species and ban the importation of whale products and seal skins. Take immediate action against battery farming, and move as rapidly as possible to abolish vivisection. Ban all hunting and coursing with hounds.

We should withdraw from the EEC. We would seek instead to establish a European Federation, non-aligned in defence matters, opposed to reliance on economic growth, with its emphasis on the regions of Europe, and not its nation states, and committed to sustainability and justice, both in Europe and the Third World. The responsible adult use of cannabis would be legalized.

The Friends of the Earth (FOE) complement this essentially parliamentarist approach with a strongly *extra*-parliamentary presence, focused on a series of diverse single issue campaigns: for example, anti-nuclear power campaigns of considerable complexity, length, and sophistication (Windscale/Sellafield; Sizewell), and campaigns against the grosser, but often microcosmic, aspects of man's exploitation of his environment (an end to the plan for a new copper mine in Snowdonia, the Schweppes campaign against 'no deposit' bottles).

FOE began in Britain in 1970/71 on the initiative of Barclay Inglis.[9] It began to capture public imagination with a series of innovative campaigns, organized by its first director Graham Searle, beginning with the famous 'direct action' at Schweppes depots all over the country in 1971. FOE differed from other more traditional environmental groups in two important ways, both of which are indicative of central Green concerns. It 'set out not merely to protect and defend certain entrenched values, but to challenge society's commitment to other, newer values, like economic growth and the marvels of technological progress'.[10] And it has laid much greater emphasis than some of the other organizations in the Green

Movement upon the importance of extra-parliamentary, decentralized, specific issue campaigns, prosecuted through *direct action* in various forms. FOE is certainly radical in its orientation but, even more than the Ecology Party, its focus is on the alternative culture of libertarian environmentalists rather than on any explicitly political, structural changes. Its major concerns have been to promote 'the conservation, restoration and rational use of the world's resources, including the recycling of materials, protection of endangered species and recognition of environmental considerations in energy policy'.[11]

With increasing concern, nationally and internationally, over the resources crisis and pollution in general, and over the dangers of nuclear power development in particular, the FOE has grown in size and influence since the late 1970s. Its membership in the early 1980s stood at approximately 18,000,[12] but, as with all such 'unstructured' extra-parliamentary groups or movements, its real strength is difficult to quantify. Undoubtedly, however, it has become a major force in the whole 'environmental debate'.

Direct policy concerns and considerations of political approach and style link together the central organizations of the Greens and the Peace Movement. In the 1980s the two Movements are integrated to a very considerable extent. Both are opposed wholly to nuclear weapons and nuclear power. Nuclear weapons are seen by the Greens as the culmination of a whole social structure fundamentally out of touch with both human needs and environmental reality. In this sense, nuclear disarmament is seen not as a single, autonomous issue, but as part of the wider struggle to reorientate and restructure human society. 'We should be creating a society based on principles and ideals where there is simply no room and no time for such things as atomic weapons . . . in the end, "the concern with nuclear weapons, and with peace, will become swallowed up or integrated within a larger movement to transform the conditions of our lives and to build a nuclear-free society".'[13]

Similarly, opposition to nuclear power development is seen by both the Greens and the Peace Movement to be central to their objectives. In part, this is because of the mounting evidence of very serious environmental damage resulting from radioactive waste emanating from nuclear power stations (viz. the beaches of the Cumbrian coast polluted long-term by the leaks from Windscale/Sellafield); and, of course, there is in the background the very real possibility of a major nuclear power disaster (viz. the 'near miss' of Four Mile Island in the USA). Opposition to nuclear power is also based in part, however, upon the now proven connection between nuclear power and nuclear weapons. 'The plutonium connection between nuclear power and nuclear weapons is so inextricable that lasting nuclear disarmament remains an improbable dream until such time as the last nuclear reactor is finally decommissioned.'[14]

Green CND has been involved in a variety of activities in recent years. It has been prominent in the Greenham Common Peace Camp in opposition to the siting of Cruise missiles in Britain, and has been closely involved in the organization of the 'Green Gatherings'. There have been four such gatherings to date (1980 to 1983) on farms near Glastonbury, attracting several thousand participants to a large number of events and workshops 'on every Green subject under the sun'.[15]

The peace issue has undoubtedly been the main factor in the wider Green Movement since 1979. Not only has it provided the link between the Peace Movement and the Green organizations, it has acted as the main focus of public attention and support. Centring on the proposed installation of Cruise missiles, the Peace Movement has swept Europe and is now the major extra-parliamentary political force in the industrialized world. In Britain CND has grown, following its decline from its earlier mass movement days in the late 1950s and early 1960s,[16] into a huge and rapidly growing political force. In early 1984 CND had approximately 90,000 members and an annual budget of over £1 million. Its membership increased by almost 1,000 per week following the installation of Cruise missiles at Greenham Common in the last days of 1983. Though CND policy is fixed at annual conference, and therefore varies over time, the Campaign's basic aims and current priorities can be seen in the following extracts from its constitution and its broadsheet *Steps to Survival*.

Aims:

The aim of the Campaign for Nuclear Disarmament is the unilateral abandonment by Britain of nuclear weapons, nuclear bases and nuclear alliances as a pre-requisite for a British foreign policy which has the world-wide abolition of nuclear, chemical and biological weapons leading to general and complete disarmament as its prime objective.

The Campaign for Nuclear Disarmament is opposed to the manufacture, stockpiling, testing, use and threatened use of nuclear, chemical and biological weapons by any country, and the policies of any country or group of countries which make nuclear war more likely, or which hinder progress towards a world without weapons of mass destruction.

Steps to Survival
1 Stop the Trident nuclear submarine
2 Refuse all Cruise missiles
3 Get rid of all other nuclear weapons and bases from Britain
4 Introduce less aggressive forms of conventional defence
5 Put our weight behind the creation of a nuclear free zone in Europe
6 Put pressure on both the USA and USSR for a freeze on the development, production and deployment of new nuclear weapons. Call for the dismantling of existing weapons on both sides
7 If the USA or other NATO countries refuse to follow this path, consider Britain's position in NATO and if necessary withdraw

8   Promote the implementation of the Non-proliferation Treaty to stop the spread of nuclear weapons to other countries
9   Call for and contribute to the redirecting of resources from arms production to socially useful production both here and in the Third World
10   Start to find ways of cutting back on all weapons of mass destruction in every country so that the world's peoples can live without violence and fear.

Although the Peace Movement, both in Britain and internationally, has fundamental problems in terms both of mass consciousness and (even more importantly) over the question of how its politics can be articulated and successfully put into practice,[17] it remains without doubt the central co-ordinating core of the Green Movement: 'Defence and the fear of nuclear war, is the common cement'.[18]

Linked to the Peace Movement, especially to its important Direct Action wing, are the various Green campaigns committed to direct action. Prominent among these is Greenpeace, which was founded in 1972 by activists from peace and environmentalist groups, in particular *Peace News* and War Resisters International. The aims of the group are explicitly linked to the Gandhian, non-violent direct action tradition. Greenpeace sets out 'to provide a non-violent libertarian focus on environmental issues, especially in opposition to the ravaging of the environment by militarism; to confront people with their personal responsibilities, oriented towards imaginative small-scale activities and direct action, rather than lobbying'.[19]

Greenpeace has mounted a whole series of well-organized and publicized Direct Action campaigns against particularly obtrusive examples of human exploitation of natural and animal resources. Perhaps the most notable of these have been the campaigns to 'Save the Whale', in which Greenpeace played a leading role, and against seal culling. In both cases Greenpeace organized direct non-violent intervention against those perpetrating the actions.

These and other Direct Action campaigns represent another central thrust within the Green Movement: that people must take action, non-violently, *themselves* to oppose the forces that threaten to destroy our planet. It is argued to be both useless and immoral, because evasive, to rely entirely or even largely on other agencies and ultimately other people (governments, parties, politicians, bureaucrats, etc.) to undertake such actions. As Ralph Schoennan wrote in the 1960s in the analogous context of the Committee of 100 Civil Disobedience Campaign, 'When, if not now? Who, if not I?'[20]

Undoubtedly, the Green Movement, in its diverse forms, has made considerable advances in recent years. How significant is this advance in the longer-term context of radical politics in Britain? At one level at least the Green Movement has been of the most profound importance for the Left. As with the Women's Movement, the Greens have compelled the wider labour movement to acknowledge that a whole range of new concerns are at least of equal importance to more traditional analyses, assumptions and priorities. Nuclear politics, the resources crisis, and the North/South divide, for example, are now accepted by most of the more progressive elements in the labour movement as being of central importance. That it took the Green Movement to stimulate such a response may be a sad commentary on the long-standing conservatism of the labour movement, but it has certainly changed the outlook of the movement (Left as well as Right) – and for the better.

The Labour Party has become involved, in a genuine and firmly based context within the localities, in the Peace Movement, the Women's Movement *and* the Green Movement. Even at leadership level the Party now has a considerably greater understanding of, and commitment to, Green policies than was ever the case in the past. Neil Kinnock, in replies to a questionnaire given just prior to his election as Party Leader, committed himself to a range of specific environmental policy objectives (e.g. banning lead in petrol, opposition to nuclear power, priority for non-motor transport, etc.), as well as making the following general statement on environmental concerns: '. . . environmental policies must take a higher place in Labour Party thinking. Ecological and environmental preservation is a major part of socialist practice and Labour must bring that achievement into the forefront of our image'.[21]

To some extent other progressive political parties – particularly the Liberals and the Communists, both of which have explicit commitments against nuclear weapons and nuclear power, and for a greater concentration on environmental issues – have also given a new priority to Green issues.[22] Overall, then, with the notable and prominent exception of the Conservative Party and government, the mainstream political parties are far more favourably inclined towards the Greens than in the past.

More than this, however, the Greens and the Peace Movement have played a major part between them in broadening the Labour Party, and moving it away from its previous heavy concentration upon parliamentary considerations. Factors other than the impact of Green politics have also been at work in this context, of course: but the Greens and the Peace Movement have been of central importance. The long-term effects of this upon the overall ideological and political orientation of the labour movement may well be of great significance. A major aspect of this process has been the involvement of the labour movement in extra-parliamentary, non-violent Direct Action (NVDA), on a whole range of issues. NVDA tactics have been inherited by the Greens from the Peace Movement of the 1950s and 1960s,[23] and have been used by increasing numbers of activists in the 1970s and 1980s. Moreover, in sharp contrast to the Direct Action movements of the 1950s and 1960s which were uniformly dismissed by the vast majority of the labour movement as being 'undemocratic' and 'coercive',[24] NVDA is now accepted as legitimate in many contexts by Labour activists.

The Greens and the Peace Movement have also demonstrated again, and perhaps more dramatically than ever before,the capacity of extra-parliamentary, single issue campaigns for mobilizing very large numbers of hitherto politically inactive people. Whilst the Labour Party (and the other Left groupings and parties) struggle to prevent the persistent fall in membership and activism, the Greens and the Peace Movement go from strength to strength. Indeed, throughout Europe there is no doubt that the Peace Movement in particular has mobilized huge numbers of people,[25] to a degree far in excess of the orthodox political parties. Such movements have been especially appealing to the radical middle class, a group of growing importance in British society since the 1950s. Whilst major sections of this class are of course opposed to radical political ideas of any sort, there has been an expansion in the number of radical, tertiary educated professional and intellectual employees, whose public sector occupations and general background of 'critical thinking' have led them into the fields of alternative politics, and specifically into support for the Green Movement.[26]

The new effect of all this has been that, on occasions, the Greens and the Peace Movement have been able seriously to challenge the power of the state, albeit within restricted areas of activity: CND in Britain, the Peace Movement and the Greens in West Germany, for example. At the very least, such activities must be seen by socialists as complementary to more centrally socialist assaults on capitalist state power.

Given all these positive factors, why have the Greens failed thus far to achieve their objectives? And what are their weaknesses, if any? First and foremost, of course, the Greens in Britain are operating within a deeply conservative political culture and a firmly entrenched capitalist socio-economic order, as indeed are all other progressive political forces. Any significant breakthrough from the left is therefore going to be difficult to achieve.[27] Over and above this problem which is common to the whole of the British left, there are several points of specific weakness for the Greens. The general problem of radical single issue movements operating within a conservative political culture (and a discriminatory electoral system) have been discussed in some detail in volume 2 of this series.[28] Such considerations apply with particular force to the Greens, disparate, and divided over priorities, as they necessarily are. Within this complex of problems three in particular stand out: the ambivalent relationship between the Greens and socialist politics; the related (and long-standing) question of political agency; and, of course, the ideological disparity between the various tendencies supporting the Greens, which makes the alliance extremely precarious in the longer term.

The first of these problems – the relationship with socialism – is far more than a difference over strategy. For the Greens the problem resides centrally in the process of industrialism *per se*. The never-ending quest for economic growth and material progress is one of the assumptions which the Greens are challenging. At most, such concerns have been tangential to socialist politics. The dismantling of the collectivist structure of the productive system, the concomitant industrial relations procedures, and the centralized and bureaucratic party system, would be anathema, at least to orthodox socialists, whether Right or Left. The Greens' emphasis upon alternative technology, the necessary reduction in material expectations, and the decentralization of both economic activity and political power, runs counter to many of the major themes within the politics of the labour movement.

Over and above these differences in general orientation, it is also significant that, on a more specific and practical level, many Green activists would incline more towards libertarian politics and philosophy than to socialism of any description. This is related closely to the problem of 'agency': of how Green politics can achieve its objectives. This is a problem for all mass, single issue, extra-parliamentary movements, and has long been of central concern to the Peace Movement in particular. In the Green Movement, as in the Peace Movement, virtually all the possible tendencies relating to agency can be identified: the advocates of apolitical moral pressure; of pressure on and through the existing, major political parties; of independent parliamentary party political activity; and of extra-parliamentary direct action of various types; or, indeed, some combination of any or all of these.[30]

Of course, such disparity over agency weakens the impact of the Green Movement overall. Indeed, the whole phenomenon of diversity is on balance a seriously weakening factor. Unlike the Peace Movement, the Greens do not even have a clear, central single issue on which to focus: the campaign is by definition macrocosmic! Moreover, the Greens' central ecological political concerns shade into a whole range of mystical, spiritual and irrationalist concerns. Eastern philosophy and religion, somewhat incongruously, have gone hand in hand with ethnicity, a belief in 'earth forces', and a tendency to reject entirely the political in favour of the spiritual and the mystical.

What then, finally, are the prospects for the Greens? If they are to move beyond their predominantly radical middle-class, alternative culture, constituency, and become a major influence on the political scene, it is essential that there should be a Green/socialist coalition. Without the involvement of the organized labour movement – both industrial and political – the Greens seem likely to remain an interesting and dynamic, but marginal, influence on radical politics in Britain. Conversely, if the Left is to mobilize popular support, and revitalize its politics (as it needs desperately to do), it is equally essential for the large number of people involved with the Greens' campaign to become integrated into socialist politics.

More important than all these tactical and strategic considerations, however, is the substantive content of Green politics. The issues of nuclear politics, the North/South divide, the energy and resources crisis, and the problem of pollution, must all become central issues for socialist politics. Equally, socialists must strive to convince Green activists that, without socialist analysis and socialist mobilization, Green objectives cannot and will not be attained.[31]

9

Northern Ireland: The Unresolved Crisis

ANTHONY ARBLASTER

The United Kingdom of Great Britain and Northern Ireland, as its convoluted title suggests, has never been completely united. Really united states or nations have no need to advertise the fact. The claim to be united almost invariably implies the opposite. Within mainland Britain three distinct nations coexist and overlap; while the separate naming of the province of Northern Ireland simply draws attention to its anomalous position. As its name indicates, it is geographically, historically and to a large extent culturally, part of Ireland – an island which has been formally divided for less than 70 years. Northern Ireland is not part of Britain, yet it remains under British authority – an outlying, neglected province of an increasingly divided and disunited kingdom.

Since the suspension of its local, quasi-independent parliament and government in March 1972, this province has had not effective civilian administration of its own, but has been governed from London, with a Secretary of State for Northern Ireland acting in effect as a colonial governor-general. Sporadic attempts to replace the old parliament, Stormont, with a new set of governing institutions have not been successful. The crisis which first erupted in the autumn of 1968, has continued until the present, with few indications that it will be speedily, or even tardily, resolved. In the past 16 years more than 2,800 people have been killed – about one in every 500 people in the province. Northern Ireland constitutes by far the most serious single problem within British and Irish politics. Yet in Britain people manage, with characteristic imperialist hypocrisy, to regard it as an 'Irish' problem, which the Irish have somehow brought upon themselves, while they are only there to perform the thankless task of keeping these primitive bloodthirsty tribes from tearing each other apart. Any suggestion that Britain itself has any responsibility for this bloody and protracted crisis is met for the most part with either indignation or blank incomprehension.

Socialists may not have fallen into *that* trap; but it cannot be said that the responses of the Left have been, for the most part, either especially well-informed, clear and cogent in their analysis, or intelligent, sensible and persuasive in their conclusions and recommendations. A number of socialist organizations, to be sure, have faced the problem squarely, and have adopted with very little reservation the view that the struggle in Northern Ireland is a straightforward conflict between an imperial power (Britain), and a national liberation organization (the Provisional IRA and Sinn Fein), in the same pattern as has been seen in many other parts of the world. But on the whole this approach has depended on ignoring some of the complexities of the situation, notably those relating to the position of the so-called 'Loyalists' in the north. On the other hand, those who have been aware of these complexities seem to have been paralysed by their awareness. The lack of serious discussion in socialist journals such as *New Left Review, Marxism Today* and, more recently, *New Socialist*, bears eloquent silent witness to this evasive uncertainty.

One of the stock accusations made (in Britain) against the Irish is that they are obsessed with history, or with the past. Yet it is hard to think of another situation in which the responses of every group and institution involved have been more clearly determined by history, or in which the past has left the present so little room for manoeuvre or innovation, as the present crisis over Ireland. And to know little or nothing of the history of relations between Britain and Ireland, and of the origins of the semi-state in Northern Ireland, is a sure recipe for failing to understand the present conflict.

No country has been dominated and exploited by Britain for longer than Ireland. No nation has had a longer and harder struggle to win its independence. No people have suffered more bitterly at British hands. And if these seem like over-partial radical judgements, consider these words of G. M. Young, Conservative historian and biographer of Stanley Baldwin:[1]

> Look at Ireland. There we have the great failure of our history. When I think of the deflexion and absorption of English intelligence and purpose by Ireland, I am inclined to regard it as the one irreparable disaster of our history; and the ground and cause of it was a failure of historical perception.

The history of English domination

Ireland was not, of course, one of those many territories incorporated into the short-lived British empire of the nineteenth and early twentieth centuries. Ireland's proximity to England determined that it would be involved in the dynastic and expansionist quarrels of England and France from their outset following the Norman conquest of England in 1066.

Engels noted that: 'As soon as the Normans had built up a powerful, unified government in England, the influence of the larger island made itself felt – in those times this meant a war of conquest.'[2] The first English, or Anglo-Norman invasion of Ireland took place more than 800 years ago, in 1169–71, and this marked the beginnings of English landlordism in Ireland, a phenomenon that was to dominate the life of the rural majority of the people until the end of the nineteenth century, and is not totally extinct even now.

But it was the Tudor monarchs who first effectively and determinedly asserted English authority and sovereignty, and accompanied it with a deliberate policy of colonization through the establishment of 'plantations'. These were based on land confiscated from those who dared to resist Tudor authority, and they were owned and worked by settlers specially brought over from mainland Britain. The most important and successful of these plantations was that based in Ulster, east of the river Bann, and it was settled by Protestants, principally from Scotland. Henceforth the division between the privileged and favoured settlers, especially in Ulster, and the expropriated and often rebellious indigenous population, tended to coincide with the division between Protestants and Catholics; for Ireland was little touched by the Reformation, so that Catholicism remained the popular religion. Thus issues of nationalism, religion, and economic and political exploitation and subordination have been entangled with each other in Ireland since the sixteenth century.

Resistance to Tudor authority was repressed with a ferocity which, the historian Lecky said, 'has seldom been exceeded in the pages of history'. In the next century, however, it was equalled by the ruthlessness and brutality with which the next rebellion of Catholic Ireland was suppressed by the Parliamentarian forces and Cromwell's armies between 1641 and 1652. The final defeat of Catholic Ireland in the early modern period took place at the battles of the Boyne and Aughrim in 1690 and 1691. These victories established the Protestant ascendancy which dominated Ireland for the next hundred years. They were soon followed by the Penal Laws, which reduced Catholics to the level of second class citizens and effectively destroyed surviving Catholic landownership.

All this explains clearly enough why the siege of Derry and the victory of the Boyne continue to be celebrated by the Orange Order in Northern Ireland. They were the events which finally cemented that dominance of Protestant over Catholic which was not successfully challenged in 'Ulster' until 1968, and which is not yet destroyed today. Hence these commemorations are not mere nostalgia, nor even gratuitous insult to the subordinated Catholics; it is a rational celebration of the historical roots of Protestant advantage.

The Catholic/Protestant divide was not yet, however, deep and irrevocable. In the eighteenth century it was the Protestants who were in the forefront of the movement for an independent Ireland; and when in the 1790s a radical nationalist movement developed under the inspiration of the French Revolution, its centre was in Belfast, and its outstanding leader the Protestant lawyer, Wolfe Tone. At this stage, in other words, it was still conceivable that Protestants and Catholics could band together in a single movement of national liberation.

It was only in the nineteenth century that nationalism became a Catholic movement – with its first campaign being for the civil emancipation of Catholics – while the Protestants increasingly identified themselves with the Union with Britain, imposed on Ireland after the suppression of the nationalist movement of the 1790s. This latter development was systematically encouraged by the British, who nurtured the Orange Order from the time of its foundation (also in the 1790s) as a valuable counterforce to the revolutionary nationalism of Tone's United Irishmen.[3]

This rift was above all a product of the extremely uneven pattern of industrialization in Ireland. A gulf developed between the more developed north east and the rest of the country; while the development of industry in and around Belfast attracted to the city many rural Catholics in search of wages and jobs. Consequently Belfast became the focus of economic rivalries and social tensions between relatively poor Protestants and even poorer 'immigrant' Catholics. Sectarian preachers were not lacking to exploit and exacerbate these tensions by endowing them with a veneer of religious legitimacy.[4]

With every decade of the nineteenth century the bitter hostility of the mass of the rural Irish to British rule and largely absentee British landlordism increased. The greatest popular leader of Irish nationalism in the first half of the century, Daniel O'Connell, led an entirely peaceful mass movement for the repeal of the Act of Union. The British authorities simply responded with repression. O'Connell's commitment to peaceful methods turned out to be a failure. That Irish nationalists should turn thereafter to violent methods was only to be expected. And hatred of Britain was terribly deepened by the most dreadful single catastrophe in Irish history, the famine of the late 1840s.

Of course the British authorities were not responsible for the famine itself. But it was their unrelenting commitment to the principles of the free market, and the consequent refusal to supply cheap or free food to the starving Irish, which made the catastrophe far worse than it needed to be.[5] Mass death, and the mass emigration of people desperate to find some more hopeful place to live, reduced the population of Ireland from eight to six and a half million in the single decade of the 1840s, and it continued to fall to around four million at the end of the century.

After O'Connell's failure and the famine, some nationalists turned, logically enough, to planning a national uprising which would drive the British out of Ireland. These were the Fenians. The planned uprising was a total failure, but their activities in England in 1867 included the rescue of two Fenian prisoners in Manchester, during which a policeman was mortally wounded; and another rescue attempt in Clerkenwell which involved an explosion which killed 12 people and maimed and wounded many more. J. C. Beckett's account of British reaction shows how little has changed in Anglo-Irish relations in more than one hundred years: 'The immediate effect of these activities was to arouse a wave of anti-Irish fury; but, when this had subsided, public opinion was more ready than before to recognise that there must be something radically unhealthy in the political condition of Ireland'.[6] Gladstone, in particular, from then on increasingly turned his mind to measures which would either ameliorate or settle the 'Irish problem', culminating eventually in the proposals for Home Rule which fatally divided the Liberal Party in 1886, and caused a major crisis in British politics 25 years later.

By this time, the Protestants of Ulster were firmly incorporated into the British economy. It was clear that their interests now lay with the British connection, and that home rule could only damage their position of relative economic privilege within Ireland as a whole. Hence the opposition to Home Rule of the Ulster Protestants became the central factor in the crisis. The readiness of powerful Conservative politicians, from Lord Randolph Churchill to Bonar Law and Edward Carson, to support, excite and exploit that opposition for their own personal or party political purposes – to 'play the Orange card', in Churchill's famous and revealingly cynical phrase – was the second decisive factor.[7] There can be no doubt that Protestant opposition was strong and genuine. It was not simply the invention of the Tory leadership. On the other hand it may be doubted how far the preparations for armed rebellion and for a unilaterial declaration of independence (UDI) in Ulster would have got without the political leadership, and ample financial support, for the purchase of arms and equipment, of the British ruling class and its principal political organization, the Conservative Party. Financial supporters included such figures as Lord Rothschild, Lord Milner, the Duke of Bedford, and Rudyard Kipling.[8] It is worth remembering, when Conservative leaders like Margaret Thatcher claim that theirs is the party of respect for law, order and the constitution, that theirs is also the *only* British political party in the twentieth century openly to promote and advocate armed rebellion within the British state against an elected British government.

The Orange state 1922–68

These are some of the more important features in the intersecting histories of England and Ireland which culminated after the First World War in the partition of Ireland, and the creation of two self-governing states coexisting in the one island; for although Northern Ireland remained part of Great Britain, and so under the ultimate authority of the Westminster parliament, the province was in effect handed over to the Unionist Party, the party of the Ulster Protestants (but allied to the British Conservative Party), to govern more or less as they pleased.

Northern Ireland's two major problems were inherent in it from its foundation. First, the most committed elements in the Irish struggle for national independence never accepted partition; and in fact even at the official level of the Anglo-Irish agreement partition was supposed only to be temporary, which explains why the aim of a united Ireland has never been formally renounced by the Irish Republic and has recently been reaffirmed by the New Ireland Forum. Secondly, a third of the population of the newly created statelet was in any case Catholic and nationalist, and two of Northern Ireland's six counties, Fermanagh and Tyrone, had nationalist electoral majorities. Not surprisingly, therefore, the inauguration of the new semi-state was far from peaceful. Over 300 people were killed in violent clashes during its first three years of life.

Since the very reason for the new state's existence was to give the Ulster Protestants a territory in which they would be dominant, it followed that the Catholic nationalists incorporated into Northern Ireland were bound to be treated as second class citizens, and, indeed, as potential 'traitors' to the new state, since it was known that they would not have chosen to live under its authority.

A more magnanimous and far-sighted group than the Unionist politicians of Ulster might have made a serious attempt to appease the Catholic minority, and win its support for, or at least its tolerance of, the new arrangements. But few Unionists have ever been magnanimous or far-sighted. The creation of the new state was a triumph for militant Orangeism: the Protestants could not resist the temptation to celebrate that triumph by inflicting every kind of humiliation upon their Catholic 'enemies'. The Eton-educated aristocrats who led the Unionist party made no attempt to curb the violent excesses of their popular supporters, precisely because they knew that their own political survival and that of their mini-state depended on every working-class Protestant believing that he or she stood to gain, materially, politically and emotionally, from the unrelenting maintenance of Protestant supremacy, by whatever means might be necessary.

So the new state sustained its authority over the Catholics from the beginning as much by force and the threat of force as by civil processes. The police in Northern Ireland were an armed force from the beginning, and they were also an exclusively Protestant force; while a Special Powers Act gave the Stormont government exceptional powers to suspend civil liberties and made use of arrest and detention without trial. These powers did not merely stay on the statute-book; they were used quite frequently. To add insult to injury, Unionist leaders regularly bragged, in Lord Craigavon's words, that 'we are a Protestant parliament and a Protestant state'; while another Prime Minister, Lord Brookeborough urged Protestants 'not to employ Roman Catholics, ninety-nine per cent of whom are disloyal'.[9] This advice did not go unheeded. Patterns of employment, housing and other services in the 'Orange state' showed clear discrimination against Catholics, who often found it hard to obtain public housing, or employment in the public sector. Added to this was the further scandal of gerrymandering of electoral boundaries, to ensure, for example, that the city of (London)Derry should be governed by a Unionist council, although Catholics outnumbered Protestants in the city by two to one.

Thus what was created in Northern Ireland was a one-party state, in which a minority of one-third of the population was permanently excluded from power, and consistently abused and discriminated against. The wonder is, not that this corrupt and brutal arrangement eventually collapsed in anger, riot and disorder at the end of the 1960s, but that it lasted for as long as half a century with so little disturbance, comparatively speaking. That it did so was due, in large part, to the isolation of the oppressed Catholic minority in the North. The Republic in the South, while never formally accepting 'the border', was careful not to intervene in the 'internal politics' of Northern Ireland; and successive British governments pursued the same hand-washing policy of non-intervention. Labour was, of course, no exception to this sordid tradition of turning a blind eye towards Northern Ireland. 'Any politician who gets involved in Ulster ought to have his head examined', that arch-cynic Harold Wilson is alleged to have said during the 1964 general election campaign.[10] Only a few small groups and individuals, including the National Council for Civil Liberties, and Andrew Boyd, the indefatigable Belfast correspondent of *Tribune* in the 1960s, persisted in trying to draw British attention to the political slum that was the Orange state.

It is true that a campaign of violence against government property by the Irish Republican Army (IRA) in the mid-1950s won little popular support. On the other hand it is also true that two Sinn Fein candidates were elected to the Westminster parliament in the general election of 1955, one of them for mid-Ulster, the seat which later elected successively Bernadette Devlin, Bobby Sands, and Owen Carron to the British parliament. Support for Republicanism and Irish unity never died among Northern Catholics.

The Catholic revolt and the collapse of Unionism

All this may seem like history which has now been more or less wiped out by the tumultuous events of the crisis that followed, particularly of the years 1968–73. But this would be to misread both the crisis itself, and the bloodstained stalemate that continues.

In the first place it is only in relation to the history of the uneven development of the Irish economy, and its political outcome in Catholic/Protestant relations in Ireland, and the Northern Irish state, that we can see the upheaval of 1968 onwards for what it was – the long delayed revolt of the Catholic minority against their subordinate and exploited status within that state and region. In its first form, that revolt marked a determined attempt to escape from the past patterns of Irish politics. First of all, it tried to avoid the republican/nationalist label, by *not* raising the issue of the partition of Ireland. Second, it tried to overcome the sectarian fissure in Northern Irish politics by forming itself as a civil rights movement, on the American model. Naturally it would attract its mass support from the Catholics, whose civil rights were being denied; but it was open to any liberal-minded Protestant to give it support as well. Third, it was committed to non-violent methods. It used peaceful occupations, sit-downs and marches, in the hope that these methods would win popular sympathy and persuade the Stormont government to respond sympathetically to its demands.

All three innovations failed, as a consequence of the implacably hostile reaction of the Protestants and the Protestant state. Marchers were beaten up, either by the club-wielding Royal Ulster Constabulary, or by the stone-throwing crowds mobilized by the Reverend Ian Paisley and the other promoters of militant Protestantism. Peaceful demonstrations were prohibited by the Unionist government, and the civil rights leaders were denounced as front persons and agents for the IRA.

What finally destroyed the hope of peaceful reform in Northern Ireland was the Northern Ireland election of February 1969. At that election the Unionist Prime Minister, Captain Terence O'Neill – the nearest thing to a liberal that Unionism ever produced – staked his position on a package of reforms designed to placate the Catholics and end the demonstrations, without antagonizing the Protestants. The gamble failed. It was clear from the results of the election that he could not carry the mass of Unionist voters with him. He resigned to make way for a leader more acceptable to the Orange intransigents, who saw, correctly, that reform threatened the whole structure of Protestant privilege and dominance within Ulster society.

After this, violent conflict between the rebellious Catholics and the alarmed Protestants and their repressive·state was absolutely inevitable. It was also predictable, given the past history of Ireland, that in this context the IRA would emerge once more as the embodiment of the most intransigent nationalist opposition to the Orange state. But it is wrong to think that the IRA would have come to dominate the opposition to Britain and Unionism in any case. It was only the manifest failure of the peaceful and non-violent campaigns of the civil rights movement which gave the 'physical force' elements in the IRA the opportunity to come to the fore.

For after the relative failure of the IRA campaign of 1956–62, there had been strong moves within Sinn Fein and the IRA to adopt a strategy of peaceful political action instead of focusing their energies on military activities. Indeed this reorientation went so far that when the Protestants launched their attacks on the Catholic ghettos in first Derry and then Belfast in August 1969, the IRA had no arms to resist the invasions – neither locally, in Belfast, nor in the Republic. On some walls in Catholic Belfast the graffiti appeared 'IRA – I Ran Away'. Out of this humiliation, and a situation in which the Protestant para-military organizations were clearly armed and active, and the British army had been introduced into Belfast and Derry, came a new organization, the Provisional IRA. This was, in fact, the old 'physical force' tradition of Irish Republicanism in a new organized form.

The two years between the first appearance of British troops in the North in August 1969, and the reintroduction, by the Unionist government of Brian Faulkner, of internment without charge or trial in August 1971, constitute a particularly complex and fast-moving period in the current crisis. On the one hand, the collapse of the Unionist government's ability to maintain control of the situation through such blatantly sectarian forces as the RUC and its notorious part-time accessories, the 'B' Specials, made the presence of British troops a necessity, and gave the British Labour government the excuse and the justification to impose upon Stormont a series of much-needed reforms which that Unionist-dominated body would never otherwise have agreed to. On the other hand these reforms were a classic case of 'too little, too late'. For the reform programme coexisted with the continuation of the Unionist Party in government, and, inevitably, with the use of the British army to prop up the discredited authority of that government, and to impose its security policies upon the resentful and rebellious Catholic communities. If anything, the enforcement upon the Unionists of some very unpalatable reforms only intensified their determination to crush the Catholic/nationalist rebellion.

This aim was not, of course, presented in those terms. As always in such situations, the public was told about the importance of restoring peace and order, and of defeating terrorism. Terrorism – if that is what it was – was being practised by Loyalist as well as Republican para-military groups; but it was plain that it was IRA terrorism which was the real target. Increasingly the British army, whose presence was at first welcomed by many Catholics as a protection against further Protestant mob attacks, became the agent of repression directed against the Catholic population as a whole. House to house searches involving much destruction and brutality, curfews, physical assaults and verbal abuse, generated a climate of tension and hostility in which the IRA, which offered the Catholics some defence as well as an active response to state-sanctioned harassment, was bound to find increasing support. As J. Bowyer Bell observed in his history of the IRA, the use of CS gas againt Catholic crowds 'did more for the Provos than all the legends of heroes and all the patriot graves'.[11]

The climax of this whole development came with the reintroduction of internment without trial or charge in August 1971. This could not have taken place without the consent of the British Conservative government; but it yielded, with supreme foolishness, to the insistent, long-standing pressure of Brian Faulkner, and during the night of 9 August the British army arrested and interned 342 people. Many more arrests on the same pattern – a total of 1,576 by December of that year – were to follow. The purpose of this action was 'to restore the morale and authority of Stormont'.[12] As could have been, and was, predicted by anyone who understood the depth and extent of the Catholic/nationalist rebellion, it had exactly the opposite effect. It produced an immediate wave of angry protests in the Catholic communities, which led, in the autumn, to a well-organized and widely supported rent and rates strike by Catholics. It also brought a fresh wave of recruits to the armed struggle of the Provisional IRA. Above all it led to an immediate and horrifying escalation of the violent confrontation between the Catholic population and the army and police. Although the increasing scale of IRA activities had been the reason offered for the necessity of internment, its entirely counter-productive effect can be gauged from the fact that whereas in the four months prior to internment eight people were killed, in the four months that followed 114 people lost their lives, including 73 civilians and 30 soldiers.

Thus in the history of violence and death in Northern Ireland, internment was a turning point. But the supreme irony was that it marked the beginning of the end for Stormont and the old system of Unionist supremacy. It turned the Catholic population even more vehemently against the old order, and if anything more was needed to complete their alienation and hostility, it was supplied by the brutal massacre of Bloody Sunday, 30 January 1972. This was the occasion when a peaceful, though (as usual) prohibited demonstration by Catholics in Derry was fired on by British paratroopers, resulting in 13 deaths. The obvious comparison was with the Peterloo massacre of 1819, and Bloody Sunday has had a similar impact and meaning for the Catholics of Northern Ireland, and indeed for nationalists throughout Ireland. Demonstrations in Dublin led to the burning down of the British embassy in Merrion Square by an irate crowd.

The Faulkner regime tried to brazen out the event, expressing no regret, and routinely blaming the IRA and even the unarmed demonstrators themselves. Those who demonstrate illegally, even if peaceably, have only themselves to blame if they are shot dead, was the barely concealed message. An extremely limited judicial enquiry conducted by the British Lord

Chief Justice, Lord Widgery, managed to blur the issue and allowed the troops to escape any legal proceedings, while also failing to discover why the troops fired, and on whose orders. But the event and Unionist reaction to it finally snapped the patience of the Conservative government in London. Within a month the decision had been taken to suspend Stormont and the whole apparatus of self-government in the province, and impose direct rule from Westminster, in the person of a Secretary of State for Northern Ireland. And so, on 24 March 1972, 50 years of corrupt and unjust rule by the Unionist party came to its final abrupt end.

This was the climactic point of the crisis which had begun less than four years before. Despite repression and murder, despite the presence of more than 20,000 British troops, the Catholic and nationalist revolt had succeeded in destroying the central institution of the Orange state, and in securing the reform of several others. Although Stormont was only officially 'suspended indefinitely', no one, on either side, believed that it would ever be restored in its old form. The Protestant community was undoubtedly stunned by this sudden and dramatic blow.

The end of Stormont was also, I believe, a lost opportunity. A more positive response from the Catholic side, and in particular from the Provisionals, who by then dominated the opposition to British army repression, might have led to a decisive move towards establishing society in Northern Ireland on a new basis – one which would have recognized the equal rights and standing of the Catholic/nationalists within the province, and also the long-term inevitability of a closer accommodation with the Irish Republic. Alas, the instransigence of the Provos at this stage, whose terrorist outrages – by which I mean the random killing of innocent citizens, as opposed to direct conflict with the armed forces of the state, which it is quite inaccurate and misleading to call by the same name – reached a climax in the summer of 1972, ruled this out. Yet the intransigence was, like so much else in the crisis, entirely predictable. The traditional 'physical force' Republicans had always been taught to see Britain as their principal enemy. Hence they could not believe that at that moment a gulf had opened up between the British Tory government and its old allies, the Ulster Unionists, and that of the two groups it was the British government which was the more amenable to reaching some sort of settlement with the forces of Irish nationalism. And indeed a meeting between the Provo leaders and the newly appointed Secretary of State, Willie Whitelaw and his assistant ministers did take place on 7 July in London. But nothing came of it. The Provos were too inflexible, and the situation in Belfast too unstable, for any 'arrangement' to stick. Yet this was the moment, when the Unionists were still reeling from the blow of the end of Stormont, when it might have been possible to enforce a relatively just settlement of the Northern Irish 'problem' on the Protestants themselves.

G

The bloody stalemate, 1974–84

By the time that the British government had devised its plan for a limited system of local administration to replace Stormont, it was too late. The structures of power-sharing offered far less to the Catholic community than many British people supposed; but while the moderate Catholic politicians of the Social Democrat and Labour Party (SDLP) were prepared to give the proposals a trial, they were overwhelmingly rejected by the Protestant community, which, under the continued protection of the the the British army, had recovered its nerve. Brian Faulkner, an agile politician who understood that no other prospect of devolved political power was on offer, was also prepared to operate the plan. But his position was virtually destroyed, as O'Neill's had been five years earlier, by popular Protestant inflexibility, expressed in the Loyalist general strike of May 1974.

It is broadly true, in my view, to say that the decade that followed the collapse of that first atttempt at a limited political settlement of the province's problems was little more than a bloody and unproductive stalemate. The one thing that it established was the hollowness of repeated British claims that the war in Ireland was all but won, and the terrorists effectively beaten. Despite the perversion of the processes of justice, the reliance on the dubious evidence of paid informers, harsh sentences, the use of interrogation methods amounting at times to torture, murders and shootings carried out by both the British army and the Ulster Defence Regiment – despite a sustained and utterly ruthless campaign, the British authorities have not succeeded in destroying the Provisional IRA, still less in dissolving the support for Sinn Fein and Irish nationalism within the Catholic community. That much is clear enough. Yet the prospect of any kind of political resolution of the conflict still seems extremely remote.

From 1974 to 1981, when a 'liberal' Tory, James Prior, arrived at the Northern Ireland Office, no British government, Labour or Conservative, took any significant political step to resolve the crisis. British handling of the Irish situation reached a nadir of militarized stagnation during the years of Roy Mason's tenure as Northern Ireland Secretary, 1976–9, and the first two years of the succeeding Thatcher government. Mason represented reliance on a purely military response at its crudest, while the response of the Thatcher government was as rigid and insensitive as one would expect from the general character of that administration.

The Thatcher government's refusal to respond in any way to the ten deaths which resulted from the hunger strike among Republican prisoners in 1981 was found especially shocking by a wide range of opinion outside Britain. The Catholic/nationalist community as a whole has had a somewhat ambivalent relationship with the Provisional IRA. Provo offensives, even against the British army, do not always win Catholic approval; but in their role as defenders of the minority community against army or Protestant attacks and harassment the Provisionals do command general support. The hunger strike, which was not even aimed at any large political demands, but simply focused on the inescapable fact that these prisoners are not, and were not, mere criminals, but are in fact *political* prisoners, was bound to arouse immense sympathy and support in both parts of Ireland, since it was the purest gesture of self-sacrifice, by which no one but the prisoners themselves (and their families and friends) could conceivably be harmed. It stood within a long tradition of such self-sacrificing gestures made in the cause of Irish national independence and unity. And it was led, initially, by a man who had actually been elected as a Westminster MP, Bobby Sands. He was the first person to die in the strike.

The unyielding British response probably did more than any other single experience in the past ten years to convince the minority community in the North that their position and their aspirations will never be understood in Britain. It is not coincidental that in the three years since the hunger strike Sinn Fein has been able to re-enter electoral politics in Northern Ireland with striking success, both at the local and national level, to the extent that they are now competing with the SDLP to be *the* political party of the Northern Catholics – whereas in the 1970s the SDLP had easily dominated minority *electoral* politics. Thus British harshness and inflexibility have greatly enhanced the standing of Sinn Fein and the IRA – exactly the opposite to what Thatcher doubtless intended by her adamant opposition to terrorism. Sinn Fein has concentrated in recent years in building up the basis of communal support upon which armed as well as peaceful opposition to the British military presence must rest, and the British response to the hunger strike strengthened that basis rather than the reverse.

Even if the British were sensitive enough to avoid such brutal miscalculations, however, there is no likelihood of the British being able to impose a military settlement upon the troubles of the province. The goal that has eluded them for the past 15 years will continue to do so. The reasons for this are political rather than military. Successive British governments have shown that they lack either the wish or the will to confront the resistance of the Protestant community not only to any hint of a closer relationship with the Irish Republic, but even to any proposals for giving representatives of the minority community a share in the government and administration of the province. So long, then, as the 'Loyalists' are effectively allowed to veto any proposals which might offer the minority safeguards against a return to the discrimination and exploitation of the past, it is clear to the Catholics that they cannot look to the British for their salvation. The very fact that the British, at every level from government downwards, interpret the whole Irish crisis in terms of a simple battle against terrorism (that is, the IRA), only confirms to the

Catholics that they are still regarded, ultimately, as the enemy which is to be defeated, and put back in its subordinate position.

Here lies the root of their support for Sinn Fein and the IRA. It is not that there is necessarily an overwhelming desire to see the North incorporated into a united Ireland. The minority simply do not want to see the achievements of their revolt since 1968 destroyed, and the whole agony of the conflict wasted in an effective restoration of the pre-crisis status quo, that is, Protestant supremacy. At present neither the intransigence of 'Loyalist' opinion, nor the incomprehension and militarist futility of the British response do anything to convince them that this dismal prospect is not all too likely – above all if the Provisionals are effectively defeated by British military might.

To say this is not to imply approval for all the tactics and actions taken by the IRA and other Republican groups. It is not an endorsement of terrorism – which, I repeat, I define quite precisely as the attempt through random killing and destruction to terrorize the civilian population, as opposed to fighting what is in effect a sporadic war against the British army and state.[13] It does not even imply that the unity of Ireland is a goal which can and should be achieved in the *near* future, regardless of opposition to it – although every socialist must hope that it *will* finally be achieved, since the division of Ireland is one of the last disastrous products of British imperial domination of Ireland. What it does imply is that as long as the other parties to the conflict, including the British and Irish governments and the Protestants of the North, fail to arrive at a settlement which guarantees the rights and equality of the minority in the North, for so long the Catholics are wholly justified in resisting the armed might of the British state and the threat of the restoration of the old, unjust order under which they suffered for so long. Continued support for Sinn Fein and the IRA reflects Britain's continued failure to devise arrangements which will secure justice for the Northern minority. Responsibility for the continuation of the war in Ireland thus rests with Britain more than with any other single participant in the conflict.

Conclusion

No study of the pre-history of the present crisis in Northern Ireland, however partial and abbreviated, can fail to make the point that the current impasse is a direct legacy of Britain's protracted imperialist domination over Ireland. Both the division of Ireland itself, and the division within Northern Ireland, are products of that domination. That being so, there can be no doubt that the only solution of the problem acceptable to socialists must be one which includes Britain's withdrawal and disengagement from Northern Ireand. The long-term future of those six counties must be as part of Ireland, not of the 'United Kingdom'. Campaigns for a British withdrawal, and in particular a British military withdrawal, therefore deserve socialist support – not least on account of the many damaging effects which the war in Ireland has had upon politics in mainland Britain – in particular, the brutalization of public opinion, and the attacks on civil liberties carried out under the all-embracing excuse of combating terrorism – which, for reasons of space only, have not been explicitly discussed in this chapter.

But if we are looking for a plausible reason for the relative uncertainty of much of the British Left's response to the Irish crisis, then it must surely lie in the unusual complexity of the position in Northern Ireland. The 'Loyalist' majority in the province is not a group calculated to arouse much sympathy among liberal or radical outsiders. It enjoyed half a century of untrammelled dominance, and it used it to impose a pattern of injustice, discrimination and repression upon the other third of the population. Its response to the Catholic revolt of 1968 and after was as brutal and bigoted as could have been expected. Many of the 'Loyalists' – perhaps the majority – still want, and even intend, to see that pattern of injustice, discrimination and repression restored. That cannot be allowed to happen.

Yet their opposition to incorporation into a united Ireland is a factor which has to be taken seriously. To point to their minority status within Ireland as a whole is not an acceptable way of resolving the issue. Minorities as well as majorities have rights: this is precisely the point that has to be made *against* the Protestants in relation to the Catholic minority in the North. The Northern Protestants are not a bunch of ex-patriate settlers with no real roots in Ireland. They belong to a community which has been settled in north-east Ireland for nearly 400 years, and it is a community not all of whose traditions and customs are to be despised. Northern Ireland is used to a degree of freedom in personal and sexual matters which does not exist in the Irish Republic. Its being a part of the United Kingdom has also enabled it to benefit from British provisions for social security and welfare which are better than the provisions in the Republic. The Republic remains an explicitly Catholic state, which reaffirmed its Catholicism as recently as 1983 by inscribing a general prohibition against abortion in its constitution. Both Protestants and those of no, or no strong, faith can hardly be blamed for disliking the prospect of incorporation into a state whose laws and constitution reflect the restrictive sexual code of the Catholic church, and in which that church occupies a privileged and highly influential position.

Furthermore, it can hardly escape notice that the Protestant/Catholic divide in the North, although it is, broadly speaking, a social and economic divide, nevertheless cuts across the class structure of the province. The working class is divided on sectarian lines. And while efforts to transcend that division and reunite it have been markedly unsuccessful, this hardly justifies socialists in disregarding or dismissing the views and wishes of the Protestant working class as being, let us say, no more than a manifestation of 'false consciousness'. That concept may be an appropriate one to invoke, but it is a mistake to suppose that a 'false' consciousness is also a shallow or insubstantial one. In any case, as I suggested in the last paragraph, some of their fears in relation to Irish unity are perfectly comprehensible and rational.

The continued dominance of the Catholic church in southern Ireland is one feature of the Republic which demonstrates the tragic incompleteness of the Irish national revolution. Undoubtedly the presence of a very substantial Protestant minority within a united Ireland would compel a secularization of the Irish state; but that process of secularization will have to be begun in the Republic as it is, if the reasonable anxieties of Northern Protestants are to be allayed. Paradoxically, the relative lack of popular support for the outlawing of abortion, as reflected in the 1983 referendum, indicates that a secularization, or liberalization, of opinion is already taking place, but it has yet to be reflected in the country's politics or institutions.

But whether we are thinking of the long-term prospect of a united Ireland, or of some kind of interim settlement of the present lethal conflict, the principal changes required lie elsewhere. They are: a significant change of attitude among the Protestants themselves, and, of course, a British withdrawal from Ireland. These two developments are, in fact, linked to each other. As long as the British give no hint of any plan or wish to withdraw, at least militarily, so long will the 'Loyalists' cling to the hope that in the end the IRA will be decisively defeated, and the way will then be clear for the restoration, perhaps in a somewhat chastened form, of Protestant supremacy. Thus almost the only chance of inducing a more realistic and accommodating attitude among the Protestants is for the British to make it clear that they will *not* remain in the province indefinitely, and to accept what is plainly true, that there will be *no* ultimate 'defeat' of the nationalist opposition. A timetable for withdrawal should be set, and accompanied by a timetable for negotiations to reach a post-withdrawal settlement. Such negotiations would, of course, have to involve all parties to the dispute, including Sinn Fein and the IRA.

It is by no means certain that a workable compromise settlement could be arrived at, or that the so-called 'Loyalists' would not then demonstrate their disloyalty by embarking on a strategy for UDI – a unilateral declaration of independence. But no policy for Northern Ireland is without risks. And the present policy-less stalemate carries its daily cost in lives lost and mutilated. It may already be too late for the British to do anything more constructive than to withdraw unconditionally and speedily, leaving the people of Ireland, south and north, to resolve matters among themselves, however dangerous such a project may seem. But the alternative ought at least to be tried. The British owe it to Ireland, and most of all to the minority in the North, to make one final, serious attempt to secure a just solution of the conflict. If this cannot be done – and Britain's credentials for playing such a role are hardly impressive at this late hour in Ireland's history – then they should finally leave Ireland.

Summary notes on Northern Ireland electoral politics

Northern Ireland: electoral politics

It is very noticeable that the professional psephologists shy away from the complexities of Northern Ireland politics, particularly since the dissolution of the Unionist-dominated system after 1969. Consequently the standard type of reference book (*British Political Facts*, general election surveys etc.) offer very little guidance through the maze.

Certain broad tendencies can, however, be fairly clearly discerned. One is the fragmentation of the previously almost monolithic Unionist Party domination of Protestant/Loyalist politics. This began at the Stormont election called by Prime Minister O'Neill in February 1969 to test the extent of support for his reform programme. He was opposed in his own constituency by the Reverend Ian Paisley, who came within 1,500 votes of beating him. A substantial number of anti-reform, anti-O'Neill Unionists were elected.

The process continued in the early 1970s. When, for example, the once hard-line 'Loyalist' Brian Faulkner reappeared at the head of the Unionist grouping which was willing to operate the new power-sharing arrange- ments proposed by Britain, this grouping was easily outnumbered by the number of Assembly members elected on the basis of 'Loyalist' opposition to power-sharing (June 1973), while in the British general election of February 1974, 11 out of the 12 Northern Ireland seats at Westminster were won by the hard-line United Ulster Unionist Council, as opposed to Faulkner's Official Unionists. The Official Unionists have recovered some ground, electorally, since then, but only by reverting to a hard-line position. In the 1983 British general election, they won 11 out of the 17 Northern Ireland seats. Paisley's Democratic Unionists won three, and an independent (Popular) Unionist one. The other two were won by Sinn Fein and the Social Democratic and Labour Party.

Like the various Unionist groupings, the Social Democratic and Labour Party is a product of the present crisis. It was formed in 1970, as an electoral expression of the predominantly Catholic campaign for civil rights and social justice. During the 1970s it usually monopolized the Catholic vote in elections, but this was partly because Sinn Fein still clung to its traditional policy of electoral abstention. (The exceptions were the two

Westminster constituencies of Mid-Ulster, and Fermanagh and South Tyrone, both of which were held at different times between 1969 and 1983 by independent nationalist MPs.)

Following the 1981 hunger strike, and the election successively of Bobby Sands and Owen Carron as MPs for the Fermanagh seat, Sinn Fein has been contesting elections with considerable success. In the 1982 Assembly elections it won five seats. In the British general election of 1983, Sinn Fein won the West Belfast seat against competition from both the SDLP and Gerry Fitt, standing as an independent. It came within 78 votes of winning Mid-Ulster, again despite SDLP competition for the Catholic vote. It won 35 per cent of the vote in Fermanagh, and 20 per cent in two other seats – thus demonstrating the considerable strength of its support in Northern Ireland today.

Summary data on the forces of the British state in Northern Ireland

Troops of the British army were first sent to the province in August 1969. They have been there ever since. In 1970 they numbered 8,100. They reached a peak figure of 20,300 in 1972, which was also the year of greatest violence in the province (see below). Since then they have been gradually reduced in number to 12,500 in 1982.

At the same time, however, the locally recruited (and overwhelmingly Protestant) forces of 'order' have greatly increased in strength. The Royal Ulster Constabulary has doubled in size, from 3,800 in 1970 to 7,500 in 1982. The RUC Reserve, a force created to replace the notorious B Specials, now numbers nearly 5,000, and the part-time Ulster Defence Regiment numbered more than 7,000 members in 1982.

Military activity – house searches

One index of military activity in the province is the *official* figures given for the number of house searches conducted by the army each year. In 1971 these numbered 17,262. In 1972 the figure had more than doubled, to 36,617; and it doubled again the following year, 1973, to 74,556, nearly one-fifth of the total number of houses in the province. There were another 71,000 searches the next year, after which the figures fall sharply, to 30,000 in 1975 and 20,000 in 1976. It is not difficult to imagine the effect of repeated ransackings on those who had to endure them. The figures also give some idea of the quantities of information which the army has collected on the population of the province over the past 15 years.

The death toll

This breakdown of the death toll was prepared in 1982 by Father Raymond

Murray of Armagh, and published in the *Irish Times* (3 September 1982) and in the Irish Freedom Movement's *An anti-imperialist's guide to the Irish War* (Junius Publications, 1983). It is possible that some of its details are not beyond dispute, but official statistics published in Britain are so inadequate and misleading that they at least cannot be relied on for a full picture.

Innocent people killed by British forces	108
Deaths by rubber and plastic bullets	14
Republicans killed by British forces	83
Republicans killed on hunger strike	10
Catholics killed by Loyalist paramilitaries	510
British forces killed by republicans	616
Assassinations by republicans	328
Civilians killed as a result of republican bombs, crossfire, accidents	194
Civilians killed by Loyalist bombs, crossfire, accidents	123
British forces killed by Loyalists	13
Loyalists killed by British forces	14
Protestants killed by Catholics in early riots	12
Catholics killed by Protestants in early riots	34
Republicans killed by premature explosions etc.	96
Loyalists killed by premature explosions etc.	26
People killed in uncertain circumstances	31
TOTAL	2,212

10

Parties in Pursuit of Socialism

DAVID COATES

The pursuit of socialism

The replacement of capitalism by socialism will constitute the most profound recasting of an entire social order ever achieved.[1] So it is hardly surprising that the many generations of socialists caught up in the pursuit of so large and daunting a task have regularly disagreed among themselves about the nature of the society they wished to create and about the character of the transformation which alone could bring it into existence. As a result, and from the beginning, both here and in every other capitalist country, those struggling for socialism have clashed with each other on a range of very fundamental issues; and those disagreements have invariably taken a quite standard (though to the uninitiated, an often totally bewildering) set of organizational forms. Indeed, from the 1860s at least it is possible to see, in each capitalist country as it industrialized, very distinct traditions of socialist politics emerging, traditions which differed from one another on questions of the following kind.

On goals

What is socialism? Is it a set of social reforms (such as welfare provision and full employment) that are to be consolidated within an economy whose major institutions remain largely in private hands? Or does that economy have to be centrally planned and directed by democratic political institutions? Does socialism involve a much more extensive replacement of private ownership; and if so, to what degree and in what sectors? Is public ownership enough; or is socialism about a much wider, and even more radical, transformation of class relations, property rights and decision-making processes in the society at large? And if it is that, what exactly are the changes which have to be made?

On strategy and tactics in relation to the state

Is socialism, however understood, to be achieved gradually, or all at one time? Is it to be achieved peacefully, or will violence be necessary? And if violence is part of any socialist change, is it a violence which the Left must initiate, or is it merely a defensive violence for which the Left must be prepared in the face of the inevitable counter-revolutionary terror of those who will oppose them? Can socialism come through the full utilization of existing political institutions (where those are already democratic) or by their democratization (where they are not)? Must those in pursuit of a democratic socialist transformation hold fast to the conventions of existing parliamentary democracy, or must they insist instead on the supplementation of parliamentary votes by extra-parliamentary struggles? (And if the latter, what exactly is the appropriate relationship between, and the relative priorities of, parliamentary and extra-parliamentary struggles in such a democratic socialist transformation?) And in either case, is parliament enough, or does socialism require the creation of new institutions of popular representation and administration? If it does, what will the relationship be between the new state forms and the old? Indeed are the institutions and personnel of the pre-socialist state amenable at all to socialist control, or must they be 'smashed' as a central element in the socialist transformation? Is the existing state, that is, to be captured, democratized, extended or replaced?

On agency

Regardless of how it is to be achieved, is socialism the project of a class or of a whole people? If it is class-based, is the agency for its achievement the working class alone? If that class is central, what exactly is its membership and what relationship do its members have to other classes (both other oppressed classes and exploiting classes) and to other groups exploited in non-class ways (to women in domestic production, to migrant workers, to Third World peoples, and so on)? And can even a fully mobilized and broadly-defined working class make a socialist revolution in one country, or must the project be international in scope and impact? Is it the agency of revolutionary change, that is, a world proletariat; and if it is, what is the relationship between struggles here and the pattern of national liberation struggles, peasant mobilizations and industrial unrest abroad?

On instrumentality

What kind of political organization, if any, is needed to bring the working class to socialism? How is that party to be organized internally, and what is to be the scope and terms of its membership? What relationship is it to have to the class as a whole (does it lead, follow, educate, or merely sustain only the advanced sectors)? And how is the party to know when support for socialism is sufficiently strong for it legitimately to act? Must it wait on a popular majority, or act on a wave of industrial unrest, or on its own sense of when the seizure of state power can spark the fire of revolutionary fervour across capitalism as a whole? Is such a 'vanguard' role for a socialist party a prerequisite to socialist success, or a guarantee of its inevitable degeneration?

Given the existence of at least this range of questions, the scale of disagreement and division on the Left is hardly to be wondered at. Indeed the idiosyncracies of many tiny groups reflect the way in which it is possible to put together a set of answers which very few others on the Left still share, or ever did. But to talk of idiosyncracies is also to imply a norm: and 'normal' packages of answers to these struggles did tend to emerge early in the history of socialist struggle, thereafter to persist. In fact, in practice it is possible to distinguish two broad traditions, around which socialists have gathered over the last century: a tradition of 'reform' and a tradition of 'revolution'; and then to notice a further division within the revolutionary current, as that current's internal development eventually set Communists and Trotskyists apart. It is possible to notice too that within each tradition disagreements persist, and developments go on, which pull sections of what were originally different traditions closer together. That is why the universe of socialist groups is so difficult to fathom when approached from outside and for the first time, in ignorance of its history and internal disagreements, and why therefore a brief résumé of that history is so vital if the contemporary situation of the Left in Britain is to be understood in full.

The tradition of reform has come to be associated in Britain with the Labour Party, but it pre-dates it by at least a century, stretching back through the radical wing of the Liberal Party to Francis Place in the 1820s and beyond. That tradition has always seen its constituency less in class than in income terms, seeking to recruit from the poor in an unequal society, and relating to the working class as it emerged in the nineteenth century primarily as just one major group which had hitherto been denied its proper political, social and economic rights. For radical Liberals the solution to the existence of widespread poverty and inequality lay through the democratization of existing parliamentary institutions and the application of pressure there for discrete reforms. In the first instance this was tried by lobbying Gladstone's Liberal Party; but by 1893 the ILP*[2] had been formed, convinced of the need to put working-class people into parliament to speak directly for the poor and deprived. At the heart of this tradition there has stood a powerful commitment to parliamentary democracy and its procedures, to the winning of popular majorities at elections, to the sending of representatives to parliament, and to the use of parliamentary power and the existing state machine to initiate and implement sets of social reforms. By 1918 the scale of reforms required was held by the Labour Party to be larger than initially thought: not just reforms within capitalism but its replacement by a socialist commonwealth based on the public ownership of the means of production, distribution and exchange. In practice, of course, Labour governments to date have fallen far short of this more radical goal, as I will show later; but the very regularity of that backsliding has called into existence and then sustained a tradition of left-wing politics dedicated to holding the Labour Party to its historic task, by winning the battle for socialism within the Labour Party. The present character and organization of the Labour Left are discussed in section II.

The alternative tradition was from the beginning sceptical of Labour parliamentarianism. It found its goals too moderate and its faith in parliamentary majorities too naïve. Instead the revolutionary current within the socialist movement looked to dispossess the owning class through a revolution which would give industrial and political power to the workers. Parliamentary action was not enough for that. Indeed parliamentary struggle took the working class away from its central area of strength, which lay in class struggles around the accumulation process in industry, and helped to defuse working-class power by subordinating it to parliamentary timetables, procedures and rhythms designed to protect bourgeois power.

That revolutionary tradition was first consolidated by the SDF (the Social Democratic Federation) and the tiny Socialist League. Left-wing rebels broke away from the SDF to form the SPGB* in 1904; and the whole revolutionary tradition gained a renewed focus in the Communist Party formed in 1920. The debates between the Labour and Communist Parties in the 1920s on the goals, strategy and tactics appropriate to socialism remains one of the clearest statements yet within the British labour movement of the choices faced by activists on the Left; and that debate continues now between the Communist Party and its own left-wing critics, many of whom are gathered in one or other of the various Trotskyist groups. For as the socialist character of the Soviet Union degenerated under Stalin, and as the Communist Party came to play the role of loyal defender of Stalinist excesses, a few revolutionaries broke away in the 1930s to form a tiny element in Trotsky's opposition to Stalin – an opposition which constituted itself as the Fourth International in 1938. It is this revolutionary current, tiny and divided, which remains the most visible face of revolutionary socialism in contemporary Britain. Developments in the Communist Party are discussed in section III, and Trotskyism in section IV.

Of course it is always possible to argue that in comparing the Labour
Party, the Communist Party and the Trotskyist sects we are not comparing
like with like – that the very way in which the Labour Party dominates
left-wing politics in Britain makes the rest of the Left largely irrelevant and
certainly trivial. There is no doubt of the electoral *un*popularity of the
Revolutionary Left. Table 10.1 gives the votes for Communist and other
Left candidates in the last five general elections, and sets those against the
vote for Labour. The contrast is dramatic. So too is the *formal* size of party
memberships. The Labour Party's individual membership at the end of
1983 was 295,344,[3] that of the Communist Party just under 16,000 and that
of the various groups discussed in section IV probably between 10,000 and
15,000.

Table 10.1   Electoral support for the Left

General elections	Communist Party	Other Left parties	Labour Party
1970	37,970	—	12,179,341
Feb. 1974	32,741	—	11,639,243
Oct. 1974	17,426	—	11,457,079
1979	14,509	14,846	11,532,218
1983	9,115	3,932	8,437,120

But it is as well to remember that the picture is not quite that simple. It is
true, as we will see, that the domination of the Labour Party means that all
other groups on the Left have to decide how to relate to its politics. But it is
also the case that the Labour Party is itself in deep crisis, with its vote
tumbling at an alarming rate. In the resistance to Thatcherism, its leadership and its politics play only one particular part. Its MPs speak out,
though often only ambiguously. Certain of its local councils offer serious
and courageous resistance in defence of local services. Many of its
members campaign in the unions, in the Peace Movement, and in public
demonstrations against the erosion of jobs and welfare provision. But in
those campaigns the Labour Party has no greater presence than does the
rest of the Left as a whole. Membership figures are very deceptive. Figures
are often inflated; and when they are not, only a proportion of the
membership are likely to be active. One can only guess at what the
proportion might be; but perhaps 10 per cent of Labour Party members are
active (in the sense of going to branch meetings), perhaps 30 per cent of
Communist Party members, and possibly 90 per cent or more of those on
the non-Communist Revolutionary Left. If those figures are in any way
accurate, that would give the Labour Party 29,000 activists to the
Communist Party's 5,000 and to the Revolutionary Left's 12,000. And
what membership involves varies considerably. There are campaigning

constituency Labour Parties of course, and there are CLPs dominated by Trotskyist politics. But in the bulk of Labour Party constituencies membership means nothing more than attending a very formal branch meeting once a month, and doing a bit of electioneering in April and in May. To be in the more dedicated of the revolutionary sects, at the other extreme, is to devote your whole life (and a considerable part of your income — Militant reportedly take £60 a *week* from supporters earning £10,000 a year) to party activity and direction, to sell papers on a weekly basis, to attend party meetings regularly, and to campaign and agitate in a variety of causes. The level of commitment required by parties of the Left differs enormously, but the Labour Party certainly demands least and the Revolutionary Left most. The Labour Party is not, in that sense, a campaigning party so much as an electioneering one. It does not even use its newspaper (*Labour Weekly*) as an agitating and recruiting document. It is the Revolutionary Left who stand outside Woolworth on a Saturday. It is they and the Communist Party who concentrate on extra-parliamentary struggle. And because they do, and because that struggle is so important, they too have a vital role to play in the creation of socialism in Britain.

The Labour Party

The Labour Party was formed in 1900 as the Labour Representation Committee, and adopted its present name in 1906. Founded in a period in which the majority of union leaders and the bulk of the then limited working-class electorate gave their political support to the Liberal Party, the new organization of Labour brought together socialists unhappy with

Table 10.2 Labour Party performance in successive general elections

Date	Seats contested	Members returned	Total votes cast	% of poll won
1900	15	2	62,698	1.8%
1906	50	29	323,195	5.9%
1910 (Jan.)	78	40	505,690	7.6%
1910 (Dec.)	56	42	370,802	7.1%
1918	361	57	2,244,945	22.2%
1922	414	142	4,236,733	29.5%
*1923	427	191	4,348,379	30.5%
1924	514	151	5,487,620	33.0%
*1929	569	287	8,364,883	37.1%
1931	491	46	6,362,561	30.6%
1935	539	154	8,325,260	37.9%
*1945	604	393	11,992,292	47.8%
*1950	617	315	13,295,736	46.1%

1951	617	295	13,948,385	48.8%
1955	620	277	12,405,246	46.4%
1959	621	258	12,216,166	43.8%
*1964	628	317	12,205,606	44.1%
*1966	621	363	13,064,951	47.9%
*1970	624	287	12,141,676	43.0%
1974 (Feb.)	623	301	11,639,243	37.1%
*1974 (Oct.)	623	319	11,457,079	39.2%
1979	635	269	11,532,218	37.0%
1983	650	209	8,437,120	27.6%

* = Labour government elected

the programme of Liberal-Radicalism and union leaders increasingly frustrated by the failure of Liberal governments to protect their organizations from the concerted attack launched on them in the 1890s by both employers and the courts. So from the outset the Labour Party was a coalition, containing within its ranks not only outright opponents of the capitalist system but also large numbers of politically moderate trade unionists and social reformers. That broad coalition has persisted, sustained by the manner in which the disintegration of the Liberal Party after 1914, and the Stalinization of the Communist Party in the 1920s, combined to leave the Labour Party as the only available political home for so many of the progressive forces in twentieth century British political life. In terms of its own criteria of success – votes won and MPs returned – the Labour Party between 1900 and 1966 was extremely successful. Since then, and particularly of late, it has been less so, as table 10.2 shows.

The Labour Representation Committee saw its initial task as that of placing a 'distinct Labour group in Parliament' to promote legislation 'in the direct interests of Labour', and that anchorage outside Parliament is reflected still in the internal life and organization of the Party. Under the terms of its 1918 constitution, the supreme policy-making body within the Labour Party is not the parliamentary group but the annual conference. MPs may attend that conference and speak from the floor, but they have no separate voting rights there, and are instead technically subject to a manifesto whose content reflects policy proposals adopted at successive conferences by delegates from the constituencies and from the trade unions – policy proposals whose implementation is supervised between conferences by a national executive committee of 28 members, 18 of whom are directly or indirectly chosen by the trade unions, and again on which MPs (other than the Party leader and deputy leader) have no automatic representation.

This set of constitutional arrangements, which are sharply at variance with those to be found in Labour's main political rivals, has helped to keep two features of Labour politics in public view down the years. The first of those features is the complex relationship between the parliamentarians and the activists in the constituencies; the second, the equally complex relationship between leading parliamentary figures and the national trade-union leadership. For from as early as 1907 Labour MPs as a group made known their unwillingness to act as the mere cipher of conference, and this struggle for parliamentary autonomy has made the issue of conference sovereignty a regular feature of internal Party disputes. Particularly when the Party has been in power, conference control has been systematically eroded by the many pressures operating on Labour Ministers; and because of that, and in the wake of the election defeat of those Ministers, the reassertion of conference control has been regularly presented by internal Party critics as *the* way of preventing similar electoral defeats in the future. Yet whether that reassertion has been successful or not has always turned on the attitude of national trade-union leaders to the Labour government that has just been defeated. For though on paper the unions enjoy enormous potential power inside the Party, through their capacity to dominate conference and the national executive committee, and because of their importance as sources of finance and sponsorship (they provide 70 per cent of Party funds and sponsor one-third of all Labour MPs), in practice union leaders have normally been willing to leave policy-making to the parliamentarians except in those areas that impinge directly on the union function and except in those periods (after 1931, 1970 and 1979) in which they have found themselves in direct conflict with the industrial and economic policies of outgoing Labour governments. So in spite of the Party's official structure, Labour politicians have generally found themselves free to take the initiative in the formulation of policy; but the existence of a constitution which gives supreme policy-making power to a delegate conference has also provided the opportunity and incentive for constituency activists to shape British political life indirectly, by the formulation of conference resolutions.

For the Left of the Party at least, those resolutions have, as often as not, been concerned with advancing the interests of 'working people and their families' and the slipperiness of that phrase, so current in Left Labour circles these days, is one index of the ambiguous relationship that the Labour Party has had, and continues to have, with the working class. In many important respects the early Labour Party was an obvious and unashamedly working-class party. The majority of its early leaders, and the bulk of its early activists, came from the working class. Keir Hardie, its first national figure, had been a miner. Ramsay MacDonald, its first Prime Minister, was the illegitimate son of a Scottish crofter and a young house-maid. Many of its early MPs were former union officials, and the Party relied heavily on working-class votes. Indeed by 1945 the Party had captured the electoral support of nearly 60 per cent of the working class, three-quarters of its own electoral strength was drawn from that class, and

Labour had become the instrument by which the socially exclusive composition of the House of Commons had been significantly diluted. As late as 1951, 74 MPs had only received elementary school education, and all of those were there as Labour members.

Yet from the outset the Labour Party was keen to capture support beyond the working class, and to present itself as more than a class (or a union-based) party; and this preoccupation with the pursuit of the 'national interest', understood as policies geared to winning the middle ground in electoral politics, became even more acute in the years following the election defeat of 1951. Since 1935 the Parliamentary Labour Party itself has become increasingly middle class in composition – teachers out-weighing miners as the single largest occupational group as early as 1945 – and Labour cabinets in particular have always shown (and increasingly have shown) a propensity to be staffed by former university students and professional people. The Wilson cabinet of 1969 contained only one (and the Callaghan cabinet of 1976 only three) former manual workers, and both had in addition only two other members who had come to political prominence after service in the trade-union movement. Moreover, four of the last six leaders of the Parliamentary Labour Party have come from professional backgrounds. This does not of itself, of course, demonstrate any automatic lack of sympathy with working-class institutions and political demands, but it does nonetheless signify the loss of those shared life styles and proletarian roots that were such a feature of the early Labour Party.

This embourgeoisification of the parliamentarians has been paralleled recently by a similar social shift amongst Party activists in the constitu-encies, (a recent survey suggested that 57 per cent of all Labour Party activists were now in white-collar occupations) and by a loss of manual working-class electoral support. The long-term trend of voting loyally has also run against the Labour Party fairly steadily since 1951 and acutely since 1966. Certainly the 1979 and 1983 elections made clear that large numbers of skilled workers could no longer be relied upon to vote automatically for the Party (by 1983 more skilled manual workers voted Tory than Labour for the first time since at least 1945). And by then it was very clear that the long years of boom and slump, the emergence of a large 'salariat' with potentially radical politics, the regular tension between Labour governments and the trade unions on wages controls, the persistent tendency of constituency parties to pick middle-class parliamentary candidates, and the long-established search by Labour cabinets for national respectability and the support of the floating voter, had all combined to weaken the traditional linkages between the Labour Party and its working-class social base.

In the early years of the Labour Party that linkage was consolidated around a particular programme. Before 1918 the Party restricted itself

mainly to acting as a parliamentary pressure group for the demands of the
unions, articulating as its programme the political demands of influential
trade-union conferences and the conventional preoccupations of Liberal-
Radicalism. But in 1918, as we have seen, the Labour Party went further
and adopted a socialist goal: 'to secure for the workers, by hand or by
brain, the full fruits of their industry and the most equitable distribution
thereof that may be possible upon the basis of the common ownership of
the means of production'. Though party policy in the 1920s remained
moderate, the traumatic events of 1931 (when Ramsay MacDonald left the
Party to lead a national government against it) prompted the Party to
adopt a distinctive set of policies that were more obviously in line with this
new aim, and which have since come to constitute what normally passes for
'socialism' in the British labour movement. That is, the Party committed
itself to extensive public ownership, to the democratic state planning of
private industry, to strengthening the legal and political rights of trade
unionists and workers, to the creation of a welfare state and full
employment, and to the redistribution of wealth and income in favour of
the poor and deprived. That programme gave the 1945–51 Labour
government its initial agenda, and it was defended as 'socialist' by left-wing
elements of the Party in the 1950s and 1960s as the Gaitskellite and then
Wilson leaderships retreated from it in favour of the creation of a high-
investment, high-growth *private* economy that could provide extensive
social services without large-scale income redistribution or tight state
economic controls. Then, as the Left in the Party regained the initiative
after 1970, the programme of the 1930s reappeared, modernized in its
detail but in all essentials similar, to provide the set of proposals on which
the Labour Party could go to the country in 1974 talking the language of
socialism again, and promising to achieve 'a fundamental and irreversible
shift in the balance of power and wealth in favour of working people and
their families'.

The radical nature of Labour Party promises at elections has been a
consistent feature of Labour politics since 1918. So too has been the
experience of frustration in office, as successive Labour governments have
fallen victim to the powerful conservative forces at work in the society they
would so drastically change. The failure of the 1924 and 1929–31
governments to solve the dominant inter-war problems of unemployment,
industrial stagnation and grinding mass poverty were often explained away
as a consequence of the Party's lack of a parliamentary majority – both
governments surviving only with Liberal support – and this thesis gained
more credibility from the initially impressive performance of Labour's first
majority government, that led by Clement Attlee between 1945 and 1951.
That government began life by taking a number of industries into public
ownership (mining, railways, gas, electricity, the Bank of England, and
eventually road haulage and steel), by continuing the physical planning of

private industry it had helped to establish in the wartime coalition, and by creating the National Health Service. But by 1948 it too went into retreat, cutting public spending plans in the wake of the 1947 financial crisis, abandoning its physical controls in the face of a heavy press campaign against it, increasing its military expenditure (at the cost of the health budget) in line with its strong identification with the USA at the time of the Korean war, and freezing wages in spite of growing trade-union opposition.

The 1964–70 government was even less successful. The Wilson leadership of 1963–4 had identified itself strongly with the achievement of economic growth through indicative state planning and the mobilization of science, and with extensive public spending, particularly on pensions, education and health. But, as with the Attlee government before it, the new cabinet's freedom of manoeuvre was heavily constrained by the competitive weakness of the British economy and by the defensive industrial strength of its trade-union allies. The weakness of the pound, with its associated financial crises and eventual devaluation, forced deflationary policies on the Wilson government, and these in turn eroded that competitiveness still further and produced heavy unemployment. Under the same set of pressures, Labour plans for social expenditure were cut and an incomes policy imposed on an increasingly unco-operative trade-union movement. Indeed relations between the Labour cabinet and the trade unions came to so low an ebb that the government attempted to win both electoral support and a revitalized economy by an attack on trade-union industrial power in its 1969 White Paper *In Place of Strife*; but, defeated in this by a backbench rebellion and overwhelmed by public sector strikes against its incomes policy, the government fell in 1970 with its policies generally discredited within the labour movement.

The initial beneficiaries of this defeat were the Left of the Party, supported on this occasion by a new generation of left-wing union leaders. They sent the Labour Party back into power in 1974 with a much more radical programme, enshrined in the Social Contract – a contract which promised voluntary pay restraint in return for 'socialist' policies on union legal rights, public ownership, state planning, pensions and industrial democracy. But that minority Labour government too was 'blown off course' after an initial short period of radical endeavour. The persistent weakness of the economy would not allow so sweeping a redistribution of power and income while remaining in capitalist hands, and the associated runs on sterling forced the government to go to the IMF, thereafter to adopt tight income controls, cuts in social expenditure, and higher unemployment. The monetarism of the Thatcher government after 1979 was foreshadowed in Labour government policy after 1976, and Labour once more left office in the wake of fierce strikes against its policies and with the distribution of class power in Britain as uneven and intact as ever.

The immediate consequence of this was the reappearance of old factional divisions within the Party, and the old call for the re-establishment of conference control. Left-wing forces inside the Parliamentary Party, unions and constituencies interpreted the events of 1976–9 as a betrayal of a viable socialist programme, and sought constitutional changes inside the Party which might prevent that betrayal in a Labour Government to come. Left-wing pressure created a momentum for change which replaced the parliamentary group's monopoly of leadership selection with an electoral college giving a role to activists and the main say to the unions; and obliged each MP to present him/herself for reselection to the constituency party at least once in each parliament. Though the Left also failed in 1980 to win NEC control over the manifesto, their campaign for internal change definitely strengthened left-wing influence in the Party, if not in the country at large, and inspired leading right-wingers to break away, to form the Social Democratic Party and to ally with the Liberals. Left-wing pressure also put men from the Centre-Left of the Party into leadership, first Michael Foot and then Neil Kinnock; and kept official policy (as specified by conference) on the economy, Europe and defence far to the left of any to which the Party had been committed since at least the 1930s.

But so far at least that is the extent of left-wing success within the Labour Party. The Left within the Party now has three main components: Trotskyist entry groups; a 'soft Left' organized around the Tribune* group of MPs; and a 'harder Left' active outside the PLP in campaigns such as the LCC* and the CLDP.* Divisions within this Left coalition on how best to push for constitutional changes after 1979 brought a major split, with many Left Labour MPs refusing to support Tony Benn in the campaign for the Deputy Leadership in 1982; and those divisions, and that campaign, helped to destroy the electoral credibility of the Party in 1983, leaving it with its lowest absolute vote since 1935, its smallest share of the total vote since 1918, and its lowest vote/candidate since 1900. Now needing a 12.8 per cent swing to win the next general election, and standing in third place to the Tories or Alliance in 309 of the 650 constituencies, the Labour Party is currently weaker in electoral terms than at any time since the war.

This weakness is reflected in the policy stance of the new 'soft Left' leadership under Neil Kinnock, whose concern to build Party unity and popular support has already produced fudging and backsliding on nuclear disarmament and EEC withdrawal. It has also quietened the 'hard Left', whose politics have been thrown into disarray by the visibly deleterious effect on the Party's voting base of their agitation after 1979. But left-wing groups remain active on and in the Labour Party. The main non-Trotskyist ones are: the Tribune group of MPs; the Campaign group of MPs; the ILP; the Labour Co-ordinating Committee; and the Campaign for Labour Party Democracy; and these (and the Labour Party Young Socialists) are discussed individually in the appendix, section VI.

The Communist Party

The Communist Party of Great Britain (CPGB) was formed in conference in 1920 and 1921 as a loose and initially reluctant coalition of small revolutionary groups who were inspired to unite both by Bolshevik success in Russia and by their own faith in the impending revolutionary upheaval within capitalism as a whole. That early revolutionary optimism was destroyed in the working-class defeats of the 1920s, and by the consolidation of Labour Party support in the inter-war years; and as a result the CPGB not only began with a small membership (initially some 3,000–5,000 people) but it has remained small ever since. Although it has managed (as few other revolutionary groups in Britain have ever done) to establish close, even organic, links with local working-class communities in particular areas, even that linkage took time to build – and with time, the politics of the tiny party changed in very important ways.

Like communist parties across the capitalist world, the CPGB 'Stalinized' between the wars. Organizationally it began to ape the Bolshevik model: becoming centralist, banning factions, expelling dissidents, and keeping tight leadership control on policy and propaganda. Stalinization also involved a subtle change in the relationship between Moscow and London. Whereas in 1920/1 both parties to that relationship agreed that the only way to defend Bolshevik gains was to spread the revolution westwards, by the 1930s that commitment to internationalism had changed into a simple 'defence of the Soviet Union', and into the subordination of party policy here to the dictates of Soviet foreign policy. By the 1930s the CPGB was a loyal acolyte of the ruling group in the Soviet Union; and altered its policy only when given approval by the Communist International (itself under Stalinist control). So the CPGB abandoned its initial anti-parliamentarianism to follow a 'united front' policy of co-operation with Labour Party members in the trade unions between 1922 and 1928, only to change its line sharply (fighting the Labour Party as 'social fascists') between 1928 and 1934, before returning to a policy of common struggle ('popular frontism') against fascism between 1934 and 1939. All these changes were dictated by the Third International, and the first two at least cost the Communist Party members and popular support. By 1930 membership had fallen to 2,500, and though it revived during the Popular Front period of the 1930s, it fell disastrously again between 1939 and 1941, when the Communist Party refused to fight against Hitler (seeing the war as one between imperialist powers of no concern to the working class). Only Hitler's invasion of Russia changed that, brought the CPGB heavily into the war effort, and enhanced its popularity significantly. By 1943 it had 56,000 members, and in 1945 even two MPs.

Since then the CPGB has been in progressive decline, a decline which now seems to threaten the very existence of the Party itself. The problems faced by the Communist Party since 1945 have been enormous. It had to react after 1948 to 25 years of economic growth and prosperity, 25 years in which living standards rose and political conservatism grew, and in which the weight of the manual working class in the social structure steadily diminished. In addition, it has had to contend with a capitalist state that has used virulent anti-communism as *the* central legitimating ideology of its own regime, and with a working class wedded, at best, to Labourism and, at worst, increasingly vulnerable to the appeal of anti-socialist ideas from Conservatives and Liberals. The Communist Party has had to operate too amid growing dissension, divisions and repression in the Soviet bloc, living in turn through the shock of Stalin's death, the events of 1956, the Sino-Soviet dispute, the invasions of Czechoslovakia (1968) and Afghanistan (1980), and the suppression of Solidarity in Poland. The impact on membership of all these things has been steadily corrosive, and latterly dramatically so. Membership fell to 30,000 by 1975 and to less than 16,000 by 1983. Active membership within those numbers also probably fell over time; and the size of the Communist vote certainly did. The Party contested seats in each general election with determined regularity, only to see its vote/candidate erode steadily – from 1,950 in 1951 to only 444 in 1979. Circulation of its daily newspaper in Britain also fell – from more than 30,000 to less than 15,000 between 1973 and 1983.

Party policy and internal disputes operated against that uncongenial background. The Party's recognition of its limited short-term potential was evident in the first edition of *The British Road to Socialism* published in 1951. In it, the Party envisaged the establishment of socialism without civil war through a combination of mass extra-parliamentary activity and the election of a socialist majority in parliament – a majority put together on the basis of an anti-monopoly alliance and still under the direction of a transformed Labour Party. That programme (and the insipid electoral and industrial politics it inspired) was insufficient to stop a slow (and at times a more dramatic) haemorrhaging of Party members through the 1950s and 1960s. In particular the Communist Party lost tiny groups of comrades to the new Maoist parties whose creation was inspired after 1956 by the growing conflict between Moscow and Peking, the force of Chinese condemnation of the Soviet bureaucracy as revisionist, and the visible moderation of local Communist Party politics. The tiny and highly sectarian world of Maoist politics in Britain lie outside the scope of this chapter, although the Appendix does list one Maoist group by way of example (the Revolutionary Communist League of Britain) and it is possible to come across others, not least the Communist Party of Britain (Marxist-Leninist) and its paper, *The Worker*. But Maoism has not made any major impact on the Revolutionary Left in Britain. Where Communism haemorrhaged more significantly in the 1950s and 1960s was to its Trotskyist and non-aligned Left. The events of 1956 in particular (Krushchev's secret speech and the suppression of the Hungarian revolution) cost the Communist Party at least 10,000 members, some of whom at least went into the Trotskyist groups or into the New Left. (On this, see the next two sections.) More importantly, the events of 1956 destroyed for ever the Communist Party's capacity to assert its hegemony on the Left. After 1956 it was just no longer posible for many revolutionary socialists to see the Soviet Union as the model for socialism, and Trotskyist critiques of Bolshevik degeneration gathered stature as a result. Indeed, as a new generation of students and workers radicalized in the 1960s, it was the Trotskyist groups which grew steadily and the Communist Party which did not. The Communist Party settled instead into a ritualistic defence of old policies and traditional socialist strategies which could not prevent its progressive marginalization from mainstream working-class politics and from the growing if still tiny world of the Revolutionary Left.

Such a crisis in British communism – which it shared even with its larger comrade-parties in France and Italy – invited a common response; and that came in the 1970s in the form of Eurocommunism. Broadly speaking, the Eurocommunist position was one which argued that neither social democratic parliamentarianism nor old-style insurrectionary politics were likely to take the Western European proletariats to socialism. Given the unpopularity of the Soviet model and experience, and the strength of the capitalist state and its supporting classes, the only route to socialism that was available in the West lay through the construction of a broad alliance of classes and strata opposed to monopoly capitalism. That alliance would have to be broad (taking in not just male manual workers, but also women in domestic production, ethnic minorities and other oppressed groups) and it would initially have to be democratic rather than socialist (not restricting itself just to the already converted or to narrowly socialist concerns). Moreover, to achieve that, the Communist Parties themselves would have to drop party claims to the monopoly of wisdom and power, and dispense with the dictatorship of the proletariat in the transition to socialism. Such a coalition of popular forces could then, Eurocommunists argued, win and democratize the existing state, and progressively shift the centre of gravity of popular consciousness towards socialism and of state power towards ordinary people.

The issue of Eurocommunism provoked bitter debates across the Communist movement, both here and in Western Europe as a whole. The appeal of Eurocommunism to Communist Party members trapped in a Left ghetto was enormous. It offered a third way between parliamentarianism and insurrection, it suggested a new way of reaching potential support beyond the working class, and it laid out a stages theory of progress to socialism which offered a long-term strategy for even a tiny party. But it also had problems on which its critics were quick to latch. By breaking with insurrectionary politics, and distancing Western European communists from the Soviet Union, the Eurocommunist strategy threatened to lose what was distinctive about communism as a tradition, and undermined the legitimacy and value of the history of each party to date. Its commitment to a broad democratic alliance offended those communists for whom the working class, industrially defined, was the key agency of socialist transformation; and its promise of a plurality of political parties in and after the transition to socialism threatened the status of the Communist Party itself, and (in the face of a large Labour Party, as in Britain) raised the question of whether a separate party was actually needed at all. As Eurocommunism established itself, therefore, it brought in its wake a spirited defence of the Soviet Union, of workerism, and of the special status of the Communist Party as an organization and of Marxism-Leninism as a science.

The CPGB has been dominated by a Eurocommunist current since at least 1977, and the latest edition of *The British Road to Socialism*, adopted that year, showed this dominance well. Developing themes prefigured in the 1951 programme, the 1977 version documented the hegemonic nature of capitalist rule and the existence of contradictions (particularly gender divisions) which could not be reduced to a simple question of class. In such a situation, and amid growing international and local economic difficulties for capital, the job of the party, according to the programme, was to link the inevitable mixture of resistance and struggle in a broad democratic alliance against state monopoly capitalism. That alliance would have as its core the working class (both manual and white-collar) but should also stretch out to small businessmen and middle management, and to other social forces and movements: women, black people, Scottish and Welsh nationalists, welfare consumers, young people, pensioners, even left-wing elements in religious circles. The programme specified the central political job for the alliance as the 'democratization' of the economy, society and the state; and conceived the transition to socialism as a lengthy process requiring majority support at each stage. It still gave the Communist Party a unique job in that mobilization, calling on it to offer a quality of political analysis and leadership which the Labour Party could never hope to produce. But the programme made no attempt to replace the Labour Party by the Communist Party; and looked instead for a Labour Party transformation under the pressure of extra-parliamentary mobilization in which the Communists would play a vital part. Yet the route to socialism was explicitly not just extra-parliamentary. On the contrary, *The British Road to Socialism* looked to an interplay of parliamentary and extra-parliamentary struggles to win a popular democratic victory which could initiate and consolidate a long process of revolutionary change.

Such a programme was insuffiently solid on traditional communist themes to inspire a breakaway by the old Stalinists in 1977, into the New Communist Party*. It also produced very bitter internal wrangling between the Eurocommunists, a faction around the internal monthly journal *Straight Left*, a group around the journal *The Leninist*, and a more fundamentalist group based mainly in the *Morning Star*. The latter tend to minimize the importance of non-class issues and of social forces other than the working class, and want the Party to radicalize its programme whilst defending the 'socialist camp' with enthusiasm. Those around *Straight Left* 'call for unconditional support for the Soviet Communist Party, and believe the party has followed a revisionist course since 1956, if not before. They deride 'bourgeois feminism' and other social movements, want to abandon the Communist Party's electoral work in order to facilitate entering the Labour Party, and are (according to their opponents) 'a CP mirror image of Militant' (*Marxism Today*, April 1984, p.28). The group around the *Leninist* see the Eurocommunists as 'liquidationists', threatening the long-term existence of the Party as such; and they fought hard at the 1983 Congress to have party control re-established over the *Morning Star*, to change *Marxism Today* (the Party's high-selling monthly journal) back to orthodoxy in place of its heavy Eurocommunist stance, and to toughen Party support for military rule in Poland. The Eurocommunist leadership of the Party survived all those arguments at that Congress – but only just. The vote on the *Morning Star*, for example, split 155 to 92; and that is just one indication of how divided the Communist Party now is, and how near to major schism it may actually be.

The non-Communist Party Revolutionary Left

Peter Sedgwick once wrote that 'we are all Trotskyists now' in the sense that an entire revolutionary generation have come to take largely for granted what were once classical Trotskyist positions shared by very few people on the Left: namely 'the identification of social democracy as an anti-working class, pro-capitalist force and of stalinism as the expression of the conservative nationalist backwardness of Moscow's rulers: . . . and a firm commitment to the development of revolutionary politics conducted outside the framework of stalinism and social democracy and necessarily on an international scale.' However there are Trotskyists and Trotskyists these days. Not all those that Peter Sedgwick had in mind would even call themselves Trotskyists, and certainly not all of them are affiliated to self-proclaimed Trotskyist internationals. The world of the non-Communist Revolutionary Left is one of immense complexity, and again it can be understood only if its history is known.

British Trotskyism, like Trotskyism elsewhere, derives from divisions within the revolutionary socialist tradition brought about in the first instance by developments in Russia after 1917. Those developments were constituted in part by a battle for power between individuals at the highest level of the new Russian state – a battle which Trotsky lost and Stalin won. But it was also a battle about the character of that new Russian state, and about the relationship of revolutionaries to it. By the 1930s Trotsky had become convinced that the revolution had been betrayed, that power had been usurped by a parasitic oligarchy, a conservative bureaucratic caste no longer interested in spreading the revolution worldwide. He had become convinced too that, though the job of revolutionaries was still to defend the Soviet Union against capitalist attack, the best way to do that was to build social revolution outside the Soviet Union and to work for political revolution in Russia itself. That in its turn, he had decided by 1938, required the construction of a new and disciplined international (a Fourth International) similar in purpose and design to Lenin's Third International before it degenerated into a tool of Russian foreign policy. Only such an international would then be able to offer revolutionary leadership to a world proletariat radicalized by the inevitable war between imperialisms which would soon mark 'the death agony of capitalism'.

The tragedy of post-war Trotskyism, of course, is that the war, when it came, did not produce the revolutionary situation envisaged by the Fourth International. Instead, workers across Western Europe gave their political allegiance in large measure to the very social democratic and stalinized communist parties against which Trotsky had railed; and in their isolation at the very margins of the class they sought to lead, the small groups of his supporters settled into a form of politics that came to have a very distinctive set of strengths and weaknesses. The strengths were those Peter Sedgwick listed earlier: a sense of the nature of Russia as a deformed workers' state, a wariness about bourgeois politics and a commitment to the revolutionary socialist mobilization of the working class. But because the groups were so tiny, those strengths were often overshadowed by less attractive features: a tendency to hang on to received dogma, and not to innovate theoretically and strategically; a tendency to split into even tinier fragments whenever any of this was tried, and an associated penchant for sectarian infighting, expulsions and the protection of organizational integrity that was reinforced by the whole communist tradition's propensity for vitriolic polemic in the style of Marx and Lenin; and a slowness to examine the relationship between the working class and other components in the coalition for socialism, projecting instead a 'workerism', even an 'economism' (a preoccupation with the wage demands and industrial struggles of organized wage-workers) which left them less able and willing to relate to the independent struggles of women, ethnic minorities and peace campaigners. Not all the groups shared these weaknesses to the same degree, as we will see, but they remain key features of the Revolutionary Left which militate against its growth. For the Revolutionary Left has grown, and grown divided, to leave us now with a myriad structure of groups, splits and intense ideological disputes. As a result, each group now has its own place in that complex structure, its own pedigree and history, which needs to be understood as part of its contemporary politics.

To clarify that, let me move briefly through the history of the main groups involved, and say at this point that what we need to remember first is that from its official creation in 1938 Trotskyism has always seen itself as an international movement in which individual parties exist merely as national sections of an internationally disciplined world organization. By 1944 the national section in Britain of the Fourth International (technically of the International Secretariat of the Fourth International – ISFI) was a tiny group of less than 400 people calling itself the Revolutionary Communist Party. Contemporary organizations on the Revolutionary Left in Britain can directly/indirectly trace themselves back to that party, not least because key figures active now were also active in the RCP. These include Ted Grant (Militant), Tony Cliff (SWP) and Gerry Healy (WRP). The RCP was riven by internal disputes on the status of the Soviet Union (was it a deformed workers' state or state capitalist?), on the significance of Tito, and on attitudes to work in the Labour Party and the trade unions. These disagreements split the organization entirely. A tiny group around Ted Grant, calling itself the Revolutionary Socialist League (RSL), went into 'deep entryism' in the Labour Party, as we will see; and an equally small group around Tony Cliff broke with orthodox Trotskyism altogether to pursue their analysis of the Soviet Union as state capitalist. It is in their journal, *Socialist Review*, that lie the origins of the present SWP, as again we will see below. What we need to establish first is what happened to orthodox Trotskyism, in the form of 'The Club' – the group organized around Gerry Healy.

Healy and his supporters retained the official support of the ISFI into the 1950s, to the point at which Healy's group (and the American SWP) decided to set up their own international (the International Committee of the Fourth International – ICFI) in 1953 because of what they saw as the ISFI's over-optimistic reading of developments in Russia after Stalin's death, and their associated unwillingness to criticize fully the repression of the East Berlin workers' rising in 1953. The ICFI remained an alternative Trotskyist international until 1963 when it too split (this time on whether the Cuban revolution was or was not a socialist one), with the American SWP rejoining the ISFI to form the United Secretariat of the Fourth International (USFI). Technically the ICFI still exists, and the Healy group is its national section; but in fact it has no other overseas affiliates of any significance.

The Healy group spent the 1950s working in the Labour Party, and was saved from extinction by the arrival of 200–250 ex-Communists after 1956 and by some recruiting success among rank and file trade unionists in the late 1950s. By then 'The Club' had turned itself into the Socialist Labour League (in 1959) and was heavily involved in Labour Party politics. It was eventually driven from the Labour Party (and its Young Socialists) in 1965, and has operated as an independent socialist party since. It changed its name again in 1973, this time to the Workers Revolutionary Party. But whatever the name, the SLL/WRP remains notorious on the Revolutionary Left for at least two things. The first is the intensely authoritarian regime which operates inside the organization, and which has produced an endles series of expulsions and high membership turnover. The second is its associated sectarianism – its refusal to work harmoniously with other groups on the Revolutionary Left against whom it maintains a steadily vitriolic condemnation. Details of its present policies are included in the Appendix, and the broad outline of the international Trotskyist structure is given in figure 10.1.

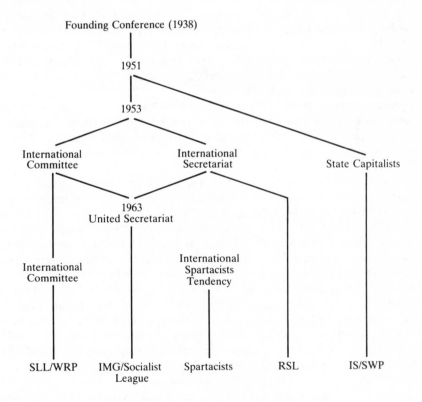

Figure 10.1   The structure of international Trotskyism

The USFI initiated its own new grouping in Britain in 1965, in the form of the International Marxist Group (IMG). This group, as the Appendix will show, attached less importance than other Trotskyist groups to the role of the working class as the vanguard of revolutionary change, and instead – and in line with USFI feeling on the question – concentrated its focus on student activism rather than on workers, looked to the Third World anti-colonial struggle as a catalyst of change rather than to industrial struggle in the First World, and proved to be as open to feminism as any Revolutionary Left group in Britain has yet managed to be. Initially wedded to the notion of universities and students as catalysts of revolutionary upsurge, the IMG quickly renounced entry work in the Labour Party to concentrate instead on Vietnam Solidarity work and on giving unconditional support to the Provisional wing of Sinn Fein in its struggle for Irish independence. The IMG was always highly democratic internally, and escaped the propensity to centralism and expulsions so characteristic of other groups on the Revolutionary Left. It also attracted to itself many socialist feminists in the early 1970s, and as a result – and like the Communist Party – was active in many key women's campaigns throughout the decade. It was also active in the search for 'socialist unity' in the mid 1970s, and its leading figures stood as Socialist Unity candidates in the 1979 general election. But the waning of student militancy, SWP intransigence in the unity discussions, its own lack of a working-class base, and the crushing defeat of Socialist Unity candidates in 1979, all left the IMG with serious problems and with major internal disagreements. Renamed the Socialist League, it too has now turned to entryist work within the Labour Party, and has in the process lost a significant number of its members and much of the public profile which made it so attractive a focus for many revolutionary socialists ten years ago.

Throughout its short life, the IMG's major competitors on the Revolutionary Left were two organizations whose pedigree stretched back in unbroken line to 1944–7 and the RCP. It found itself in competition in the first instance with the International Socialists, Cliff's group which had grown from a handful in the 1950s to more than 1,000 members by 1968. The International Socialists remained in those years the most theoretically fertile and organizationally open of all the formally Trotskyist groups. They abandoned any obligation to defend the Soviet Union by dismissing it as state capitalist, adopting as their slogan instead 'neither Washington nor Moscow but International Socialism'. That in its turn set them apart from official Trotskyism, which continued to see the Soviet Union and its allies as worthy of defence as deformed or degenerate workers' states. IS also abandoned the short-term catastrophism endemic to official Trotskyism, and developed a theory of 'the permanent arms economy' to explain the long post-war boom. They developed too a new explanation of industrial militancy, by concentrating on the role of shop stewards in the face of an 'employers' offensive' and a necessarily conservative trade-union bureaucracy; and they used this view of rank and file industrial strength as a way of underwriting what little remained of their official Trotskyism – namely a faith in the revolutionary potential of the working class and in the associated need of revolutionary socialist parties to concentrate their main energies there.

Yet IS was also sufficiently flexible in those years to throw its energies into the Vietnam Solidarity Campaign, and to involve itself (less easily, it has to be said) in support work on the question of Irish independence. Active inside the Labour Party until 1967, the International Socialists grew rapidly in the early 1970s, turning the organization into the Socialist Workers Party in 1976, and setting up rank and file newspapers in 15 industries in an attempt to politicize and link up struggles across industry as a whole in the expectation of the impending radicalization of the working class under a Labour government visibly in decline. Membership stagnated when that failed to happen, and the scale of the SWP's rank and file newspapers was reduced accordingly; but the party still remains the largest revolutionary socialist party in Britain with about 4,000 members. Indeed it has to be said that it was the SWP's commitment to this very growth that blocked the establishment of any wider unity on the Left in the negotiations of 1976–7. For the SWP remains committed to 'unity in action' (in individual campaigns) whilst resolutely opposing any move towards organizational unity between itself and what it sees as tiny and politically dissimilar groups on the Revolutionary Left. The Party has become more 'Leninist' of late, reorganizing itself internally to give greater control to its central leadership at the cost of expelling or losing many of its former leading figures. Traditionally bad on the question of feminism – it actually closed its women's newspaper (*Women's Voice*) in 1982 – the SWP, for all its lack of any official linkage with international Trotskyism, is today extremely orthodox on some of the defining themes of that tradition: stressing as it does the need for a vanguard party, and for concentrating its energies on the defence and advancement of the interests of the working class at the point of production in preparation for an upsurge of working-class militancy and radicalism in the crisis to come.

The WRP, SWP and Socialist League also faced a challenge from the much more secretive Revolutionary Socialist League, now entrenched in the Labour Party as the major Trotskyist group still committed to entryism of a 'deep' kind. By that I mean a policy of entering a party not as a raiding exercise (to recruit and leave) but as a long-term strategy of waiting for the crisis to open up the possibility of that party's mass radicalization – a radicalization then to be achieved from within. The RSL began such an entryism in the early 1950s, committing itself to over 30 years of waiting for social democracy to 'go into ferment', from which to extract a 'revolutionary tendency'. Using a theory of the labour aristocracy to explain

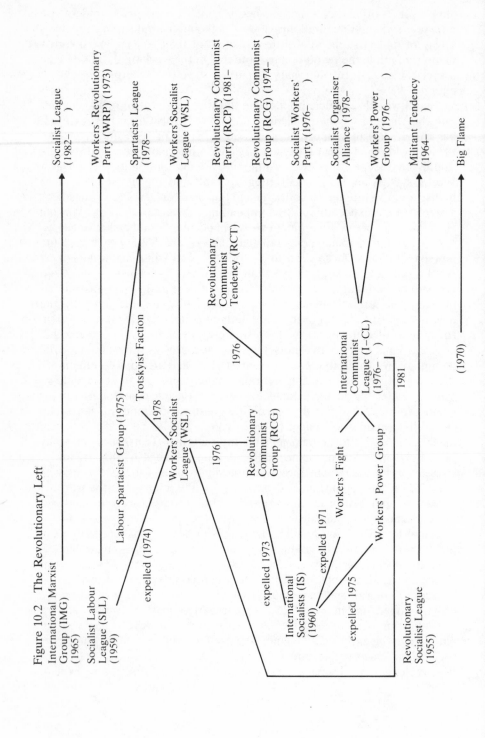

Figure 10.2   The Revolutionary Left

working-class conservatism, and a view of the PLP leadership as politically corrupt, all that the Militant Tendency (as the RSL became) saw itself as having to do was to wait for the crisis of capitalism to destroy the material basis of the first, and its own activism to expose the latter. Militant has always taken a highly sectarian line on other Trotskyist organizations, dismissing them as 'the sects' and as anti-Marxist; and it still tends to discount all non-working-class mobilizations (anti-racism, feminism, even the peace movement) as distractions and irrelevancies. Against them, and the Labour Party leadership, the Militant Tendency poses its series of transitional demands while consolidating its place in constituency Labour Parties, using its newspaper, *Militant*, as the main vehicle for both processes. That consolidation has worked to a degree. For in the absence of any serious theoretical challenge within the Labour Party from the organs of the Labour Left, Militant has established its space as *the* Marxist current within the Labour Party, and has benefited from the general radicalization of Party activities in the era of Tony Benn. Though its actual membership size is difficult to locate, it has definitely grown dramatically of late; and its growth has been so successful in fact as to stimulate moves within the Labour Party to proscribe the organization and to expel its members. Its five leading figures were expelled at the 1983 conference, and individual expulsions periodically occur at constituency level; but this still leaves the Tendency with two MPs and with genuine regional and party strength, particularly in Liverpool and in the Labour Party Young Socialists. The Militant Tendency is now the best placed and most publicized of all the Trotskyist groups engaged in entry work within the Labour Party, but its organization, membership and policy-making processes remain necessarily hidden and difficult to locate. Informed opinion would suggest, however, that there could be as many as 5,000 members in the RSL and as many again as sympathizers in the Labour Party Young Socialists; and the latest published work on the Tendency – that by Michael Crick – reports Militant's annual income at over £1 million and the number of its full-time workers at 140. If this is true, Militant now has an income in excess of the SDP and more full-time workers than the Liberals and SDP together.

These then are the main Trotskyist and semi-Trotskyist groups and parties now active in Britain. From them, at various times and for a multiplicity of reasons, a number of other smaller organizations have broken away. Figure 10.2 charts the main routes of those divisions; and the particular policy stance of each is given in the appendix, section 6.

The non-aligned Left

Finally, a brief note on a non-aligned current on the British Left – one

H

organized around discussion groups and educational activities, and peopled primarily by intellectuals. These groups were at their most extensive in the late 1950s, when a number of ex-Communist Party members joined with university-based radicals to form New Left Clubs, from which to create and disseminate a democratic and humanistic socialism that was neither Stalinist nor social democratic. A similar initiative in 1968 produced a May Day Manifesto, an analysis of British capitalism and a suggested programme for socialist reconstruction. In similar vein, Centres for Marxist Education were established briefly in the mid-1970s in places such as Manchester, Leeds and Newcastle. The most recent example of this current is the Socialist Society formed in 1981.

The aim of the Socialist Society is to help to create a new socialist popular culture – to make socialism the common sense of the age – by educational and agitational initiatives, and by reseach and debate. The Society is open to socialists aligned to particular political parties and groups, and to socialists aligned to none. It came into existence because of a sense that Thatcherism was winning not simply the political battle for popular support but also the ideological battle for popular consciousness. That in its turn was seen as an indication of how weak the Left had allowed itself to become – weak because of the visibility of its own internal disagreements and weak because of the paucity of its own specification of contemporary socialist alternatives. The Society saw itself as one possible part of the answer to that weakness. It offered itself as one arena within which the Left could meet together to discuss (and hopefully to resolve) some of its internal disagreements. The hope was that, in the process, the Left could work together to clarify problems of socialist transition and to prepare the material on which the case for such a transition could be generalized. In other words, the Society saw itself, and still does, as a catalyst for unity on the Left, which it interprets as involving four things:

1   the creation of a framework within which socialist intellectual work and socialist political activity can come into mutually beneficial contact;
2   the encouragement of political co-operation and debate among socialists in the Labour Party and those outside it, whether organized or not;
3   systematic efforts to develop the relationship between socialism and feminism, with the aim of creating a Left integrally committed to women's liberation and politically equipped to fight for it; and
4   a struggle against GB chauvinism and racism both domestic and international – against the oppression of minority nationalities and ethnic communities, and imperialist domination of the Third World.

In the event, the Socialist Society's highest ambitions remain as yet unfulfilled and the Society itself is still much smaller than first was hoped. Though it began work with hopes of rapid growth country-wide, the Society remains heavily London-based, though regional groups are active in such places as Liverpool, Manchester, Cardiff, Brighton, Derby and Leeds. The bulk of the Society's work has gone into the organization of study groups, summer schools, conferences and publications; and current membership is probably no more than 500. Yet for all that, the needs to which the Society saw itself responding remain of vital importance to the Left as a whole; and the series of which this volume is a part is our attempt to make a small contribution to the project for which the Socialist Society was created – namely of turning socialism into the common sense of the age. That remains still a vital task facing the Left in the rest of the century.

11

Class Conflict and Socialist Advance in Contemporary Britain

ROBERT LOOKER

Introduction: the current crisis of the British labour movement

For many sections of the Left in Britain, Labour's second successive defeat by the Thatcherite Conservative Party in June 1983 was not merely an electoral setback of major proportions for the Labour Party. Rather it is seen as indicative of a crisis of historic proportions in the British labour movement as a whole. On this view, the elections of 1979 and 1983 together constitute a watershed in the history of British capitalism, comparable at the very least to Labour's 'great leap forward' of 1945. Indeed, to take the long view, the transformations now taking place in the balance of class forces as a consequence of these defeats have been compared to those of the crisis decades from the 1880s to the 1920s which saw the birth of Labourist politics and modern trade unionism in the first place.

At first sight, this may appear to be a somewhat overblown reaction to two electoral defeats, however painful that experience may be for the Labour Party itself and however depressing – in all senses of the word – the experience of the Thatcherite alternative has proved for most of us. Indeed, when we examine the detailed explanations offered to account for these defeats by the various factions within Labour – the Bennite 'civil war' vs. the 'treason' of the Gang of Four; the Falklands factor; a weak and divided leadership equivocating over its own equivocal policies on defence, Europe, economic policy and much else; organizational and policy weaknesses in the election campaign further exacerbated by the Party's viciously hostile reception in the mass media etc. – one might be reluctant to be persuaded that Labour is faced with anything more than a temporary decline in its electoral fortunes. Given a new leadership and a degree of party unity, surely recovery may be just around the corner? Incidentally, the emergence of the Kinnock-Hattersley 'dream ticket' leadership and its enthusiastic reception by the bulk of Party activists must surely write the political obituary of those on the 'hard Left' in the party who saw electoral defeat this time round as the necessary price paid for the internal power struggle to ensure that next time, Labour would be offering a real socialist programme, leadership etc. to the electorate. Alas for Labour's socialist activists, next time never comes.

Yet if the language of watersheds and historic crises is somewhat overstated, the crisis for the Labour Party revealed by the electoral results is far more deeply rooted than might be evident from the Micawberish 'something will turn up' optimism which currently pervades the Labour leadership, at least if one judges it by its public utterances. For when these electoral defeats are placed within three appropriate contexts of analysis, each one raises real and continuing doubts about whether the politics of Labourism, in any of its Left, Right or Centre variants, will ever again be able to present itself to the electorate with any chance of success. Not just as the embodiment of 'the parliamentary road to socialism' but even as a party of modest social reform, Labour's days seem numbered. Indeed, the sense of dismay, even despair, which has overwhelmed Labour and its supporters has reached a point where the eminent Marxist historian and Communist Party theorist, Eric Hobsbawm, can advocate virtually any policy compromise and electoral accommodation, including an alliance with the Alliance, in order to oust the Conservatives and restore Labour's electoral credibility.[1] It should be said that within the electoralist logic that he shares with the Labour Party, Left as well as Right, Hobsbawm is undoubtedly correct. Much of the anguish and outrage with which his proposals have been greeted flows precisely from the unwillingness of the electoralist left to face the political implications of that logic. Equally, it is precisely the inexorably rightward pull of that logic which constitutes one of the main grounds on which others on the Left reject the electoralism.[2]

The first context within which the electoral defeats must be interpreted is perhaps the most obvious one, that which is provided by the economic crisis of British and world capitalism. For unlike the electoral defeats of the 1950s which took place against a background of economic growth and general prosperity, those of 1979 and 1983 must be situated in the context of a slump – in the latter case, of a slump presided over by a Tory government whose policies have deliberately accentuated its impact on production and unemployment while simultaneously cutting away at the limited protection offered to its victims by welfare provision, low pay legislation and the like. In the face of such conditions, it might not seem unreasonable to expect that any political alternative which offered even a modest degree of amelioration in these conditions would sweep to power. Yet it was under *these* circumstances that Labour's share of the vote plumbed to a depth not sounded since 1918, and in an election in which the Labour Party received a minority of the support not only of the working class as a whole but even of trade-union members! As we wrote in an earlier volume in the Socialist Primer series prior to the election, 'That four years of mass recession, cuts in public services and government attacks on working-class organization and industrial power, has not radicalized the broad mass of workers to a reinvigorated socialism must stand as the most glaring indictment of the bankruptcy of reformism as it has been practised by the British Labour Party . . .'[3]

The defeat of 1983 was no sudden and unlooked for catastrophe induced by some combination of special circumstances in the election campaign or in the four years of opposition that preceded it. Such special factors as were present served mainly to reinforce a long-term process of erosion in the party-class relationship established in the historic 'social contract' which underlay the victory of 1945. This is the second context in which 1983 must be read. For the story of the post-war years, at least since 1951, has been one of long-term electoral and organizational decline, as Labour has proved unable either to hold on to its traditional base in the manual working class or to extend its support into major sections of the growing white-collar salariat. From a highpoint in 1951 when it secured the support of nearly 49 per cent of the votes cast, almost 14 million people or over 40 per cent of the total electorate, Labour has declined almost continuously until its nadir in 1983 when barely 28 per cent of the votes or 20 per cent of the electorate, some eight and a half milion people in all, gave their support to Labour.

To some observers, this long-term decline may serve simply to confirm a view that secular changes in both the nature of the class structure and in the significance of class as a major determinant of political loyalties and voting habits have rendered Labour's compact with the British working class, and the reformist politics on which it was based, historically irrelevant.[4] Such views need not detain us here. As this and previous volumes of the Socialist Primer series have been at pains to argue and document, British society today is still based upon a capitalist mode of production and continues to exhibit all the antagonistic relations of class exploitation and oppression integral to that system. While the composition of the working class and its boundaries with other classes have changed – particularly through the rela-tive decline of the 'traditional' industrial proletariat and the growth of a white-collar/white-blouse salariat – and while this has complex implications for class politics, it does not of itself render such politics either redundant or irrelevant.[5]

As I have argued elsewhere,[6] the key to the erosion of the party-class relationship lies not in the nature of the class as such but rather in the working out of the reformist logic of its relationship with the Party. Key sections of the working class in the post-war years have found that their practical experience of Labourist politics, as much in its successes as in its failures, has not generated enthusiasm for a 'new socialist commonwealth' so much as a complex set of responses ranging from disappointment to cynicism and de-politicization, or even downright hostility to 'socialism' and a consequential openness to rightist politics. Indeed, far from setting the direction and pace of some 'forward march of Labour', the logic of Labourist political practice within an ailing British capitalism has increasingly driven it to discipline, abort or combat attempts by the organized labour movement that created it to defend or advance their position within capitalism.

I shall return briefly to this theme later. For the moment, I must turn to the third context in which the electoral defeats of Labour must be read, for it is provided by their reciprocal outcome, the triumph of Thatcherite Conservatism. For it is Thatcherism above all which is taken by many on the Left to embody and demonstrate a decisive shift in the political terrain of British capitalism comparable to that accomplished by Labour in 1945. 1945 was a watershed precisely because it was then that Labour (a) established itself as the 'natural' party of the great mass of the British working class; (b) constituted itself as a viable party of government, and (c) entrenched the assumptions and values of reformist social-democracy into the terrain upon which parties of both the Left and Right would have to vie for majority support. 1983, by contrast is increasingly read on the Left as the year that confirmed the scope and the scale of a veritable counter-revolution, initiated by the Conservative victory of 1979, which has (a) built a powerful national majority for New Right politics on the basis of mobilising important segments of the working class behind an ideology of authoritarian populism; (b) effectively marginalized Labour to the status of a pressure group for the old, predominantly northern, decaying industrial areas and inner-city ghettoes; (c) inscribed the 'free market, strong state' perspectives of Thatcherism into the very common-sense definitions of reality in public and popular consciousness. On this view, the threat posed by Thatcherism is that it proposes not merely to halt but systematically to roll back the march of Labour; to discredit and dismantle the institutions and practices won and defended by the British labour movement over the past century.

These are large claims indeed, whether the voices articulating them express Right hopes or Left fears. If we are to consider the prospects for class conflict and socialist advance in the coming years under a Thatcherite Conservative government in Britain – and this is the main purpose of this chapter – then we need first to consider their degree of plausibility. Crabwise, we will proceed via (a) some brief observations on the historic achievements, and limitations, of the British labour movement; (b) a look at the nature and extent of the Thatcherite challenge to it (c) the possible lines of response by the Left to that challenge.

A sideways glance at the 'forward march of Labour'[7]

It is doubtless salutory periodically to remind ourselves that 'the basic freedoms that so many English men and women now accept . . . as their birthright are . . . neither so firmly established nor so proof against attack that we can afford to take them for granted or believe that they are to be maintained, let alone extended without constant vigilance and constant effort.'[8] And it is important to recognize that such 'freedoms have been won for us over the centuries by the determined efforts of others, people who had to fight, often against overwhelming odds, for every inch of the ground'.[9] We certainly need to insist on what several generations of socialist historians have convincingly argued, that by far the most substantial contribution to that struggle in the past two centuries has been made by the working class in and through the movements, institutions, ideas and practices they have generated and sustained in the long continuing conflicts against the realities of capitalist oppression and exploitation. Those freedoms, then, were the outcome of 'the forward march of Labour'.

More specifically, it is argued that during the course of the nineteenth century, the working class of Britain both made itself and actively sought to remake the industrial capitalist environment which gave it birth. At times through violent confrontation, more frequently as the century progressed by a process of institutional entrenchment in trade unions, co-operatives, trades councils etc. the emerging labour movement first warrened the capitalist structure from end to end – to borrow John Saville's suggestive image – and then embarked upon a programme of super-structural alterations designed to transform not merely the facade but the very fabric of that edifice.[10] In a series of struggles stretching from the Chartists to the Suffragettes, democratic institutions and practices were quarried out of an oligarchic state structure which had hitherto served to express and legitimate the political and social ascendancy and economic power of the British ruling class. And within the arena thus cleared for representative democracy, the challenge posed by the aspirations and institutions of the labour movement compelled the ruling class and its political agents to pay ransom rather than to rely on repression for decades before the watershed victory of 1945 placed government power firmly in the hands of the Labour Party as the chosen political instrument of the mass of British working people. With that outcome, the long march of Labour reached its climax, with the foundations of the welfare state, a mixed economy built upon a substantial state owned sector, and legislative recognition of the legitimate rights and power of organized labour.

Taken at a sufficiently brisk pace, and choosing the point at which to conclude it with care, this tale of 'the forward march of Labour' can be stimulating and uplifting. And in contrast to some capitalist cant which portrays freedom, justice and democracy as by-products of market forces – or some Tory cant, which sees them as some natural expression of the spirit of the nation, a gift to us from princes and oligarchs to be defended and advanced by judges and lawyers and police and soldiers – in contrast to this, our tale expresses an essential truth. The right to free speech, the right to vote, the right to organize, had to be won with the blood and sweat and tears of ordinary working men and women in struggles with precisely those market forces, princes and oligarchs, judges and police. Yet the tale is more panegyric than history, and as we move closer towards the latter, the need for qualification and modification grows progressively greater.

In the first place, those struggles, though often intense and protracted, were rarely if ever as clear and self-conscious in their goals as the tale might suggest. Nor were they, either in their scope or in their support, characteristically the struggles of a whole class as such. Frequently sectionalist in their social base and aspirations, defensive and reactive in their responses, they never directly and consciously confronted the power and rule of capital. However much they sought to alter the fabric of their capitalist context, they assumed that its structure could only be adapted, not abolished.

Eric Hobsbawm has observed that 'In Britain, where the working class has been for almost a century far too strong to be wished away by the ruling classes, its movement has been enmeshed in the web of conciliation and collaboration more deeply, and far longer, than anywhere else.' The responses of our rulers he compares to 'that of the lion-tamer rather than the big game hunter'.[11] Yet the condition for this containment by the ruling class is, in large part, the contained character of the aspirations of the working class. Nowhere has this dialectic of containment and self-containment been more pervasive than in the case of the bourgeois democratic state in Britain. The struggle for the vote, for 'participation in politics', was long and hard, yet the political system has been remarkably successful at hedging, containing and controlling popular democratic impulses within institutions, social practices and power relationships which remain profoundly oligarchic even by the standards of bourgeois democracy. To have won the six points of the Charter in the 1840s might well have revolutionized Britain: for that very reason, defeat was probably inevitable. But the slow filtration of sections of the oppressed and exploited into the political system – the skilled male manual workers in the 1860s, the unskilled in the 1880s, women in the 1920s – facilitated that strategy of containment and conciliation precisely because each challenge came separately and already sectionalized. The results are most visible today in a political system whose archaic form — from the monarchy and the House of Lords to the judge-invented common law – obscures their very contemporary role as part of the mechanisms of ruling-class containment and control of any impulses towards mass democracy.

Seen at this level, there is a marked contrast between the oligarchic and secretive British state structure on the one hand and, for example, the much more open and accessible system at work in the USA. But then, US capital has been able to corral its working class at a much greater distance from direct participation in representative democratic institutions than was possible in the case of Britain, given the size and historical development of our working class. In the latter case, the system of capitalist containment necessarily involved some representation of the working class as an essential part of its operations. Historically this has taken the shape of the ideologies and institutions of Labourism. One does not need to deny or denigrate the real benefits that have flowed to the working class from the proximity to governmental power of the Labour Party in our century, in order also to recognize that, from its origins until the present day, Labour has been an agency for the political self-containment of the working class as an instrument for its economic and social advance. Analysts from Ralph Miliband to David Coates have explored in great detail the intricate connections between the reformist perspectives and parliamentary practice which propel the Labour Party in the direction of accommodations to capitalism and into opposition to anything that raises the prospects of real working-class power, and the arguments need not be repeated here.[12] It is sufficient for our purposes to stress that if the British state is a key agency for the incorporation and containment of the working class, then the Labour Party has, from its inception, proved a more or less willing instrumentality for the 'self-containment' of that class.

And yet, there have been real and tangible advances for both organized labour and the wider working class arising from the Labour connection. Indeed, it is not only apologists for the Labour Party who point for instance to the achievements of the 1945–51 Labour government – admittedly with an increasingly bitter-sweet nostalgia for an heroic past apparently now firmly behind us. Yet it is necessary for socialists to take a cool look at such achievements, for as with so much else in Labour history, panegyric often substitutes for analysis. It is not simply a matter of arguing that 'Labour didn't go far enough' – what was needed was more nationalization, a more comprehensive and universalistic welfare state structure etc – though that is undoubtedly true. Certainly there were 'external' constraints – from the opposition of the medical profession to the economic threats of big capital – which could have been challenged more vigorously. But of at least equal importance were the internal contradictions and deformations in the structure and purpose of the measures themselves. The bureaucratized state industries which constituted the nationalized sector were not thus constituted because of some personal predilection of Herbert Morrison's. They flowed directly from a perspective and a practice which accepted without real questioning the 'capital logic' of such enterprises within the framework of a still dominant capitalist mode of production.

For the miners, transport and power workers and many others whose unions had formed the very backbone of the Labour Party, 'socialism' in 1945 may not have had a very sophisticated theoretical content, but it was centrally about 'public ownership' which embodied real and practical solutions to the felt problems of their working lives. For such workers, the experience of the realities of nationalization marked the beginnings of the long process of disillusionment with the project for socialism. Precisely because the one option for translating aspirations into reality, workers' control based on workers' power, was closed off from the start by the very nature of the Labourist enterprise, socialism came to represent at best an 'ideal' which, precisely because it was 'impractical', had no leverage on the 'here and now' consciousness of workers. At worst, it became equated directly with the bureaucratic practices that were organized in its name by Labour. Nor is this story confined to the nationalized industries. For the vast bulk of the working class, the experience of Labourist socialism *at its best* has been all too frequently dispiriting and disillusioning, as anyone who has found themselves on the receiving end of the hospital system, or the council housing structure, or 'the welfare' can testify. Attempts at redistributive and ameliorative measures to compensate for the consequences of capitalism without decisively challenging and destroying the engines sustaining that system are bound to have a temporary, transient and 'make do and mend' quality. The institutions and practices which formalize those attempts necessarily deform themselves also into bureaucratic agencies of discipline and control. To call the result 'socialism' is simply to contribute to the discrediting of that project. In this respect, the very successes of Labour have, alongside and as a necessary accompaniment of their ameliorative consequences, contributed mightily to that process of discrediting the socialist goal.

At the end of the day, the very image of 'the forward march of Labour' is a reformist mirage, encapsulating as it does some vision of a sustained advance by the working class onto the terrain of capital and its progressive constriction of the power of capital through the agency of the democratic state. The reality is that capital cedes no permanent territory to labour, no victories for 'the political economy of labour' which cannot be challenged and reversed by 'the political economy of capital' so long as the rule of capital persists. And if 'the forward march' is a mirage, so too is the view that its halt can be equated with a decline in the electoral fortunes of the Labour Party. The real basis for any gains that have been won by the labour movement over the past century has been the industrial strength and combativity of the working class, and its instruments have been at least as much those of the strike, the mass agitation and direct actions as the ballot box. And in that struggle, it has not infrequently been confronted by the coercive face of state power, often wielded by Labour governments. Indeed, the gains won at the ballot box and by Labour in parliament, though real, have more often than not worked to undermine the combativity of the class, as much through the disillusioning results of their 'successes' as in the disappointments produced by their 'failures'. Moreover, they have been purchased at the price of accepting the hegemony of a Labourist ideology and practice which is as much about the self-containment of the working class and its aspirations as it is about its advance.

I will examine both the question of state coercive power and of the Labour Party's approach to the issue of extra-parliamentary action at a later point in this discussion. For the moment it is sufficient to refer to Labour's record with regard to manifestations of the core of working-class power, its industrial strength, where the recent decades have seen the Labour Party not merely seeking to contain that power, but rather to undermine and roll it back as a necessary condition for the renovation and restructuring of a British capitalist haemorrhaging under the lash of international competition. If Thatcherism represents a sustained strategy by capital drastically to redraw the lines of class power in Britain (and if it is, this in itself exposes the fallacies in the reformist assumptions which surround the 'forward march' image), then the measures it pursued from 1979 on were on ground already cleared for it by the previous Labour government. Far from the strength of the labour movement depending on the electoral strength of the Labour Party, its position has been increasingly dependent on a readiness to use its industrial strength to resist the attacks of a Labour government. And the condition for survival and advance in the face of the Thatcherite attack may well depend on the labour movement rejecting and transcending the logic of Labourism, along with all its mechanisms and institutions of containment and control.

The nature of the Thatcherite challenge

If 'the outstanding achievement of Thatcherism has been to disorganise the opposition',[13] then one of the areas in which this has been most evident is in the diagnosis of the nature of Thatcherism itself by various sections of the Left. For the new-style Conservatism which came to power in 1979 both fascinates and bewilders many of its opponents to the point at which they offer us not analysis, but rather responses in need of therapeutic psycho-analysis; the snake has so hypnotized the monkey that the outcome is often noises which tell us more about the deep-seated fears of the monkey than the intentions of the snake.

Interestingly enough, the initial responses to Thatcherism, particularly from the neo-Keynesians who form the core of Labourist politics, was to view it as some kind of ideological idiocy, a mad monetarist dogma pursued far beyond the bounds of economic sense by a dogmatic woman and her docile cabinet. The assumption was that the 'realities of the situation' – as viewed through the corporatist spectacles of the neo-Keynesians – would compel a 'U-turn' of the Heath kind sooner or later; or, if 'the woman' proved totally obdurate, the electorate would deliver a crushing punishment on such lunatic politics at the first opportunity it got.[14]

Long before 1983, such scornful superiority had come to be replaced by an overpowering fear that 'the woman' meant what she said, and was bent on something far more sinister than the testing of some arcane economic dogma. At the extreme, we were treated to a fair bit of windy rhetoric about Thatcherism constituting some kind of incipient fascism, an attempt to destroy the whole fabric of the British welfare state democracy and replace it with a brutal and authoritarian regime. On the lips of Labour leaders like Kinnock and Hattersley, such rhetoric served the convenient purpose of evading the need to come to terms both with the essential rationality and coherence of the Conservative strategy, and the extent to which that rationality exposed Labour's own political incoherencies, and subverted their assumptions about the nature of modern capitalism and its politics. In the mouths of more straightforward comrades, it suggested some basic confusions about both fascism and the nature of bourgeois democracy.

Even when the crassness of the fascism tag is avoided, there remains a powerful impulse on the Left to treat Thatcherism as 'the great Satan', a scourge of reaction sent to punish the Left for its internal divisions, and which can only be defeated if we sink our sectarian differences in some great anti-Thatcherite Popular Front crusade. I do not have space here to examine with the seriousness they deserve the kind of arguments developed by Eric Hobsbawm in the wake of the 1983 defeat.[15] I can only note that his treatment of Thatcherism as a reactionary politics whose victory was made possible largely as a result of the internal civil war between Right and Left in the Labour Party involves (a) no serious or sustained analysis of the logic of the Thatcherite strategy as a solution to the problems of British capitalism which could then be compared, not only in its methods but also in its goals, with those of the Labour Party leadership – they are simply assumed to be fundamentally opposed one to the other; (b) an assumption that the Labour Party/working class connection is one of the axiomatic accepted facts of British political life, rather than an historically contingent outcome, at least as far as the existence of alternative options *on the Left* are concerned; (c) that in so far as that connection is being eroded *from the Right*, this is a product of the sectionalism of the labour movement or the sectarianism of the Left, rather than a consequence flowing directly from working-class disillusionment with the logic and direction of precisely that Labourist politics which the Left within the Labour Party had sought, however vainly, to reverse. It is the contention of this chapter that Hobsbawm is fundamentally wrong on all three assumptions.

Some of the most serious and sustained attempts to grasp the essence of the New Right politics of the Thatcherite Conservative government have been undertaken by those on the Left, like Stuart Hall, who discern there a programme which is as much concerned to transform the ideological landscape and political loyalties of British capitalism as with undertaking its material economic and social reconstruction. On this view, Thatcherism is best encapsulated by the phrase 'authoritarian populism'. It is seen as a fusion of 'the resonant themes of organic Toryism – nation, family, duty, authority, standards, traditionalism – with the aggressive themes of a revived neo-liberalism – self-interest, competitive individualism, anti-statism'.[16] Or, in another widely cited usage, 'the free economy and the strong state'.[17] Yet for all the subtlety and insight of these dissections of Thatcherism-as-Ideology, there is a consistent tendency to loosen the strands entwining the ideological and the material and to re-focus the discussion at the level of a battle for the hearts and minds of the working class rather than on the level of direct material practice of the regime, and the class and economic context within which it takes place. If we are therefore to re-balance the discussion on this and other matters raised by this brief glance at the responses of the Left to the task of 'reading' Thatcherism, we need to touch on four themes: ideology; economic strategy and context; state power; and Thatcherite political practice.

1. First, with respect to *ideology*, there is a danger that too great a focus on and fascination with the appeals of Thatcherism-as-Ideological Struggle can result in a massive over-estimation of its actual potency, particularly as far as the working class is concerned. For capitalism and its political agents have no imperative need to mobilize the active consent of the mass of people, either for a general vision of the social world or for specific and detailed policy measures. It is sufficient that they be acquiesced in as facts of life. In this sense, the real power of Thatcherism lies not in some authoritarian populist reconstitution of the world of common sense — or what is by no means the same thing, of public media discourse – but in a widespread acceptance of the view that there is no alternative. And the power of *that* conviction derives not from the overwhelming momentum of the Thatcherite ideological juggernaut, but from the palpable failure over the previous decades of Labourism to offer such a viable alternative in either theory or practice. One of the fundamental asymmetries of the capitalist system is that capitalist practice does not need to create and sustain a conscious acceptance of it in order for it to work, whereas the socialist challenge to that practice depends centrally on winning conscious support from the working class. In so far as Thatcherism has, as a matter of fact, gained the backing of sections of that class – in the more prosperous South and among the skilled and white-collar strata – it probably has a lot to do with its critique of Labourist practice as bureaucratic, inefficient, long on promises and short and disappointing on delivery. And that critique is successful primarily because it speaks directly to the experience of such Labourist practice by wide sections of the working class.

2. Second, with respect to *economic strategy* and the *context* within which it is formulated, it is necessary here to revisit briefly matters dealt with more extensively in volume II of this series.[18]

The widest context determining economic strategy is the world capitalist system itself.[19] Here, in marked contrast to the inter-war experience of stagnation and protectionism, the pattern of general economic expansion in the post-war years known as the Long Boom was firmly associated with trade liberalization and the restoration of competition within the world market. In the process, the dominant trend in the major industrial capitalist economies was towards increasing inter-dependence and synchronization at the levels of trade, finance and even production.

Even in the expansionist phase of the post-war economy, British capitalism was ailing; its growth rates were lower than its competitors, as were its rate of investment and its level of profitability. The reasons for this pattern are too complex to investigate here — once again see volume II of this series – but it meant that the modernization of British capital, and its restoration to competitiveness and profitability, increasingly became the central preoccupation of successive governments, Labour and Conservative, from the 1950s on. And for these governments, a key part of the process involved removing what was seen to be the central obstacle to the task of capitalist renovation, namely the entrenched power of organized labour, particularly in the industrial and manufacturing sectors of the economy. As we argued in volume II, organized labour's 'ability to resist cuts in real wages designed to restore profitability, its refusal to abandon the degree of defensive and negative control it enjoys over the work process, and its consequential ability to thwart managerial strategies for raising productivity and increasing the rate of exploitation in the interests of profit, have been the rocks upon which the "modernizing" strategies of Labour and Tory governments alike have threatened to founder'.[20]

The dominant trend in the economic strategies developed by both Labour and the Tories to tackle this task of capitalist reconstruction in the post-war years has been in a corporatist direction. Underpinned by a faith in the efficacy of Keynesian techniques of economic management, the state saw its role as intervening on a sustained and continuous basis both to steer the economy and stimulate the modernization of industry in an effort to restore profitability and competitiveness to British capitalism. Alongside other panaceas and nostrums – going into Europe, the National Plan, arguably Labour's 'Alternative Economic Strategy' today – and as a necessary accompaniment of them, strategies were developed for containing the strength of organized labour through the incorporation of the union leaderships within a complex web of consultative relations with the government and management. The object of these strategies was to secure union co-operation in achieving wage restraint, ending 'restrictive practices' and restoring managerial control over the labour process. Though such policies occasionally required resort to direct state compulsion – from as early as Labour's use of troops to break dock strikes in the 1940s to wage freezes and pay policies in the 1960s – the main thrust of this policy was to stimulate the trade union organizations themselves to act as agencies for the self-containment of organized labour. In other words, within the context of this very specific period and strategy, some considerable weight was placed on winning an ideological battle for the minds and hearts of the working class, or at least to rally its trade-union leadership, in order to get them to discipline their own memberships in the name of 'the national interest'.

By the late 1960s and early 1970s, such strategies had proved to be of limited value either in terms of securing the self-containment of organized labour or in generating the economic benefits expected to flow from this. Whatever gains had been made were more than offset by the increasing bite of competition from more efficient national capitalisms like West Germany and Japan, and this was still further accentuated by the slump after 1973. During the course of the 1970s, further nails were driven into the coffin of corporatism: the collapse of the Heath government in the face of the miners' strike of 1973–4; the inflationary 'fiscal crisis of the state' generated largely as a consequence of Labour's attempts to utilize orthodox Keynesian measures to insulate the British economy from the consequences of the slump in 1974–5; the collapse of the social contract phase of the Callaghan government in the 'winter of discontent' of 1978/9. Faced with these experiences, significant sections of the capitalist establishment – financiers and businessmen, journalists and civil servants, and politicians within both the Labour and Conservative parties – became increasingly convinced that a major change of strategy was needed. Given the combination of the structural weakness of British capitalism and its high degree of interdependence on, and synchronization with the rhythms of, the world economy, reliance on market forces was increasingly seen as the only realistic option for the renovation of the system. This was still further confirmed in the early 1980s by the collapse and reversal of the Mitterand attempt at 'reflation in one country' in France. All this implied a marked shift in the nature of state involvement in the economy in general and in relationship to the problem of organized labour in particular. This shift in strategy was already under way in the later years of the Callaghan government, though the practice still wore a predominantly corporatist face. It was to find its fullest practical expression and ideological justification in the policies and proclamations of the Thatcher Conservative government from 1979 on.

The Conservative Party, even in the heyday of corporate ideology and practice, had always included a wing committed to market solutions to the problems of British capitalism, and Conservative governments have been tempted from time to time to take that path – not only the Heath government policies of 1970–1, but also the early years of the Churchill government after 1951 show this pattern to some degree.[21] However, it was in the context of the continuing world and British capitalist crises of the 1970s and in the wake of the policy failures already described above, that this wing gained control of the Conservative Party. Under the leadership of Margaret Thatcher it began to argue for a major shift away from the corporatist strategies that had predominated in the post-war years. For our purposes, three key targets of the New Right strategy need emphasizing: (a) to utilize the changed market conditions for labour produced by the slump – falling production, rising unemployment etc. – drastically to undermine the strength and combativity of organized labour and to facilitate and entrench this re-drawing of class power by a progressive state-organized constriction of areas of legitimate trade-union action; (b) since it is seen as a costly burden on capital, to curb, and if possible reverse, the growth of state expenditure and the levels of state intervention and social provision associated with the corporatist 'welfare state-managed economy' pattern, and within the overall pattern of spending, to reinforce the state coercive apparatus – police, army, judiciary etc; (c) to legitimate this programme in terms of an eclectic mixture of ideas culled from nineteenth century liberalism – the virtues of market competition; freedom of the individual; of enterprise and so on – along with some selective borrowings from some of the symbolic values of traditional Conservatism – respect for authority; law and order; the Victorian values of morality, the family and the nation etc. – shorn of the paternalism and 'one nation' rhetoric which had accompanied them in more traditional Tory presentations of their philosophy.

It is, of course, important to recognize that the package, taken as a whole, does involve a significant break with the post-war corporatist strategy in terms both of practice and its legitimations. Yet there remains an underlying continuity of goals – the restoration to profitability of British capitalism – and of the means to achieve it – re-drawing the balance of class power in Britain in the interests of capital by rolling back trade-union power. And both the corporatists and the New Right ultimately have to rely on what Gramsci called 'the combination of force and consent' in order to maintain capitalist hegemony. What is striking, in view of all the attention paid by the Left to the ideological dimensions of Thatcherism, is that the New Right strategy actually involves a shift in the balance away from consent and towards force, and towards associated material pressures. In place of the corporatist stress on winning the consent and co-operation of organized labour, there is a readiness to place a much greater weight of the attack on the 'dull compulsions of economic necessity', orchestrated and reinforced by the threat – and occasional judicious use – of state power to achieve the desired results. It is a strategy best encapsulated in a sexist phrase from one of Nixon's aides, on how to deal with opponents, 'when you have them by the balls, their minds and hearts follow'!

3. This emphasis on the relatively greater weight placed on compulsion in the New Right strategy brings us to our third thematic observation, concerning *state power*. It cannot be denied that the period of the Thatcherite government has seen a significant increase in the range of weaponry available in the state armoury, particularly with regard to measures designed to sap the power of organized labour. As well as direct legislative acts (the Prior Act of 1980 and the Tebbitt Act of 1982) there have been a series of administrative measures (banning union membership at GCHQ Cheltenham; changes in social security procedures for strikers and their families) and new uses of the courts and police (the *de facto* criminalization of mass pickets during the course of the miners' strike in 1984–5 is an outstanding example) along with encouraging what amounts to extra-legal police harassment and violence against workers. But does this really all add up to what Stuart Hall has called a move towards 'an exceptional form of the capitalist state' in the shape of authoritarian populism,[22] or what in more extreme language has been characterized as incipient fascism? Surely not. Marxists have always insisted that state violence is one of the fundamental underpinnings of the capitalist system. While bourgeois democracy is no mere facade, either with regard to the scale of state violence it normally exhibits, or to the degree to which it is kept under legal control, it is surely a liberal illusion to believe that parliamentary democracy and civil liberties have fundamentally altered the class logic of state power and replaced force with consent.

There is always a gap between the image of government by consent and the reality of that power. Nor is that gap a product only of exceptional moments of crisis which can be later written out of the history books, the way we are taught to remember the football match between miners and police in the 1926 General Strike but not about the warships with their guns trained on the working-class districts of our industrial ports. For certain groups – the blacks in the inner-city ghettos, extreme Left groups, gays, women faced with domestic violence – the realities of harassment, or indifference to their legal rights by police and courts, have been everyday occurrences for as long as anyone can remember. For the mass of the poor and socially deprived, the daily degradations involved in being 'administered' by central and local state bureaucracies is another, and scarcely more subtle, form of state coercion and control. And for some 'special situations' like Northern Ireland, state violence on a day-to-day basis and with or without the dubious benefits of 'due process' has been literally a matter of life and death for over a decade and a half. It was the hardly radical *Irish Times* rather than some left-wing 'extremist rag' which compared the 'shoot to kill' policy of the RUC and the British army in Ulster with the operations of the right-wing military 'death squads' in Latin American countries.[23] What is qualitatively new about the deployment and use of state coercion in its various forms by the Thatcher government is that it is not now contained and peripheralized in special situations and confined to particular groups but is being mobilized against the organized labour movement itself on a fairly continuous basis.

Yet even so, the effectiveness of such measures depends at least as much on the cowing effect of their threatened use as on their actual deployment. This is no 'exceptional' state, still less a quasi-fascist one. It is the 'normal' bourgeois state, facing one of its central tasks of controlling working-class resistance to the needs of capital. If the balance has tilted from a relative reliance on compromise, conciliation and manipulation in the name of 'consent', to a somewhat greater emphasis on coercion and direction in the name of 'force', it is because the scale of the crisis of British capitalism is greater, and the space for softer strategies correspondingly less than in past decades. It is also because the Thatcher regime thinks that the time and circumstances are right for victory.

4. Turning to the level of detailed policy measures, therefore, it is important to recognize that Thatcherite political practice, despite all the rhetoric about 'conviction politics', is necessarily pragmatic and opportunistic. Media fascination with Mrs Thatcher's personal style of political leadership, with images of a will-power – 'determined' or 'obstinate' depending on the point of view – triumphing over obstacles which would have turned aside lesser mortals from their goals, should not be allowed to obscure this point. It is not simply that Thatcher's 'toughing it out' style in the face of opposition has in fact had more than its share of luck. The Falklands war, both in its origins and in its actual unfolding, was an enormous political gamble to retrieve something from a situation with potentially disastrous electoral consequences for the Conservatives and which could have been lost with a few well-placed Argentine torpedoes.

Nor is it a matter of pointing to the banana skins upon which the government has slipped from the Parkinson affair to the Oman contract, though it does no harm to remind ourselves of the many hypocrisies and incompetences which pervade this government and its ministers and limit its effectiveness. Nor is it simply to point to the undoubted fact that like all politicians, Mrs Thatcher's convictions have as much to do with perceptions of electoral advantage as with ideological commitment. Where the latter gets in the way of the former, it can get very short shrift, not simply at the level of rhetoric – the 'NHS is safe with us' pledge in the 1983 campaign – but also at the level of practice: drains on state resources are one thing but the political costs of withdrawing tax relief on mortgage interest payments for house owners is quite another matter!

The Thatcherite political style is ultimately merely an extreme example of the illlusions which are shared by all bourgeois politicians. They range from a Micawberish 'something will turn up' optimism, to a belief that will power and resolution are all that is necessary to overcome all obstacles. (Remember Harold Wilson and his self-confidence?) Yet as Marxism has surely taught us, the realities of bourgeois democratic politics are very different. Ultimately, a Tory controlled state is no more in command of the capitalist environment within which it operates than is a Labour one. It has to react to events as much as dictate their course. It has to respond to pressures and demands from the situation which are not simply conflicting but contradictory – the complex equations linking interest and exchange rates with the balance of trade and payments and the profitability of British capital are one example, the apparently insoluble problem of controlling the money supply is another. Indeed on some very plausible views on the pattern of development of the post-war international economy, the trends towards integration, synchronization and competition discussed earlier have markedly reduced even the limited scope open to state power to control and direct the economy in even advanced industrial capitalisms like Britain.[24]

In a very real sense, the character of the Thatcherite regime in the coming years will depend less on its own policy choices or the determination with which it seeks to pursue them than on two major forces which are only partially affected by them. First, as the widely leaked scenarios being considered last year by the Treasury and government Think Tank made clear, the Tories' room for political manoeuvre around issues of state spending, tax cuts, levels of real wages and employment and the like – and hence on the balance of force and consent – are heavily dependent on the rates of growth actually achieved by British capitalism. Whatever the government claims, this has mainly to do with whether or not the world capitalist economy is capable of sustaining the slight recovery begun in 1983 for a number of years, or whether it is set to peter out into renewed stagnation under the impact of high interest rates and a global debt crisis by 1985 at the latest.

If the first force is largely outside the control of any of us, short of a revolution designed to smash that world capitalist system, the second is much closer to hand. What the Thatcherite government is prepared to attempt, and what it is able to achieve, will be profoundly affected by the power and character of the resistance generated to those policies, and the perspectives which inform both the goals and the tactics of that resistance. While these matters will ultimately be determined by a very complex series of class and other forces at work in Britain, they may be influenced to a not inconsiderable extent by how, and whether, socialists seek to intervene in such struggles. It is therefore to the possibilities open for intervention by the Left and the perspectives which shape it to which we must now turn our attention.

Conflict and resistance in Thatcherite Britain

As this and previous chapters in the book have sought to map out, the British social formation is the nexus of multiple and interrelated crises – its ailing and uncompetitive capitalist economy, its location within a system of world imperialistic rivalries and the nuclear arms race that generates, the legacies of its own imperialist history particularly in Northern Ireland and in relation to the black community, the implications of the transformations of the labour market from the Long Boom to the current and continuing slump, particularly for blacks and women and the inhabitants of the decaying industrial cities of the North. All of this guarantees that conflict and resistance – from the trade-union struggle to the peace campaigns, from the battles against sexism and racism to those against British troops in Northern Ireland, from resistance to the central state from local councils to civil liberties campaigners against Police and Criminal Evidence Bill and other authoritarian statutes – will be the order of the day over the coming thousand or so days of the second Thatcherite Reich. Equally inevitably, and only partly because of the parliamentary weakness and internal disarray of the Labour opposition, the focus of these struggles will be upon direct action and extra-parliamentary conflict, to some degree quite independently of the ideological commitments, or lack of them, of those drawn into opposition to Thatcherism and what it represents.

In orienting themselves to those struggles, socialists need to start with a clear awareness of their own weaknesses and limitations. Nowhere is it a matter of waving the banner and waiting for the troops to rally around. On the contrary, socialists will find that in none of these struggles, even in those that are seen as on the Left, will they constitute more than a minority

BRIGHTON POLYTECHNIC
LEARNING RESOURCES

presence. Moreover, socialists will have no guarantee of even a moderately sympathetic hearing for their views among the mass of people involved in those struggles. On the one hand, they will have to overcome the widespread popular identification of socialism with 'what Labour politicians say and do', and the widespread antipathy to socialism, and even politics, that often flows from that equation. On the other hand, they will be working both alongside and in competition with more committed groupings – radical feminists, black activists, Irish nationalists etc. – who are deeply suspicious of assertions about the nature of the linkages being made between socialist goals and strategies and their own particular struggles and concerns.

In order to be able to justify their presence within, and attempts to influence the direction and outcome of these struggles, socialists need to achieve both clarity in their own minds and complete honesty in their dealings with others on a number of important issues. Three matters in particular need clarification. The first turns on the question of the nature of the linkages between socialists and others in these struggles, a question upon which there are profound and far-reaching divisions between different sections of the Left. Second, there is the argument over extra parliamentary struggle in Britain today. Finally, there is the matter of priorities as between the various struggles as areas for socialist participation and intervention. We shall briefly examine each question in turn.

1 Popular Front or United Front? If we exclude the option of isolation from concrete struggles on the grounds of ideological purity – surely the test of sectarianism today – then socialists have to confront the question of the terms of reference on which they, *as socialists*, are to involve themselves in the conflicts we have been discussing. One way of examining the options is to see it as a choice between a Popular Front and a United Front strategy, to borrow from the language of the inter-war Communist International. In terms of organizational advocacy, the former is most closely associated today with the Communist Party, particularly its Eurocommunist wing, while the latter accords with the views of the Socialist Workers' Party. In so far as the Labour Left has a view beyond 'join the Labour Party', it is inclined towards the former rather than the latter.

The terminology of the Popular Front derives from the Comintern policies of the middle-late 1930s when it was arguing for the construction of a broad coalition of popular and progressive forces – revolutionary, reformist, liberal, progressive conservative – around a programme for the defence of liberal democracy against the threats of Nazism and fascism. In the post-war period, it has been intimately intertwined with the 'state monopoly capitalism' perspective and its most publicized expression came in the 'historic compromise' period of the Italian Communist Party under the Eurocommunist leadership of Berlinguer which advocated a coalition stretching from the PCI to the Christian Democrats. The specific context for this proposal was the PCI's belief that any attempt by the Left alone to seek electoral power in Italy might well precipitate a Chile-style military coup. However, the general theoretical underpinnings for this approach have been provided by an interpretation of the ideas of the Italian Marxist theoretician, Antonio Gramsci (1891–1937) and in particular his notion of the 'historic bloc'. Characteristically, it is in this Gramscian language rather than in the older Comintern usage that the strategy is advocated today as providing a general guide for socialist participation in the broader struggles.[25]

The virtues claimed for this approach are many. It is argued that this stress on broad alliances and democratic rather than specifically socialist objectives enables it to put together the largest possible constituency from among contrasted groupings impelled into action by very different motives and perspectives. The result is to maximize the forces available, by avoiding precisely those divisions and disagreements which would emerge within the broad front if specifically socialist perspectives were argued for within the movement. This in turn increases the chances of a successful outcome in the struggle, and in the process, gains socialists a broader credibility as a leading part of 'the broad democratic alliance' spoken of in *The British Road to Socialism*.

The strategy can undoubtedly achieve some successes within its own terms of reference. To take but one current example, Ken Livingstone's ability to win the campaign to 'defend local democracy' and defeat the so-called 'Paving Bill' abolishing elections in the GLC, will certainly owe a great deal to building a broad popular front stretching from the 'broad Left' to 'progressive' Tory peers in the House of Lords. Indeed, even the Queen got a walking on part in the campaign to provide the GLC with its democratic as distinct from socialist credentials at the opening ceremony of the Thames barrage in 1984.

Yet the very successes achieved by this strategy already begin to indicate its problems as a strategy for *socialist* advance. Its short-term strengths – the ability to put together a very broad coalition – are also the key sources of its long-term weakness. It is precisely in the course of struggle that the incoherences built into such fronts – that they span strata and groupings with radically opposed perspectives on what the struggle is about and how it should be fought – come to the fore, and the resultant confusions and divisions frequently result in internal disintegration, capitulation and defeat. By reining in their political analysis and perspectives in the name of popular unity, socialists disarm themselves of precisely that which socialism claims to be its fundamental strength: the ability to grasp the overall logic of the context of the struggles within capitalism and, on the basis of this, to have a clear view of both the goals, strategy and tactics involved in each particular struggle. This is a claim that cannot be vindicated in the abstract. It requires demonstration in each and every situation. But it is the essence of the socialist claim nonetheless and to refuse to make it involves both self-deception and the deception of others. The practical result is that the politics which win out are those of the most moderate, the most timid, the most conciliatory. For this is the price to pay for the very breadth of the Front.

Though the Gramscian language within which the Popular Front strategy is advanced on the Left today is intended to provide it with an impeccably revolutionary Marxist pedigree, the logic of its theory and practice is in reality that of reformism. This is not the place to consider directly the rich but ambiguous legacy we have received from Gramsci's writing,[26] though it is exceedingly dubious that he would have accepted the construction put upon them by many of his self-proclaimed disciples today. What we can do is point to the revisionist core at the heart of Popular Front analysis. It tacitly takes its point of departure from the assumption that class exploitation and class conflict are not the fundamental facts of capitalist existence. On the contrary, on a whole series of issues, it assumes that there is an important degree of common interest transcending merely sectional class divisions which provides the basis for a coherent programme of common action by disparate strata in pursuit of wide-ranging goals. Yet as we argued in volume II of the Socialist Primer series, this is the very essence of the reformist analysis and strategy. However much it may evoke the language of direct action, its analysis is rooted in a view of the democratic state as the framework for achieving popular unity and consensus, and hence as the agency for socialist advance, and its practice is intimately bound up with the politics of electoralism, with all the consequences that such politics entail.[27] Eric Hobsbawm's advocacy of an electoral pact with the SDP/Liberal Alliance is no aberration of analysis. It is a self-conscious and logical outcome of his commitment to the strategy of the Popular Front.[28]

Our purpose here is not to assess the question of Popular Front strategies in the wider historical context, but specifically in relation to the struggle against Thatcherism in Britain today. However one may judge its record in the 1930s – and from Spain to France many see that record as little short of disastrous in its effect on the anti-fascist resistance – it involves a major irony when applied to our present situation.[29] For the strategy in the 1930s had as its lynchpin the need to draw a very sharp distinction between bourgeois democratic and fascist regimes. As I have argued above, the blurring of the real differences between these alternatives is precisely what enables today's advocates of the Popular Front to throw the word 'fascist' at the present Tory government in an entirely promiscuous way!

If we turn, more briefly, to the alternative United Front strategy, we may note in passing that the terminology derives from Comintern strategy from 1921 onwards when, in the context of capitalist restabilization particularly in Europe after the revolutionary surges of the 1917–19 period, Communists found themselves in a tiny minority in relation to the reformist social-democratic parties which commanded the support of the mass of workers. That reformist leadership had contributed considerably to containing the revolutionary upsurge and assisting in the processes of restabilizing capitalism, and in clearing the ground for a shift to the Right in European politics, particularly in Germany. The question was therefore one of how to respond to the concrete struggles and resistance with which predominantly social-democratically influenced workers and others responded to their experience of these trends. The answer was the United Front tactic adopted at the Third Congress of the Comintern. The purpose here is not to review the historical experience but to consider the relevance of such an approach to the situation in Britain today.[30]

Taken at its widest scope, as a broad orientation to the general problem of linkages rather than as a specific tactic, we can highlight some of the issues it raises by discussing it in the context of socialist involvement in 'non-class' struggles. My starting point is that capitalism is fundamentally built upon class exploitation and necessarily produces class conflict in a variety of contexts and guises, most notably in the form of the trade-union struggle. However, in the articulation of the capitalist mode of production into a complex social formation, there are generated a whole range of relationships of oppression – of race, gender, nationality etc. – which though they are anchored in the reproduction of relationships of exploitation, do not necessarily map directly or immediately onto the basic class divisions. Within advanced capitalism, the experience of those complex relationships of oppression will impel large numbers of people into activity, including many who are not 'objectively' part of the working class, whether this is understood in its widest sense or confined more narrowly to those directly engaged in processes of social production as wage-labourers. In so far as these movements develop any popular base at all, they will find that they become Popular Fronts, in that they contain contradictory potentialities, not least because they reproduce within themselves a conflict of class interests and class perspectives.

If we postpone the question of orientation to the industrial class struggle until later, we can now draw out the implications of the United Front strategy in relationship to these 'non-class' struggles in the women's and black movements. In such contexts, revolutionary socialists seek to assert both solidarity with the struggles against the oppressors in concrete circumstances and actions, and also hegemony within those struggles. What is involved in this? It is not an electoralist strategy concerned with aggregating together disparate interests which can then be represented through a party. Nor is it a strategy which involves either suppressing or diluting the fundamental Marxist conviction that the class struggle is at the core of the process of destroying all the oppressions and exploitation anchored in capitalism. It is an approach which recognizes the *two-way* interconnectedness of class struggle with struggles against oppression, both in its theory and its practice: active solidarity with struggles against sexism, racism, and imperialism cannot involve treating them as mere side-shows, distractions or some mere reformist patching up of the system. At the same time, it also involves attempts to win those movements to socialist perspectives as the only ones which provide either an adequate explanation of the oppressions involved or how they can be linked to the wider struggles against the capitalist system that sustains them. And this necessarily means being involved in conflicts *within* these movements. It involves ideological struggle with those who wish to generalize their experience into a theory of oppression which denies the primacy of capitalism in its determination: hence the debates with radical feminists, black nationalists and others. And it involves the real risk of splitting those movements, for while it acknowledges that there are sections of the oppressed who in class terms may be on the other side, it argues that they can be won to a radicalized struggle only in spite of rather than because of this, and only then on the basis of grasping and accepting a socialist explanation of their oppression.

To its many opponents, the United Front strategy of simultaneous solidarity with, and conflict within, the specific struggle is arrogant, sectarian and divisive. And while there are soft answers to all these accusations – concerning the sensitivity with which socialists should try to apply the tactics, pointing to successes like the Anti-Nazi League – the charges do have an objective basis in the very logic of the way the strategy will be experienced by those who, at that point in the struggle, do not share the perspectives that underlie it. Yet if socialists are to take seriously their own analysis and prescriptions, it is difficult to see how they can avoid being arrogant in an objective sense. If Gramsci has provided much of the language within which the Left today debates its options, then it is salutory to remind ourselves that his conception of hegemony was consciously borrowed from the Russian Bolshevik usage, and was centrally concerned to assert the *leadership* of socialist and proletarian perspectives within the 'historic bloc' of workers, peasants and others which he saw it as the task of the Communist Party to construct. And it was no electoral alliance, but an alliance built on struggle in which revolutionary perspectives would be fighting to gain hegemony. Real arrogance indeed!

2 The extra-parliamentary struggle. Nowhere is the choice of strategy going to be more crucial in the coming years than in the context of extra-parliamentary action. For as I observed earlier, the struggles and conflicts of the next few years against Thatcherism will necessarily be extra-parliamentary, almost irrespective of the perspectives of the participants.

This is not to say, however, that the nature of those perspectives may not themselves crucially shape the course of these battles and their chances of success. We must therefore examine more closely the views on extra-parliamentary action that will be competing to assert leadership in the coming years. In practice, there are three more or less clearly defined alternatives.

The first, which is that associated with the traditional Right and Centre of the Labour Party and the trade-union leadership, views with profound suspicion *any* manifestation of extra-parliamentary action as involving a potentially dangerous challenge to parliamentary democracy and the constitution. Even such modest activities as mass lobbies, peaceful demonstrations, petitions to parliament etc. receive at best grudging consent, and usually involve the participation of such leaderships largely to ensure that any tendency to exceed the limits of constitutionality and legality are vigorously suppressed. This is perhaps the deepest and most long-lasting response of the Labourist tradition to manifestations of class and other struggles outside the parliamentary arena. From its foundation, through its opposition to the syndicalist agitations of the pre-1914 period, through its responses to the General Strike in 1926, through its open hostility to the Hunger Marches of the 1930s as 'communist inspired', from its opposition to the squatters movement of the 1940s to the anti-nuclear, anti-war actions and right to work marches of more recent decades, distrust of extra-parliamentary activity and hostility and opposition to extra-parliamentary struggle and assertions of power has been unremitting. Whether it is Michael Foot's denunciation of Peter Tatchell when he expressed anodyne views on the subject in 1982, or the TUC's opposition to the NGA 'defying the law' at Warrington in 1983, or Neil Kinnock's opposition to Liverpool Labour Council's 'illegal' budget in 1984 and his silence on the miners' strike, one thing is perfectly clear. If the perspectives of the Labour leadership and the bulk of the trade-union leadership win out, there will be no effective extra-parliamentary struggle, and certainly no victories.

Not all Labour leaders in parliament and in the unions subscribe to this view. Many of those on the Left, including Tony Benn, subscribe to an apparently more favourable account of the legitimacy of such struggles, though within clearly defined limits. It is a perspective which fuses together assumptions derived from the corporatist theory and practice of Labourism in earlier years with the Popular Front perspectives of the 'broad Left' today. In essence, it argues that in the kind of pluralistic democracy which was assumed to be in operation in Britain prior to 1979, organized labour and other significant interests had a right to be consulted, to have their views taken into account, and above all, the right not to have their legitimate interests challenged at a fundamental level. If parliament and governments fail to honour these claims – and the core of the fascism jibes about the Thatcher regime and references to its minority and undemocratic nature is precisely that it refuses to do this — then it is legitimate to take extra-parliamentary action in defence of those interests. This point of view was perhaps best articulated by David Basnett, when, speaking in his capacity as chairman of the TUC Economic Committee on 11 December 1982, he made the much quoted observation that 'another five years of the exclusion of the trade-union movement from influence on economic affairs could convert us into an insurrectionary trade-union movement, committed to civil disobedience. This is not what we want. We want to play our role with a government working towards agreed consensus objectives within a pluralistic democracy.'

Leaving aside the willingness to co-operate with the Thatcher government if only it would listen to the unions – there would be an 'historic compromise' indeed! – we need to note the way in which the rhetoric of insurrection rapidly decays into the language of civil disobedience. For the essence of this viewpoint is that it legitimates extra-parliamentary action only as a form of protest, not as a method of achieving results won by the use of mass action and industrial power. Precisely because the protest is ultimately made only on behalf of a sectional interest, it must, afterwards, bow to the rulings of those who sit in government and who therefore speak, however imperfectly, on behalf of the whole nation.

If such a perspective were to win out in the ensuing struggle for leadership, it would not, like that of the Labour leadership, result in the abortion of all struggles before they could get off the ground. On the contrary, it could well stimulate demands for mass action and mass protest, and because the words appear on the lips of some of the most powerful leaders in the trade-union movement, they could for a while convey to the activists some sense of being part of a broad and powerful Popular Front with which the Thatcher government will be forced to come to terms. And indeed, on some issues it might, though if the government's responses to the campaign of protest against the banning of union membership at GCHQ Cheltenham in early 1984 are anything to judge by, this is an unlikely result in the current situation. But just as that refusal to compromise by the government led to the collapse of the protest, so too does the logic of this perspective point in the direction of acquiescence. For too many failed protests pave the way for a move towards the 'new realism' of Len Murray, with its quietist philosophy of 'what can't be cured, must be endured' and its readiness to co-operate with any government on virtually any terms, provided it is consulted first.

For the struggle over GCHQ to have succeeded, it would have required a readiness to mobilize support and industrial action on the widest scale, not least of all at Cheltenham itself. But for this to have occurred, a very different perspective would need to have won leadership in the conflict.

Ultimately, only the revolutionary socialist analysis of the class character of state power under capitalism equips the struggle with such leadership. For, to repeat once more, the fundamental realities of a system based upon the capitalist mode of production are those of exploitation, oppression and struggle. Within that context, the institutions and practices which make up bourgeois democracy are neither irrelevant nor merely cosmetic, but they are still fundamentally about achieving the most effective combination of force and consent with which to sustain the rule of capital. As such, they have no overriding claim to legitimacy in the eyes of those subjected to that class rule. Nor are they, ultimately, democratic in any socialist sense of the word. The real struggle against capitalism is that of the masses. It is the parliamentary struggle which lacks centrality, and which can at best merely endorse victories won in struggle elsewhere.

It may with some justice be objected that even if this perspective is granted legitimacy in the abstract, it is the exercise of an ostrich for it ignores the deeply rooted attachment of the mass of people in this country to the virtues of parliamentary democracy, however ill that system is currently serving them. There is much truth in this, but it in turn ignores the extent to which the long post-war crisis within the British labour movement has begun to erode the influence of one of the major mechanisms in maintaining that attachment, namely the loyalty of the mass of the working class to 'the parliamentary road to socialism'. A crumbling at the edges, perhaps, and as productive of apathy and cynicism as radicalization. Even so, the conflicts will continue, and in their experience of the capitalist state which that involvement brings to those who participate in industrial struggle, in anti-nuclear protest, in movements in defence of women and blacks etc., the possibilities for making a point of relevant connection with the revolutionary socialist perspective is present in the existing situation. In the context of the current crisis and the Thatcherite strategy for dealing with it, the resultant sharpening of the antagonisms and the concrete experiences of state practice they are likely to entail – of police harassment and violence, of legal bias and arbitrariness, of bureaucratic bullying, as well as of political dishonesty, corruption and self-interest – open up possibilities for exposing that gap between the image of consent and the reality of class power of which we wrote earlier. And with the perception of that gap, the way is opened for a potentially fruitful fusion between the experience and the Marxist perspectives which interpret it and direct it to action. It may be no more than a possibility, yet without it, and without some victory for the perspective on extra-parliamentary action it embodies, the coming conflicts will be deprived of their best chance of success. That is why co-operation in the struggle must also involve a battle for the hegemony of socialist ideas within the struggle.

3 *The Question of Priorities*. I come, finally, to the question of the order of priorities which should guide socialists in making choices about where to concentrate their efforts and interventions. In one sense, of course, socialists are not free to choose. The choice will be made for them by the actual patterns of conflict and levels of mass involvement in the struggles that develop in the coming years, whether the issue is bombs or jobs, pay or union rights, sexual harassment or racial attacks. However, even if the very limited resources of the Left today did not of themselves dictate some concentration of effort, we would still need to determine our strategic priorities, however much these may be amended on a day-to-day basis in the light of events.

The logic of the argument in this chapter points directly to a focus on the industrial and trade-union struggle as the central priority for socialist intervention, and it does so for a number of different reasons. At the most fundamental level, it rests upon an acceptance of the Marxist assertion that it is the working class which constitutes *the* potential agency of revolutionary change in capitalism, and that, in Marx's famous phrase 'the emancipation of the working class is the act of the working class itself'. But this perspective bites on the real world only to the extent that the experienced realities of exploitation and oppression generated by capitalism impel the working class into struggle and resistance in ways that open up real possibilities for connecting socialist politics with those conflicts in the consciousness of the class. The argument of this chapter has been directed to the assertion that such a situation exists in Britain today. As we have seen, the issue of the organized industrial power of the working class lies at the very heart of the crisis of post-war British capitalism and it has been at the centre of the strategies of both Labour and Conservative governments for dealing with that crisis. More specifically, I have argued that it is a combination of the very severity of the current phase of that crisis and the specific character of the Thatcherite strategy for attacking the trade unions which has led to an escalation in the scale and scope of the roll-back of union strength envisaged, and the costs to the working class of failing to defeat it. If Thatcherism is to be defeated, only the organized industrial strength of the labour movement is capable of ensuring that defeat, and only if the working class is ready and willing to use its strength. And that in turn brings us back to the question of socialist politics and the possibilities and problems faced by socialists in seeking to make their intervention.

It should hardly need to be said that assertions about the centrality of the class struggle in general and industrial struggle in particular do not of themselves take us much further towards a grasp of the hows and whys of socialist intervention. For industrial struggles are no simple or elemental fact of capitalism whose political significance is fixed immutably by that general context. This is an error most frequently encountered in the case of those – usually reformists but also some revolutionaries who ought to know better – who seek to characterize such struggles as necessarily economistic. What is required is a correct reading of each conflict and of the wider but still specific historical conjuncture within which it is located and which defines its political potential. Only on the basis of such readings can we determine the pattern of socialist intervention.

Such readings are necessarily beyond the scope of this discussion, but I cannot close without some brief observations on the extent to which the coming period opens up real possibilities for socialist advance in the context of interventions in industrial struggle. At one level, there is the fairly obvious fact that the nature of the Thatcherite attack on organized labour, with its greater reliance on the threats of state coercion to back up the compulsions of the market, contains within itself potentialities for radicalizing and politicizing the trade-union struggle which were far less developed when the main thrust of the attack was placed on corporatist strategies by previous governments. Yet at another level, both the political and market contexts which have shaped the relationship of politics and economics in the consciousness of most workers in Britain are themselves in a process of alteration in ways that also open up possibilities for socialist advance.

'Pure and simple' trade unionism has never been deeply entrenched in the British working class. For well over a century, organized workers have sought to connect their industrial experience with wider political perspectives, whether this was at the level of trade-union leaderships looking for political protection for their organizations, or of a mass membership giving their electoral loyalties to one party rather than another, or of militants who sought for a politics which could sustain their commitment to struggle and help to generalize it. And just as the basis of the need for politics has been diverse, so also have the types of politics chosen and the manner of the connections made between politics and economics varied widely. The broad mass of union leaderships and mass memberships have, for much of the time and with varying degrees of active enthusiasm and passive habituation, chosen a politics of radical reform rather than revolution – Labourism in our century, radical Liberalism before that – with its emphatic insistence on the constitutional necessity of the separation of industrial struggle from, and subordination to, the politics of parliamentary competition. It was precisely this tradition of politics with its attenuated practice and eroded electoral support among the working class that was offered as the key evidence for the view that we confront some crisis of socialism in the 1980s. Yet for socialists facing the challenges of this decade, it is a crisis to be welcomed, for it is visibly a politics which has been tried overlong, and which has equally been found wanting by an increasing number of those who gave their loyalties to it.

Even in their heyday, Labourist politics have never held unchallenged sway or totally monopolized the loyalties of socialists in the working class. In each generation, at least from the 1880s onwards, minorities of workers – and characteristically they have included many of the best industrial militants of their generation – have sought for socialist alternatives to Labourism, often specifically looking for a perspective which made a different kind of connection between the industrial and political struggles of the working class. From the time of the SDF in the 1880s and the BSF and syndicalists prior to 1914, through the CPGB from the 1920s onwards, to the various Trotskyist groupings after the Second World War, minorities of industrial militants (fluctuating in both numbers and industrial influence, and with varying political perspectives) have tried to relate the two struggles to each other, often with very little help from the perspectives involved. Arguably, both the SDF and the BSP effectively isolated themselves from the possibilities for socialist advance through their own electoralist politics. In a very real sense, the continued presence of this minority of working-class militants within the workplace has kept open the possibility that a socialist alternative to Labourism would be able to assert leadership as and when Labourism's own internal contradictions threatened to undermine its hold on the loyalties of the mass of workers.

The paradox of our epoch is that the conditions which have accentuated the long decline of Labourism over the past decades have been accompanied by a simultaneous, albeit separate and temporary, distancing of militants from the need for alternative socialist politics, or indeed any politics at all. For the industrial militancy of the 1950s and 1960s was formed within quite unusual and temporary market conditions which in turn sustained uncharacteristically economistic perspectives. Briefly, the quite peculiar conjunction in those decades was one of boom conditions generating full employment, and an expansion of oligopolistic manufacturing sectors – cars, chemicals, engineering generally – which had not yet encountered the growing international competition that was to overwhelm many of them from the 1960s onwards, and were therefore faced with comfortably expanding and largely non-competitive markets. It was in this context that shop floor militancy associated with the growth of shop stewards committees came to dominate the situation in many sectors of manufacturing in Britain. Yet the very conditions that created it and made it successful in terms of winning significant wage rises and exercising a degree of negative control over the labour process itself were ones which were least likely to encourage an awareness of the need for politics among militants. The localized and fragmented bargaining, the pay-offs to be achieved through pure and simple militancy and the purely instrumental solidarities which could be sustained on an 'it pays for itself' basis, all lessened the need to build national connections on either an industrial or a political level. Quite uncharacteristically, for a while, objective market conditions effectively marginalized politics, whether reformist or revolutionary, in relation to the self-activity and combativity of important sectors of militants and the wider organized working class. At the extremes, the result was the West Midlands syndrome, a combination of intense labour industrial militancy with a political consciousness so attenuated that voting Conservative seemed perfectly compatible with that militancy.

The changed market conditions from the 1960s onwards – of rising unemployment, fierce market competition for products, capital's imperative need to reassert managerial control over the work process etc. – did produce something of a turn back to national and political perspectives at the trade-union and Labour Party level among militants and the wider rank and file. Yet this was to result in further disillusionment and retreat as the experience of the Social Contract years of the 1970s sapped both shop floor organization and the economistic militancy which had sustained it. But if the downturn of the middle-late 1970s severely weakened the self-confidence and industrial militancy of organized labour, it also served to undermine the pervasive hold of pure and simple economistic perspectives upon the militants.[31] In the changed market conditions of the 1980s, any revival in industrial struggle would have to be based on something more than do-it-yourself reformism on the shop floor. Negatively, this means that the solidarities upon which struggle in the 1980s will depend – solidarities within the workplace, between factories, across industries, between skilled and unskilled, white-blouse and blue-collar etc. – will be much harder to build and sustain. They certainly cannot be generated on the basis of the pure and simple economistic militancy of previous decades, though that is not to say that where the struggle is determined enough economic gains cannot be won and market forces bent by the power of organized labour. Rather it is to argue that objective need for socialist politics as the basis for sustaining solidarities in struggle has never been more pressing, nor the claims of Labourism to fill the gap less persuasive in the minds of large numbers of workers.

Writing in the early months of the 1984 miners' strike, it is evident that we are in the middle of perhaps the most crucial industrial confrontation of the decade. Victory for the miners against a determined Thatcherite government and in defiance of both 'the market' and 'the forces of law and order' will rebuild the self-confidence and combativity of organized workers, and also of every group and strata – women, blacks, ghetto dwellers, peace marchers – who are on the receiving end of this capitalist system. Yet such a victory cannot be won without rejecting and transcending the politics of Labourism – or of the trade-union leaders vacillating between Len Murray's new realism and Basnett's limits of legitimate protest, and of Labour Party leaders preaching conciliation and compromise while distancing themselves from the militant tactics that alone can win the strike. Victory here, and elsewhere, will depend on

J

rejecting these perspectives and upon finding a very different political language in which to argue for support and solidarity in struggle. Victory here, and elsewhere, will therefore be profoundly affected by the success with which socialists can intervene, argue for, and demonstrate the relevance of their politics to workers within those struggles. The objective need for politics is there and is visibly being felt by miners and others. A triumph for the miners will not, of itself, be a victory for socialism. But it could well be a vital moment in the process of turning the decade of the 1980s into one of sustained socialist advance, on the basis of a real socialist politics of class struggle.

The argument of this chapter is about the need to make a commitment to involvement in an organized struggle for socialist advance. The nature of the organization and the commitment readers choose will obviously depend upon a complex range of issues – from the choice between reform or revolution, to their analysis of the situation of the class and other struggles in Britain today. But when it comes down to cases, it is centrally about the practical choices that have to be made – about the order of priorities involved, about approaches to the nature of extra-parliamentary struggle, and between Popular Front and United Front modes of intervention in struggle. The anatomy of the Left carried out by David Coates in the previous chapter, and the information offered in the Appendix following this chapter, are intended to assist in the process of making these choices. One thing is certain, however. The need for making the right choice has never been more crucial for socialists in Britain than it is today. For the possibilities for socialist advance are present in ways which we have not seen for decades. The time has come for some optimism of the intellect as well as of optimisim of the will.

Appendix
Addresses and Further Information: The Constituency of the Left

Addresses and Further Information: The Constituency of the Left

1 The trade-union movement

Largest British unions: head office addresses
and main membership coverage

TGWU, Transport House, Smith Square, London SW1P 3JB.
Recruits workers in the majority of industries and occupations, organized in 'trade groups' each possessing a degree of autonomy.
AUEW-E, 110 Peckham Road, London SE15 5EL.
Covers all grades of engineering production and maintenance workers, though still oriented to male craft workers.
GMBATU, Thorne House, Ruxley Ridge, Claygate, Esher, Surrey KT10 0TL.
Wide range of industries and occupations; particularly strong in local government and public utilities.
NALGO, 1 Mabledon Place, London WC1H 9AJ.
White-collar staff in local government and some other public services and utilities; majority of members female.
NUPE, Civic House, 20 Grand Depot Road, Woolwich, London SE18 6SS.
Mainly lower-paid grades in local government and NHS; two-thirds members female – largest number of women in any British union.
USDAW, Oakley, 188 Wilmslow Road, Fallowfield, Manchester M14 6LJ.
Shop workers primarily; traditionally strongest in co-op sector.
ASTMS, 79 Camden Road, London NW1 9ES.
Mainly supervisors and technicians in public and private sectors; recent initiatives in financial institutions.
EETPU, Hayes Court, West Common Road, Bromley BR2 7AU.

Mainly electrical engineeering and electricity supply.
UCATT, UCATT House, 177 Abbeville Road, Clapham, London SW4 9RL.
Most construction occupations, particularly crafts.
NUM, St James House, Vicar Lane, Sheffield S1.
All mineworkers, except supervisory and clerical occupations.
COHSE, Glen House, High Street, Banstead, Surrey SM7 2LH.
Hospital workers, mainly nurses and ancillaries.
SOGAT 82, Sogat House, 274/288 London Road, Hadleigh, Benfleet, Essex SS7 2DE.
Paper industry and mainly non-craft occupations in printing.
NUT, Hamilton House, Mableton Place, London WC1H 9BD.
Teachers, especially in primary schools.
CPSA, 215 Balham High Road, London SW17 7BN.
Lower administrative and clerical grades in civil service and related employment.
UCW, UCW House, Crescent Lane, London SW4 9RN.
Postal workers and some telecommunications occupations.
AUEW-TASS, Onslow Hall, Little Green, Richmond, Surrey TW9 1QN.
Major base in drawing offices and related technical staff.
BIFU, 17 Hillside, Wimbledon, London SW19 4NL.
Principally bank staff.
NUR, Unity House, Euston Road, London NW1 2BL.
All railway workers, though minority among footplate and non-manual occupations.
POEU, Greystoke House, 150 Brunswick Road, London W5 1AW.
Technical grades in telecommunications.
NGA, Graphic House, 63–7 Bromham Road, Bedford MK40 2AG.
Traditional printing crafts.
NAS/UWT, 22 Upper Brook Street, London W1Y 2HD.
Mainly secondary teachers.
GMBATU-B, Lifton House, Eslington Road, Newcastle-on-Tyne NE2 4SB.
Mainly craft occupations in shipbuilding.
APEX, 22 Worple Road, London SW19 4DF.
Mainly private-sector clerical and administrative staff.

2   The women's movement

Information on women's organizations

The Spare Rib Diary (27 Clerkenwell Close, London, EC1) carries an extensive list of women's organizations and activities. There is also a

National Information Service and Newsletter: WIRES, PO Box 162, Sheffield 1DU, Tel. 0742.755290.

Below are the main campaigns and groups mentioned in chapter 6:

Equal opportunities: Women's rights

Rights of Women, 51–4 Featherstone Street, London EC2.
Equal Opportunities Commission, Overseas House, Quay Street, Manchester 3.
Equal Pay and Opportunities Campaign, c/o Suzanne Lawrence, 59 Canonbury Park North, London N1.
National Council of Civil Liberties, Women's Rights Unit, 21 Tabard Street, London SE1.
Campaign for Financial and Legal Independence, 214 Stapleton Hall Road, London N4.

Childcare

National Childcare Campaign, 17 Victoria Park Square, London E2.

Women and the Labour Party and trade unions

Joyce Gould, National Women's Organiser, The Labour Party, 150 Walworth Road, London SE17.
Women's Action Committee, Ruth Raymond, 16 Milverton Crescent, Leamington Spa, *or* Ann Pettifor, 39 Calderuane Road, London SW4 9LY.
Women's Fightback (organizes around women's work in the trade unions and the Labour Party), 41 Ellington Street, London N7.

Peace/nuclear threat

Women oppose the nuclear threat. Central Contact, Box 600, Peace News, 8 Elm Avenue, Nottingham.

Media

Women in Media, BMWIM, London WC1N 3XX.

Lesbians

For information and advice write to BM, Box 1514, London WC1N 3XX.

Black women

OWAAD, c/o Black Women's Centre, 41 Stockwell Green, London SW9.

Reproductive rights

National Abortion Campaign, Wesley House, 70 Great Queen Street, London WC2B 5AX.
Abortion Law Reform Association, 88A Islington High Street, London, N1.
Co-ord (Co-ordinating Committee in defence of the 1967 Abortion Act), 27-35 Mortimer Street, London W1.
The Women's Reproductive Rights Information Centre, 51–4 Featherstone Street, London EC2.

Campaigns against male violence

Women Against Violence Against Women, c/o A Woman's Place, Hungerford House, Victoria Embankment, London WC2.

Battered women

Women's Aid Federation, 51–4 Featherstone Street, London EC1 *and* 18 Park Row, Leeds 1.

Rape

Women Against Rape, c/o Caroline Barker, 23 Fairlawn Road, Bristol, *or* PO Box 287, London NW6.
Rape in Marriage Campaign, c/o ROW, 51–4 Featherstone Street, London EC1.
Incest Survivors Campaign, Hungerford House, Victoria Embankment, London WC2.
Rape Crisis, PO Box 69, London WC1.

3   Resistance to racism

Principal UK based organizations working
in the field of race and immigration

All Faiths for One Race, Lozells Social Development Centre, 1 Finch Road, Birmingham B19 1HS.
All London Teachers Against Racism and Fascism, 66 Littleton Street, London SW18.
Board of Deputies of British Jews, Woburn House, Upper Woburn Place, London WC1H 0EP.
British Council of Churches (Community and Race Relations Unit), 2 Eaton Gate, London SW1W 9BL.
British Refugee Council, Bondway House, 3–9 Bondway, London SW8 1SJ.

Campaign Against Racism in the Media, PO Box 50, London N1.
Catholic Commission for Racial Justice, Church Hall, 1 Amwell Street, London EC1R 1UL.
Commission for Racial Equality, Elliott House, 10-12 Allington Street, London SW1E 5EH.
Counter Information Service, 9 Poland Street, London W1.
Institute of Race Relations, 247–9 Pentonville Road, London N1 9NG.
Joint Council for the Welfare of Immigrants, 44 Theobalds Road, London WC1X 8SP.
London Voluntary Service Council (Migrant Services Unit), 68 Charlton Street, London NW1 1JR.
Minority Rights Group, 36 Craven Street, London WC2N 5NG.
National Association of Community Relations Councils, Mary Ward House, 5–7 Tavistock Place, London WC1H 9SS.
National Council for Civil Liberties, 21 Tabard Street, London SE1 4LA.
Policy Studies Institute, 1–2 Castle Lane, London SW1E 6DR.
Quaker Community Relations Committee, Friends House, Euston Road, London NW1.
Race Today, 165 Railton Road, London SE24 0LU.
Runnymede Trust, 37a Gray's Inn Road, London WC1 8PP.
Searchlight Publishing, 37B New Cavendish Street, London W1M 8JR.
United Kingdom Council for Overseas Student Affairs, 60 Westbourne Grove, London W2 5FG.

Black women's groups/organizations in the UK*

Asian Women's Resource and Refuge Centre, 134 Minet Road, NW10.
Battersea Black Women's Group, c/o York Gardens Community Centre, Lavender Road, Battersea, London SW11 2UQ.
Brixton Black Women's Group, c/o BWC 41 Stockwell Green, London SW9.
Camden and Islington BWG, c/o 7b Ospringe Road, London NW5.
East London Black Women's Organization, c/o Haleem Thomas, 285 Romford Road, London E7.
North Paddington Black Women's Group, c/o N. Paddington Women's Centre, 115 Portnall Road, London W9.
Eritrean Women's Association, PO Box 7007, London WC1.
Peckham BWG, c/o St Giles Community Centre, Benhill Road, London SE5.
Shepherd's Bush BWG, c/o 139 Becklow Road, London W12.
Southall Black Sisters, 86 Northcote Avenue, Southall.
Somali Women's Group, c/o Oxford House, Derbyshire Street, London E1.
SWAPO Women's Council, 96 Gillespie Road, London N5.

Tamil Women's League, 23a Sumatra Road, London NW6.
United Black Women's Action Group, c/o Wood Green Community Centre, Stanley Road, London N15.
West Indian Women's Organization, 71 Pound Lane, London NW10.
Women for Palestine, c/o Oxford House, Derbyshire Street, London E1.
Woolwich BWG, c/o Simba Project, 58–60 Artillery Place, Woolwich, London SE15.
Birmingham Black Sisters, c/o The Link Centre, 4 James Watt Street, Birmingham B4 7NB.
Manchester 'Abasindi' Co-op, Moss-Side Peoples Centre, St Mary's Street, Moss-Side, Manchester.
Wolverhampton Black Women's Co-op, c/o Wolverhampton Council Community Relations, 2 Clarence Road, Clarence Street, Wolverhampton WV1 4HZ.
Liverpool Black Women's Group, c/o Charles Wotten Centre, 248 Upper Parliament Street, Liverpool.
Black Women's Centre, 41 Stockwell Green, London SW9.

* Feminist Review, No. 17, 1984.

4   The Green Movement

Principal Green Movement organizations

Ecology Party, 36/8 Clapham Road, London, SW9 OJ9, Tel. 01.735.2485.
Friends of the Earth, 377 City Road, London, EC1V 1NA, Tel. 01.837.0731.
Socialist Environment and Resources Association (SERA), 9 Poland Street, London, W1V 3DG, Tel. 01.439.3749.
Greenpeace, 36 Graham Street, London, N1, Tel. 01.251.3020.
Greenline (journal), c/o 14 Alexandra Road, Oxford, OX2 0DB, Tel. 0865.246079/245301.
Campaign for Nuclear Disarmament (CND), 11 Goodwin Street, London, N4 3HQ, Tel. 01.263.0977.

5   Northern Ireland

A list of some of the most important political organizations

This list is necessarily selective. It is also part of the turmoil and uncertainty of politics in Northern Ireland that organized groups do not always have a very long life: many have faded away, been absorbed by others, or have changed their names. This is particularly true of the many militant 'Loyalist' groups which have emerged since the collapse of official Unionism.

'Loyalist' organizations

Official Unionist Party (OUP).
The most important inheritor of the tradition of the pre-Direct Rule Unionist Party. Its current official leader is James Molyneux, but it would be foolish not to recognize the important role played within it by the ex-Conservative, Enoch Powell.

Democratic Unionist Party (DUP).
Founded in 1971, the DUP has always been dominated by the Rev. Ian Paisley, whose position was once again reinforced by his personal success in the 1983 European Election. It is intransigently opposed to any moves towards rapprochement with the Irish Republic, let alone Irish unity.

Ulster Defence Association (UDA).
The largest and most inclusive of the 'Loyalist' paramilitary organizations, founded in 1971. It staged the very effective 'Loyalist' general strike against power-sharing in May 1974.

Ulster Volunteer Force (UVF).
Possibly the nastiest of the various 'Loyalist' groups committed to a policy of sectarian murders – i.e. the murder of Catholics for being Catholics. Set up in 1966, it thus pre-dates the beginning of the present crisis in 1968.

Orange Order.
The Unionist or 'Loyalist' equivalent of the Freemasons. Its origins go back to the 1790s. It has provided the ideological and organizational backbone of Unionism throughout the history of the province.

Protestant based organizations

Northern Ireland Labour Party (NILP).
An attempt to create something analogous to the British Labour Party within the context of Northern Ireland. But its commitment to the union with Britain confined its support to a minority of Protestant working class. The formation of the SDLP (see below) effectively dealt the NILP a death blow. It died in the 1970s.

Alliance Party.
Launched in 1970 as an avowedly non-sectarian and liberal or moderate party, it has therefore often been looked on with approval by outsiders, particularly in Britain. But the real conflict of interests and struggle for power in Northern Ireland have doomed it to remain an ineffective

minority group. Its support comes almost entirely from liberal-minded Protestants.

Nationalist organizations

Social Democratic and Labour Party (SDLP).
Founded in 1970, the SDLP's deliberately non-sectarian title barely conceals the fact that it is, and was intended to be, the mass party of moderate, constitutional Catholics and nationalists. As such it commanded general electoral support from the minority community throughout the 1970s (except in Fermanagh and Tyrone), but since 1982 Sinn Fein has mounted an increasingly strong challenge to the SDLP even in the electoral/parliamentary sphere. Leading figures in the SDLP have included Gerry (now Lord) Fitt, John Hume, Ivan Cooper, Austin Currie and others. They were civil rights campaigners in the late 1960s. Their denunciations of the IRA have won them British admiration but lost them support in their own community.

Irish Republican Army (IRA).
Today this title refers only to what was originally the Provisional IRA, which broke away from the Official IRA towards the end of 1969. For a while both IRAs were engaged in military action against the Unionist state and the British troops. But the Official IRA has now (I think) been formally dissolved. There has, of course, always been an IRA of some kind since the civil war of the early 1920s. Before 1968 it used to be regarded by the British, and many Irish, as something of a joke. Not now.

Sinn Fein (SF).
As with the IRA, there used to be two Sinn Feins. Now there is only one. British media commentators invariably refer to it as the 'political wing' of the IRA, just in case we might be tempted to take its evident popular support (including at the ballot box) seriously. But Sinn Fein, like the IRA, has a 60-year history, and has always commanded support from the Nationalist community in the North – and South.

Irish Republican Socialist Party/Irish National Liberation Army (IRSP/INLA)
Formed in 1974 as a breakaway from the Official Sinn Fein/IRA. They have been engaged in bitter and sometimes murderous feuding with other Republican groups; but the INLA has also committed some audacious political killings, including that of Airey Neave MP at the House of Commons in 1979.

Northern Ireland Civil Rights Association (NICRA)
NICRA was founded in 1967, and led the fight for equal rights for Catholics during the first months of the crisis in 1968–9. As its title

suggests, it was modelled on the black example in the USA in the 1960s, and it tried to avoid raising the traditional nationalist issues – in vain.

Parties in the Irish Republic

Fianna Fail
The official heirs of the Republican tradition in the Irish struggle for independence. But also the 'natural party of government' in Ireland, until the 1970s. It has therefore been divided and ambiguous in its response to the crisis in the North; but it remains committed to the ultimate goal of a united Ireland.

Fine Gael
More conservative and less Republican than FF. But its basically weaker position means that it has only been able to govern in a bizarre alliance with the Irish Labour Party.

Irish Labour Party
Has made enough electoral headway in the past decade or so to be indispensable to Fine Gael if the latter is to govern. One of its leading figures, Conor Cruise O'Brien, has endeared himself to the British by his repeated denunciations of Irish nationalism and all its works.

Workers' Party
This party is the outcome of the conversion of the one-time Official IRA and Sinn Fein to Marxism and class-based politics. It has already established itself within the Irish political system.

Relevant organizations in mainland Britain

These are remarkably thin on the ground.

National Council for Civil Liberties
The NCCL has monitored much that has happened in Northern Ireland over the past 15 years, and has produced some valuable pamphlets on the erosion of civil liberties and basic principles of justice in the province.

Troops Out Movement
Campaigned vigorously for the withdrawal of British troops in the late 1970s, but now appears to be defunct.

Irish Freedom Movement
Run by the Revolutionary Communist Party. Currently active in staging meetings and producing publications.

6 British political parties of the Left

BIG FLAME, Room 265, 27 Clerkenwell Close, London EC1R 0AT.

Publications. BF used to publish a magazine, *Revolutionary Socialism*, but now brings out intermittently a paper *Big Flame* and a magazine *Anti-Nuclear Action*. It also publishes pamphlets including *Ireland: rising in the North*, and *The Past against our future: fighting racism and fascism*.

History, organization and membership. BF began in Liverpool in 1970 as a Merseyside socialist newspaper, and continued after the paper's demise as a small group committed to mass politics within rank and file industrial and wider social struggles. It went national in 1975, and now has groups in Liverpool, Sheffield, Birmingham, Coventry, Nottingham, London, Bristol, Newcastle and Manchester. It co-ordinates itself through an annual conference and a national committee, and through commissions around which work is organized. These are currently anti-nuclear, Ireland, workplace struggles, women, anti-racism and international questions. Heavily involved in the search for socialist unity in 1976–9, the group split in 1981 on the question of entry into the Labour Party. BF remained outside, much reduced in size; and is probably now no more than 100 people in total.

Programme and perspectives. BF has long sought to establish a unity between revolutionary groups on the basis of an anti-imperialist, pro-feminist socialism. It has seen its job as one of servicing autonomous struggles: particularly industrial struggles, the struggle for Irish independence, and struggles against gender and racial oppression. It was therefore very active in Troops Out, in the Anti-Nazi League, and in the peace and women's movements. It works to establish a communist current within those struggles, and to link each struggle consciously in the overall move to socialism. It remains opposed to Labour Party entryism, preferring to concentrate on mass politics and class mobilization.

CAMPAIGN FOR LABOUR PARTY DEMOCRACY, 10 Park Drive, London NW11.

Publications. Newsletter.

History, organization and membership. The CLPD was founded in 1973 by activists who had been involved in the Socialist Charter campaign of 1968-72 to democratize the Labour Party, and who saw themselves as involved in a slow and steady campaign to educate party members in the need for greater accountability. The CLPD is open to individual membership, and to affiliation by organizations; and by 1980 807 individuals had joined, and affiliations had come from 107 Constituency Labour Parties, and 161 trade union branches. The CLPD operates through an AGM and elected executive, and works by suggesting model resolutions that CLPs can submit to conference, and by issuing a newsletter and other agitational material. In its heyday in the late 1970s it also lobbied hard at trade union branch meetings to win resolutions favourable to internal constitutional change.

Programme and perspectives. The initial programme of the CLPD focused on making conference decisions binding on the Parliamentary Labour Party, on keeping the Labour Party NEC to its task as the custodian of conference policy, and on ensuring that the manifesto of the Party at each general election accurately reflected policy as laid down at conference. Then in December 1973 the CLPD adopted the policy of the mandatory reselection of MPs, and by 1976 was pressing for a change in the method of electing the party leader. The Campaign is formally committed in its constitution to the task of working through constitutional channels for the implementation of policies to give effect to the 1974 and 1979 election promise to 'bring about a fundamental and irreversible shift in the balance of wealth and power in favour of working people and their families'. But in practice the CLPD has maintained its focus on questions of internal party democracy and constitutional change, and has avoided taking public positions on actual policy debates within the Party.

CAMPAIGN GROUP, c/o Alan Meale, 106 Savernake Road, London NW3.

History, organization and membership. A group of Socialist MPs within the Labour Party, set up in September 1983.

Programme and perspectives. The group exists to link the politics of the parliamentary party to campaigns carried out by the labour movement *outside* parliament, by participating in trade union struggles and by carrying into the PLP the views and concerns of activists in those struggles.

COMMUNIST PARTY OF GREAT BRITAIN, 16 St John Street, London EC1M 4AL.

Publications. Daily paper, *Morning Star* (technically not the official organ of the Party, but editorially it still expresses party views). Monthly journals: *Marxism Today* and *Communist focus.* Quarterly journal: *Link.* For futher details, see section III of chapter 11.

FABIAN SOCIETY, 11 Dartmouth Street, London SW1H 9BN.

Publications. Fabian Tract series (eight per annum) including recently Raymond Plant, *Equality, Markets and the State*; Bernard Crick, *Socialist Values and Time*; Anthony Wright, John Stewart and Nicholas Deakin, *Socialism and Decentralisation.* Books in association with commercial publishers, including Nick Bosanquet and Peter Townsend (eds) *Labour and Equality: a Fabian Study of Labour in Power, 1974–79*, 1980; Howard Glennerster (ed.), *The Future of the Welfare State*, 1982; Ben Pimlott (ed.), *Fabian Essays in Socialist Thought*, 1984; also, *100 Years of Fabian Socialism*, Centenary Pictorial history; *Fabian News*, members' newsletter; periodic *Briefings.*

History, organization and membership. The Fabians are the oldest socialist society in Britain, and the only one to have remained affiliated to the Labour Party since participating in its foundation. Its early members included Bernard Shaw, Sidney Webb and Graham Wallas – all contributors to the influential *Fabian Essays* of 1889. Fabianism has often been identified with the outlook of Beatrice and Sidney Webb, especially in view of the latter's influence on the Labour Party as a drafter of the Party's 1918 Constitution and programme *Labour and the New Social Order*. But intellectual influences within the Society have been diverse, with leading contributions in Fabian pamphlets by Leonard Woolf on *Imperialism*, R. H. Tawney on the *Acquisitive Society* and G. D. H. Cole on *Guild Socialism*. In the 1930s the Society was in decline and Cole established the New Fabian Research Bureau, with Attlee as its Chairman; this in effect took over the Fabian Society in a merger in 1938.

During the war, the Fabian Colonial Bureau began to plan the dismantling of imperialism; the International Bureau brought together those who hoped to build a Socialist International when the war was over; and the essays *Social Security*, edited by William Robson, paved the way for the Beveridge report. The post-war Society has maintained the strong Fabian social policy tradition, in the work of Richard Titmuss, Peter Townsend and Brian Abel-Smith; its leading politician-pamphleteers included Tony Crosland, Richard Crossman and Tony Benn. Two of its post-war General Secretaries, Bill Rodgers and Shirley Williams, were among the leading defectors to the SDP, and a ballot of the Society's members adopted a rule change to exclude them from full membership. A consequent loss of members was, by mid-1984, replaced: current membership is about 5,000, comprising 3,300 national members plus 1,700 who are members of local societies without being national subscribers. The Society is run by an Executive Committee elected by annual ballot and with representation from local Fabian societies.

Perspectives. When the Fabian Society and the NFRB merged in 1938, the rules incorporated the 'self-denying ordinance' which precludes the Society from adopting a collective position on any matter of policy beyond its socialist objectives. It thus exists to promote research, writing and debate from different democratic socialist perspectives; its publications represent the views of their authors and not of the Society, which merely commends them as worthy of consideration within the labour movement. This said, the Society has remained essentially within the non-Marxist British socialist tradition of its founders, while reflecting a diversity of tradition – for example, between the centralist philosophy of the Webbs and the decentralist philosophy of G. D. H. Cole – within it.

INDEPENDENT LABOUR PUBLICATIONS, 49 Top Moor Side, Leeds LS11 9LW.

Publications. Monthly paper, *Labour Leader*, founded by Keir Hardie; also pamphlets and books, including recently E. Preston, *Labour in Crisis*;

P. Schofield et al., *Youth Training: the Tories Poisoned Apple*; H. Barnes, The *Public Face of Militant*; and B. Winter, *The ILP – a brief history*.

History, organization and membership. Independent Labour Publications is descended from the Independent Labour Party which played so dominant a role in the creation and early development of the Labour Party. The ILP was the leading socialist group in the Labour Party from 1900 to 1932, and provided from its ranks the major figures and the bulk of the activists in Labour's first generation. But the ILP became increasingly uneasy with the rightward drift of policy in the two inter-war Labour governments, and disaffiliated in 1932. Its membership then collapsed, and thereafter it remained as a tiny independent current on the Left, equally resistant to Labour Party moderation and Stalinist Communism. In 1975 it reorganized itself as Independent Labour Publications, and returned to the Labour Party. The ILP has a current membership of about 400, and is organized on a branch basis, with an AGM and a democratically elected National Administrative Council. It is an active registered group inside the Labour Party.

Programme and perspectives. The ILP uses its publications to develop socialist ideas and policies within the labour movement, and to win the Labour Party to a socialist perspective. It sees its role as one of building a coherent socialist base in the Labour Party with clear perspectives and democratic practices. The ILP sees the crucial issue as how to shift the Labour Party to the left, in a conservative culture, without destroying it. It argues that the Labour Party will become a vehicle for socialism only after a fundamental transformation of its present practices; but that such a transformation is essential, in that popular support for socialism will only be harnessed by socialists working within and through the existing institutions of the labour movement.

LABOUR CO-ORDINATING COMMITTEE, 9 Poland Street, London W1.

Publications. Occasional broadsheet, *Labour Activist*; (with SERA) a bimonthly newsletter, *Local Socialism.*

History, organization and membership. The LCC was formed at a fringe meeting of the Labour Party Conference in 1978, to link up 'like-minded left activists in the party and unions'. It is open to any member of the Labour Party. It has an annual policy-making AGM and a 20 person executive elected by postal ballot. It has regional and local groups, and at national level a women's committee and a trade union one. Its current membership is 856, plus affiliations from 85 organizations on the Left (mainly Constituency Labour Parties and trade-union branches).

Programme and perspectives. The LCC is committed to the creation and electoral success of a revitalized and socialist Labour Party. It opposes those who wish to split the party (to drive out non-socialist elements), and seeks a new party unity on the basis of genuine tolerance and debate. But in its own input into that debate the LCC stresses the need to develop a strategy for socialism which fuses parliamentary and extra-parliamentary action. It pursues popular support for the Labour Party through three routes: the internal democratization of the party; the adoption by its leadership of left-wing positions (on the AES, women's rights, industrial democracy, health and welfare provision); and the involvement of the Party in locally-based mass campaigns. Recognizing the enormous impact of Thatcherism on popular consciousness, the LCC looks to the Labour Party to become an equivalent hegemonic phenomenon; and argues that such a counter-hegemony will be created only if the party lifts its sights off mere electioneering, confidently asserts the socialist credentials of such popular values as equality, liberty and democracy, and involves itself in public campaigning and in the daily lives and struggles of its potential supporters (in every street and workplace). The LCC supports the view that the Labour Party should participate regularly in common campaigns with other groups and organizations on the Left in the construction of a popular majority for socialism.

LABOUR PARTY YOUNG SOCIALISTS, 150 Walworth Road, London SE17.

Publications. Monthly paper, *Socialist Youth*, also pamphlets and leaflets, including recently *Youth for Labour, End Arms Scandal, The Battle against Racialism and Fascism*, and *Northern Ireland, the way forward*.

History, organization and membership. Formed in 1960, the LPYS now have more than 500 branches mainly organized on a constituency basis. They are also grouped into 11 regions, each with an annual conference which elects a committee and one representative to the LPYS National Committee. Nationally, the LPYS has an annual policy-making conference, from which it elects one representative to the Labour Party's NEC. It runs regional schools and summer camps, and is affiliated to a wide range of campaigns (including CND, Anti-Apartheid and Chile Solidarity). Membership is open to all Labour Party members who are between 15 and 25. It was once dominated by the SLL, and is now an important base of power within the Labour Party for the Militant Tendency.

Programme and perspectives. The LPYS exists formally to win the support of young people for the Labour Party, and to express the views of the young within the Party itself. In practice the LPYS try to create a socialist youth movement and to win the main Labour Party to a fully socialist programme. To that end, it publishes policy statements on issues affecting young people particularly, and on general issues such as Poland, the bomb, racism and so on. The socialist programme it currently presses on the Labour Party includes full implementation of Clause 4, unilateral nuclear disarmament, a guaranteed job for all school leavers, a 35 hour week without loss of pay, a £90 a week minimum wage, a crash building programme of schools, houses and hospitals, equal pay opportunities for women, and the repeal of all immigration laws.

THE MILITANT TENDENCY, 1 Mentmore Terrace, London E8 3PN.

Publications. Weekly paper, *Militant*; theoretical journal, *Militant International Review*, plus a whole range of pamphlets, details of which can be obtained from World Socialist Books at the above address.

History, organization and membership. For details, see section IV of chapter 11; and also M. Crick, *Militant*, London, Faber and Faber, 1984.

Programme and perspectives. The Militant Tendency understand capitalism to be a system prone to crisis, and now in deepening contradiction. Capitalism will therefore move towards a pre-revolutionary situation under its own logic; and the only question for the Left is where they can best put their energies in order to be able to capitalize on that situation when it rises. Militant's answer is to be inside the Labour Party: because that is where the working class is, because that is the only place in which to avoid marginalization as a revolutionary, and because the Labour Party can be transformed into a revolutionary party if the existing 'rotten' leadership can be removed. Militant's politics reduce back to a question of party leadership with remarkable speed; with Militant's strategy being one of posing a series of transitional demands (35 hour working week, no redundancies, nationalization of the top 200 companies, and so on) in order to expose the inadequacy of existing party leaderships. The Tendency expect that a radicalized Labour government would use an Enabling Act to achieve a peaceful transition to socialism, underpinned by the support of a wholly mobilized labour movement. Militant sees itself as the agency which will transform the Labour Party, and is highly dismissive of all other groups on the Left (which it dismisses as 'sects'). Its need for secrecy has kept Militant out of the mass campaigning beloved of those 'sects'; and this has been easy because of the Tendency's view that women's struggles, anti-racist mobilizations and (until lately) peace campaigning are at best peripheral and at worst distracting from the main job of Labour Party transformation and socialist mobilization.

NEW COMMUNIST PARTY OF BRITAIN, PO Box 73, London SW11 2PQ.

Publications. Weekly paper, *The New Worker*; theoretical journal, *New Communist Review*.

History, organization and membership. The NCP was formed in July 1977 as a formal split from the CPGB by a section of the Party who were convinced that the leadership of the Party were irretrievably revisionist. The NCP is organized on Bolshevik lines and attaches particular importance to the recruitment and building of party branches in industry. As part of this, it attaches importance to elevating industrial workers to key positions in the party. The NCP is organized in nine geographical regions (South London, North London, South East, Midlands, North West, Yorkshire, North East, Scotland, Wales). It claimed 1,000 members in 1977 but is now probably considerably smaller than that.

Programme and perspectives. The NCP left the CPGB because of major differences over the application of 'scientific socialism' and the associated need to build a revolutionary party on Marxist-Leninist lines. The NCP rejected as 'unscientific' the theory of Eurocommunism, seeing it as the abandonment of the class struggle, as rejecting the need for a revolutionary party and working-class internationalism, as spreading illusions about capitalism's reformability, and as a surrender to anti-socialist ideas canvassed against the working class by its enemies. The NCP sees itself as concerned with the proper revolutionary task abandoned by Eurocommunism: of building a vanguard party on Leninist lines which can equip the working class with the theory and organization necessary to take state power in a revolutionary situation.

The NCP participates fully in all the campaigns of the broad trade-union and labour movement, and supports movements of a progressive kind. It places particular importance on strengthening the peace movement. believing that the struggle for peace is inextricably linked to the struggle for socialism. It sees its involvement in such movements as based on the adoption of principled positions, specifically working to overcome anti-sovietism and to strengthen working-class unity. It recognizes the Labour Party as the mass party of the working class, and seeks affiliation to it with its own paper, organization and programme. The NCP refuses to stand candidates against the Labour Party in elections, irrespective of agreement or disagreement with the particular candidate.

REVOLUTIONARY COMMUNIST GROUP, BCM Box 5909, London WC1N 3XX.

Publications. Monthly paper *Fight Racism! Fight Imperialism!*, 20p; books, *The Revolutionary Road to Communism in Britain*, RCG Manifesto, 1984, £1.50; David Reed, *Ireland: the key to the British Revolution*, 1984, £3.95.

History, organization and membership. The RCG was formed in 1974 by a group (the Revolutionary Opposition) expelled from the International Socialists (now SWP) for criticizing what they took to be IS's abandonment of the materialist basis of Marxism. Convinced of the need to apply Marxism to current conditions if the working class is to break the grip of opportunism and reformism which holds back its struggles, the RCG developed a Marxist analysis of the contemporary crisis and modern imperialism. This appeared in the journal *Revolutionary Communist* and in the RCG's manifesto. It currently organizes its small membership through geographical branches and a national conference. The bulk of its members are now young workers, including black and Irish workers.

Programme and perspectives. The RCG believes that communism will come in Britain only through an alliance of British workers with national liberation movements fighting imperialism, particularly in the case of Ireland which it regards as 'the key to the British revolution'. It believes that the key force for revolution in Britain lies outside the organized Labour/trade union movement, in the most oppressed layers, particularly black workers. Black workers are seen as an important link between the class struggle here and national liberation movements abroad. The RCG supports all working-class struggles and urges unity with the Irish and anti-racist struggles. In addition to campaigning on the questions of racism and imperialism, the RCG supports struggles for prisoners' rights and other struggles for democratic rights, such as Greenham Common. It is Leninist rather than Trotskyist and sees the Soviet Union, its allies and China as socialist states.

REVOLUTIONARY COMMUNIST LEAGUE OF BRITAIN, c/o New Era Books, 203 Seven Sisters Road, London N4.

Publications. Monthly paper, *Class Struggle*; theoretical journal, *October*.

History, organization and membership. The roots of the RCL are to be found in the early 1960s with former members of the CPGB who had supported Peking in the Sino-Soviet dispute, and who had opposed the concept of peaceful transition as laid out in the 1951 programme of the CPGB, *The British Road to Socialism*. The RCL was formed in 1977, as a uniting of the Communist Federation of Britain (M-L), the Communist Unity Association (M-L) and the East London Marxist-Leninist Association. During 1980 the RCL was joined by the Birmingham Communist Association and the Communist Workers Movement, the latter made up of former members of the CPB (M-L) which had been amongst the earliest of the Maoist Parties. The RCL is run on democratic centralist lines and has a tiny membership.

Programme and perspectives. The RCL supports the Theory of the Three Worlds and recognizes the absolute necessity for communists in an oppressor nation such as Britain to support unconditionally the oppressed nations and peoples of the world. In particular it wholeheartedly supports the right of the Irish people as a whole to self-determination. It recognizes how important it is to carry out more theoretical and practical work on understanding the relationship between class struggle and national struggle in England, Wales and Scotland. It sees the fight against all forms of chauvinism and opportunism within the working class – and the fight against women's oppression – as essential at this early stage of its development. The RCL sees the Labour Party as an imperialist party, believes that parliamentary democracy is but one form of the dictatorship of the bourgeoisie, and argues that social democracy represents the ideas of the ruling class within the ranks of the working class. The ideology of the RCL is described by the League as Marxism-Leninism-Mao Ze Dong Thought, and the League lays great emphasis on the relationship between theory and practice, on the need for the mass line, and on the ideas of criticism and self-criticism.

REVOLUTIONARY COMMUNIST PARTY, BM RCP, London WC1N 3XX.

Publications. Monthly paper, *The Next Step*; books and pamphlets, *Preparing for Power* (the programme of the RCP) and *Revolutionary Communist Papers* (an occasional theoretical journal).

History, organization and membership. The RCP was formed in 1981, emerging from the earlier Revolutionary Communist Tendency which had split from the RCG in 1976. The RCP now has branches in parts of London, Birmingham, Cardiff, Coventry, Liverpool, Manchester, Sheffield, Bradford, Leeds and Glasgow. It has several hundred members nationwide.

Programme and perspectives. The RCT were expelled from the RCG as 'chauvinists' – condemned that is, for filtering their attitude to the South African Left through their own domestic concern to criticize the CPGB. That itself indicated the RCT's greater concern with local class struggle and its political leadership. The RCP sees no common interests between workers and employers, and insists that workers' interests must be pursued unambiguously without regard for their consequences for the capitalist class and its state. The RCP sees reformist leadership in the Labour Party and the unions as the main problem facing the Left. It regularly stands against the Labour Party in elections, opposes union bureaucracies, encourages broadly-based mass struggles against the state's encroachment on workers' hard-won rights, and attaches importance to women's struggles, black resistance and gay battles as well as industrial conflict. Its Irish work has been central to its politics throughout, first through the Smash the Prevention of Terrorism Act Campaign (SPTAC) and then through the Irish Freedom Movement. The RCP has defended the right of the Provos to adopt any tactics, including the use of bombs against civilian targets in England, and has earned some opprobrium even on the Left for doing so.

SOCIALIST LEAGUE (formerly the *International Marxist Group*), PO Box 50, 328 Upper Street, London N1 2XP.

Publications. Weekly paper, *Socialist Action*; theoretical journal, *International*.

History, organization and membership. For details, see section IV of chapter 11.

Programme and perspectives. The IMG's formative years were concentrated on student politics from a perspective which downplayed the revolutionary potential of the Western European working class and stressed instead the catalysing role of single-issue struggles outside the class. For this reason the IMG was the Trotskyist group most open to autonomous organization and struggle by the women's movement and to immersion in support work here for Irish independence. Far from seeing these as a distraction from class struggle, the IMG saw them as first stages in a strategy of movement 'from the periphery to the centre' that would in the end revolutionize the working class as a whole. Priority was attached too to the achievement of socialist unity (negotiations on this in 1977–8 were blocked by SWP intransigence); and less weight was given to industrial struggles, though periodic 'turns to industry' (in 1972, and recently) saw IMG comrades taking manual jobs and becoming shop stewards (most famously at British Leyland, Cowley, from which they were hounded by the national press in 1983). The Labour Party was thought of as barren territory by the IMG between 1968 and 1979, as the group tried to mobilize radical forces independently. The dismal results of the 1979 election brought a rethink, a change of name in 1983 (to the Socialist League) and of paper title (from *Socialist Challenge* to *Socialist Action*), and a re-entry into the Labour Party, with heavy and public support for the Benn faction.

SOCIALIST ORGANISER ALLIANCE, 28 Middle Lane, London N8 8PL.

Publications. Weekly paper, *Socialist Organiser*; occasional pamphlets, including *Where We Stand*, 1978; and *Labour Democracy and the fight for a Workers' Government*, 1980.

History, organization and membership. The Socialist Organiser Alliance was launched in 1980 as an offshoot of the Socialist Campaign for a Labour Victory founded in 1978 as a coalition (in which Workers' Action was the major initiating force), wanting to put an alternative Left voice within the Labour Party campaign at the 1979 election. SOA is organized in local groups, with an AGM to fix the general line of the paper and the campaigning priorities of the membership. Membership is open to all Labour Party members, and involves a commitment to selling a number of copies of the paper, to meeting regularly, and to participating in campaigns in the Party and the unions. Membership is about 300.

Programme and perspectives. SOA are a Trotskyist group operating within the Labour Party, holding conventional Trotskyist views on the Soviet Union and on the need for revolution. They believe that revolution will never be achieved by groups who stand outside the dominant institutions of the labour movement. They work inside the Labour Party and the unions (a) to transform them internally by democratizing them, and (b) to equip the broad mass of workers with a renewed understanding of the content and relevance of revolutionary socialist ideas. SOA aims to be 'in the party and on the streets', campaigning vigorously on all left-wing issues within the Labour Party whilst participating fully in campaigns and struggles outside. Inside the Party it argues against the reformism (as it sees it) of the Tribune group and the LCC; and outside it struggles against what it terms 'the cancer of sectarianism', seeking 'collaboration in action and serious honest dialogue about our differences' between different Marxist groups. Committed to maximum left unity in action wherever possible, SOA argues against the call for British withdrawal from the EEC – rejecting that position as nationalist – and calls instead (without endorsing the EEC) for a united European workers' government.

SOCIALIST PARTY OF GREAT BRITAIN, 52 Clapham High Street, London SW4 7UN.

Publications. Monthly paper, *Socialist Standard*; also many pamphlets and tapes of public meetings, all of which can be inspected at Head Office.

History, organization and membership. The oldest of the revolutionary groups active on the British Left, the SPGB was formed in 1904, when a section of the then SDF were expelled for their opposition to what they termed the 'electoral opportunism' and moderation of the SDF proramme. Currently, the Party has 18 branches (eight in London, others in Lancashire, the North East and Scotland) and 12 groups in areas in which membership is insufficiently strong to sustain a branch. The internal structure is extremely democratic – all meetings are open to the public, all policy is decided at annual conference, and there is no full-time paid official. Current membership is approximately 600. Individuals are admitted only after a period of probation and the completion of a set of examinations on socialist theory and practice.

Programme and perspectives. The SPGB focuses exclusively on the single issue of socialist transformation, and does not participate in movements (such as CND) which – though useful in alerting workers to the dangers of capitalism – are seen as reformist (and hence in the end bound to fail). Socialist transformation will come, according to the SPGB, only when a majority of workers understand and want it, when they recognise that the existing state will have to be captured and used to dispossess the capitalist class. The job of the party is to educate the working class, by recruiting members and debating the issue of socialism at every opportunity and with every shade of political opinion. The SPGB sees Russia as state capitalist (and has done since 1918); and is opposed to Leninism, Stalinism, Trotskyism and Maoism. It is explicitly not a vanguard party in the Leninist sense, but a party seeking to educate the working class in the need for socialism through education and political debate.

SOCIALIST SOCIETY, 9 Poland Street, London W1.

Publications. Pamphlets such as Anthony Arblaster, *The Falklands: Thatcher's War, Labour's guilt*; Mike Rustin, *Comprehensive Education after 18: a socialist strategy*; Raymond Williams, *Democracy and Parliament*; Socialist Education Group, *The Youth Training Scheme – a strategy for the labour movement*; and West London Group, *The mass psychology of Thatcherism*. Books published in collaboration with Penguin include Lynne Segal (ed.) *What is to be done about the family* and Elizabeth Wilson (ed.) *What is to be done about violence against women.*

History, organization and membership. For details see last section of chapter 11.

SOCIALIST WORKERS' PARTY, PO Box 82, London E2 9DS.

Publications. Weekly paper, *Socialist Worker*; monthly magazine, *Socialist Review*; quarterly journal, *International Socialism.*

History, organization and membership. For details,, see section IV of chapter 11.

Programme and perspectives. The SWP believes that the task of revolutionaries is to build a revolutionary party outside and in opposition to the Labour Party, by supporting working-class struggles, attracting and educating socialist militants, and propagating socialist ideas. The SWP rejects the possibility of a parliamentary road to socialism, or of socialism in one country. Seeking the overthrow of capitalism, the Party argues for independent working-class action under a revolutionary party, as a national component of a world revolutionary movement. Internationally, the SWP supports movements of national liberation, opposes racism and imperialism, and supports working-class struggles in the Soviet bloc against the bureaucratic ruling class in power there. Domestically, the SWP is these days publicly committed to ending sexual inequality and to supporting autonomous black organizations engaged in communal self-defence; but in fact the question of how to relate the socialist struggle particularly to the feminist struggle has never been fully resolved by the SWP – and indeed the Party was slow to recognize even the importance of the issue. Though the instigator and major force in the Anti-Nazi League, the party has been uneasy with other campaigns of a single-issue or cross-class nature, and has preferred to concentrate instead on working-class aspects of those campaigns. Nor has the SWP followed Left fashion on Ireland – keeping its distance from Republicanism and supporting instead the attempt of the Socialist Workers Movement to radicalize the Irish proletariat north and south. Though in general the SWP has been willing to work with other left groups in common campaigns, it has been reluctant to pursue socialist unity to the point at which that unity threatened its own organizational integrity and distinctiveness.

SPARTACIST LEAGUE, PO Box 185, London WC1H 8JE.

Publications. Monthly paper, *Spartacist Britain*; other publications include, *Spartacist* (publication of the International Spartacist tendency), *Workers Vanguard* (fortnightly) and *Women and Revolution* (Spartacist League/US publications distributed in Britain).

History, organization and membership. The Spartacist League emerged as a fusion in 1978 between two groups: one that had formed itself as the London Spartacist Group in 1975; the other, the Trotskyist Faction, that had broken from the WSL, and was centred on former members of the RCG who had joined the WSL in 1976. The new organization became the British section of the international Spartacist tendency, which believes it is the only genuine Trotskyist tendency and seeks the rebirth of the Fourth International. While the group is small, it has members and supporters mainly in London, Sheffield and Birmingham.

Programme and perspectives. The Spartacists believe that a central task for revolutionaries today is championing unconditional military defence of the deformed/degenerated workers states (primarily the Soviet bloc, including Cuba) in the face of a NATO imperialist war drive. They support the Russian intervention in Afghanistan ('Hail Red Army') and said 'Stop Solidarity's counter-revolution', arguing Solidarity had become a 'Polish company union for the CIA and bankers'. They oppose the peace movement's call for a nuclear-free Europe with their own slogan, 'Smash NATO, Defend the Soviet Union'. The Spartacists see this as quite orthodoxly Trotskyist, and link it to their condemnation of the Stalinist bureaucracy; they say a political revolution is needed in Poland, the USSR etc. to ensure defence against counter-revolution and extension of socialist revolution throughout the capitalist world.

They seek to build a revolutionary party through a combination of 'revolutionary regroupment' (winning to their politics comrades now in organizations seen as 'centrist' or 'left reformist', e.g. CP, SWP, IMG), and fighting for revolutionary leadership in the trade unions and of the key struggles of workers and the oppressed. Their publications pay much attention to polemics with other left organizations around the key issues of the class struggle. While saying 'Drive out the SDP fifth column' (the 'NATO/CIA/IMF-loving' right wing of the Labour Party), they also politically oppose and seek to break workers from the Labour Left, saying a mass revolutionary party will only be built when the working-class base of the Labour Party is split away from what they call the Party's pro-capitalist misleaders. They pay much attention to the fight against racial oppression, opposing capitalist immigration controls and racist deportations and seeking to initiate the mass trade-union/minority mobilizations to smash fascist/racist attacks. They politically oppose feminism, saying they stand for 'women's liberation through socialist revolution'. The Spartacists also have a special position on Ireland, demanding the immediate, unconditional withdrawal of the British army and opposing Orange supremacy, but citing Leninist precedents to oppose politically the IRA as 'Green nationalists', and to oppose any forced unification of Ireland against the wishes of the Northern Protestants. While defending IRA military campaigns against the British army and police, they advocate the creation of integrated workers' militias 'to combat imperialist rampage and sectarian terror' and a Trotskyist party north and south whose goal would be a workers' republic in Ireland as part of a socialist federation of the British Isles.

TRIBUNE GROUP OF MPs, c/o Jeannette Gould, House of Commons, London SW1A 0AA.

History, organization and membership. The group was formed in 1964, as a successor to the Bevanite group of Labour MPs. In December 1983 its membership consisted of the following:

Norman Atkinson	Michael Foot	Lord Molloy
Richard Balfe MEP	John Fraser	Martin O'Neill
Guy Barnett	Reg Freeson	Stan Orme
Kevin Barron	Norman Godman	Terry Patchett
Margaret Beckett	Bryan Gould	Peter Pike
Gerry Bermingham	Harriet Harman	John Prescott
Syd Bidwell	Eric Heffer	Jo Richardson
Roland Boyes	Stuart Holland	Allan Roberts
Jeremy Bray	Doug Hoyle	Allan Rogers
Gordon Brown	Bob Hughes	Jeff Rooker
Lord Bruce	Neil Kinnock	Ernie Ross
Janey Buchan MEP	Ron Leighton	Clare Short
Norman Buchan	Terry Lewis	John Silkin
Richard Caborn	Oonagh McDonald	Chris Smith
Ann Clwyd	Kevin McNamara	Peter Snape
Frank Cook	Max Madden	Clive Soley
Robin Cook	John Maxton	Gavin Strang
Ron Davies	Michael Meacher	Jack Straw
Alf Dubs	Bill Michie	Stan Thorne
Ken Eastham	Ian Mikardo	Bob Wareing
Bob Edwards	Maurice Miller	David Winnick
Mark Fisher		

Programme and Perspective. The group does not seek to establish positions which are binding on its members. Broadly on the Left of the party, it monitors business in the House and movements of opinion within the wider labour movement, holds regular meetings of its members, and makes whatever contributions it can to strengthening the cause of democratic socialism.

WORKERS POWER GROUP, BCM 7750, London WC1N 3XX.

Publications. Monthly paper, *Workers Power*; theoretical journal, *Permanent Revolution*; books and pamphlets include *The degenerated revolution: the origins and nature of the Stalinist states*, 1982; and *The Death Agony of the Fourth International*, 1983.

History, organization and membership. The WPG originated as the left faction of IS in 1972, as part of an internal dispute on how to react to the Aldershot bombing (and hence to the struggle in Ireland). Expelled in 1975, the Left faction fused briefly with the Workers' Fight group to form the International Communist League. But the two elements within the I-CL disagreed on whether priority should be given to trade-union work (the WPG) or to activity in the Labour Party (Workers Fight). The League split in 1976. Since then the WPG has existed as an independent group, organized on democratic-centralist lines around an annual conference. It has approximately 60 members.

Programme and perspectives. WPG sees the prime task of revolution-aries as to build a revolutionary party, because capitalism is ripe for overthrow, and because revolution is blocked by the dominance of reformist and centrist leaderships in the working-class movement. The Labour and Communist parties are characterized as 'reformists' (aiming to reform capitalism whilst actually reconstituting it); and the bulk of Trotskyist groups are characterized as 'centrist' (hot on revolutionary rhetoric, but vacillating and opportunistic in their politics). The WPG feels that a revolutionary party will only come through the persistent and uncompromising development and presentation of a revolutionary pro-gramme. The WPG attach great importance to support work for national liberation struggles, and to work among the oppressed and super-exploited (especially women and ethnic minorities) as well as among industrial workers. In its participation in all this it makes a virtue of lack of compromise: in the peace movement, for example, it argues for the replacement of CND with a working-class anti-militarist movement which is not pacifist but which favours class war to nuclear holocaust. However WPG does not make acceptance of its point of view conditional on its involvement in particular campaigns, and is in fact committed to the politics of the united front – 'marching separately but striking together'. It continues to take its inspiration from the writings and political practice of Lenin and Trotsky, from what it sees as 'the old and unfalsified tradition of Bolshevism and Trotskyism'; and remains committed to the notion that socialism requires a vanguard party, transitional demands, and the smashing of the state.

WORKERS REVOLUTIONARY PARTY, 216 Old Town, Clapham, London SW4 0JT.

Publications. Daily paper, *The News Line*; monthly journal, *Labour Review*.

History, organization and membership. See section IV of chapter 11.

Programme and perspectives. The WRP is in many ways ultra-orthodox in its Trotskyism. Its own analysis rests on the belief that capitalism is in danger of imminent collapse (at the moment because of an impending collapse of international banking) with a resulting abandonment of democratic rights by the capitalist class and a period of prolonged civil war. Against this scenario, the party's internal authoritarianism is justified as vital to the moment, since divisions only introduce bourgeois complications into what is clearly a polarizing class struggle. The WRP's Trotskyist orthodoxy is also evident in its insistence on the primacy of class in all social analysis and political practice – a 'reductionism' which enables it to dismiss all criticism as necessarily bourgeois (since the correct line is obviously proletarian in derivation) to reject any strategy (such as that of the CPGB) which seeks a broad alliance of all the oppressed, and therefore to keep the WRP distant from the women's movement, student mobilization or involvement in Ireland.

Instead the party's job is to recruit and educate young workers. Since time is too short for reforms, all the party must issue are maximalist demands. Since these are pre-revolutionary times, only one party is required; and so all other left groups are to be fought against as a threat to the revolution (and that includes the SWP and Militant no less than the Labour Party and the CPGB). The WRP sees itself as alone capable of preserving the truth of the Leninist international (before its Stalinist degeneration) that the task of establishing a 'new socialist order . . . can only be done by firmly taking the revolutionary road, mobilising the working class under revolutionary leadership, smashing capitalism and building a socialist planned economy under workers power'.

THE WORKERS SOCIALIST LEAGUE

The WSL was formed in 1974 by a group (around Alan Thornett) expelled from the WRP. Numbering initially perhaps 200 people, it had a strong industrial base in British Leyland at Cowley, and published a fortnight (and eventually weekly) paper *Socialist Press*. The group were particularly keen to apply the Trotskyist strategy of 'the transitional programme' to industrial struggles, concentrating on encouraging groups of workers to co-ordinate their strike action as a context within which to raise more general political demands. The WSL was active in a number of strikes in the late 1970s, and built a series of small but significant international contacts. However the group failed to grow or to widen its industrial base, and in the changed conditions after 1979 turned its attention more to the rising left-wing forces within the Labour Party. By 1981 it had fused with the International Communist League, which had an industrial presence at Longbridge and was already active within the Labour Party in the Rank and File Mobilizing Committee. This new WSL was also active in the Labour Party, working through the Socialist Organiser Alliance (on this, see earlier in the Appendix). But the fused organization has now disintegrated in a series of expulsions; and many of the original group are now poised to reorganize as a tiny independent force again. Their contact address is 31 Bartlemass Road, Oxford.

YOUNG COMMUNIST LEAGUE, 16 St John Street, London EC1.

Publications. Bimonthly magazine, *Challenge*; theoretical journal, *Real Life.*

History, organization and membership. Created in 1921, the YCL is organized through local branches on democratic centralist lines. It has about 750 members.

Programme and perspectives. The YCL accepts the general view of socialist strategy embodied in the 1977 version of the Communist Party's *The British Road to Socialism*, details of which are given in the text of chapter 11. The YCL's task within the construction of the Communist Party's 'broad democratic alliance' is the creation of a viable youth movement committed to the CP's programme.

Notes

Editorial Introduction

1 A. Sampson, *The Changing Anatomy of Britain*, London, Hodder and Stoughton, 1982.
2 In this volume Britain/British is used to denote England, Scotland and Wales. The United Kingdom incorporates Northern Ireland.

Chapter 1

1 I am grateful to Ben Fine and Jerry Coakley for discussing and developing the ideas in this chapter.
2 For a discussion of Marxist theories of economic crisis and the periodisation of capitalism see B. Fine and L. Harris, *Re-reading Capital*, London, Macmillan, 1979, chs 5,7,8. The arguments in this chapter are developed more fully in B. Fine and L. Harris, *Peculiarities of the British Economy*, London, Lawrence and Wishart, 1985.
3 See K. Middlemas, *Politics in Industrial Society*, London, Deutsch, 1979, chs 7,8,9.
4 F. Blackaby (ed.), *De-industrialisation*, London, Heinemann, 1978, p.1.
5 Sheriff and Brown in Blackaby, *De-industrialisation*.
6 See J. Coakley and L. Harris, *The City of Capital*, Oxford, Basil Blackwell, 1983, pp.4–5.
7 Coakley and Harris, *The City of Capital*, pp.97 and 160.
8 Restrictions on the City's operations have been abolished, with the exception of supervisory controls, for banks and others have (minimum) requirements on their operations to protect investors.
9 See S. Aaronovitch, *Monopoly*, London, Lawrence and Wishart, 1955.
10 See M. Kalecki, *Dynamics of the Capitalist Economy*, Cambridge, Cambridge University Press, 1971; P. Baran and P. Sweezy, *Monopoly Capital*, New York, M.R. Press, 1966; J. Steindl, *Maturity and Stagnation in American Capitalism*, Oxford, Oxford University Press, 1952; M. Cowling, *Monopoly Capitalism*, London, Macmillan, 1982.
11 J. H. Dunning, *International Production and the Multinational Enterprise*, London, George Allen and Unwin, 1981, table 6.1, p.146.
12 Dunning, *International Production*, table 6.2, p.147.
13 Dunning, *International Production*, pp.153–8.
14 *British Business*, 3 July 1981, quoted in B. Fine 'Multinational Corporations' and B. Fine and L. Harris, *Peculiarities of the British Economy*, London, Lawrence and Wishart, 1985.
15 Fine, 'Multinational Corporations'.
16 Blackaby, *De-industrialisation*; A. Singh, 'U.K. Industry and World Economy: a case of de-industrialisation?' *Cambridge Journal of Economics*, June 1977; A. Glyn and J. Harrison, *The British Economic Disaster*, London, Pluto Press, 1980; R. Caves and L. Krause, *Britain's Economic Performance*, Washington, D.C., Brookings Institute, 1980; A. Glyn and B. Sutcliffe, *British Capitalism, Workers and the Profit Squeeze*,

Harmondsworth, Penguin, 1972; A. Kilpatrick and T. Lawson, 'On the nature of industrial decline in the U.K.' *Cambridge Journal of Economics*, March 1980; D. Coates 'The Character and Origin of Britain's Economic Decline', in D. Coates and G. Johnston (eds), *Socialist Strategies*, Oxford, Martin Robertson, 1983, ch.2.

17 Glyn and Sutcliffe, *British Capitalism*; Glyn and Harrison, *The British Economic Disaster*; Kilpatrick and Lawson, 'Industrial Decline in the U.K.'

18 R. Bacon and W. Eltis, *Britain's Economic Problem: Too Few Producers*, London, Macmillan, 1978.

19 Coates, *Socialist Strategies*, ch.2; I. Gough, *The Political Economy of the Welfare State*, London, Macmillan, 1979; B. Fine and L. Harris, 'State Expenditure in Advanced Capitalism, A Critique' *New Left Review*, No.98, 1976.

20 W. E. Martin and M. O'Connor, 'Profitability: a background paper' (Chart B2c) in W. E. Martin (ed.), *The Economics of the Profit Crisis*, London, HMSO, 1981.

21 Martin and O'Connor, 'Profitability'.

22 Commission of the European Communities, *The Competitiveness of the Community Industry*, Luxembourg, 1982, p.38.

23 Commission of the European Communities, *Competitiveness of Community Industry*.

24 D. C. Smith, 'Trade Union Growth and Industrial Disputes' in Caves and Krause, *Britain's Economic Performance*.

25 Quoted in Smith, 'Trade Union Growth', pp.110–111.

26 A. G. Hines, 'Trade Unions and Wage Inflation in the United Kingdom, 1893–1960' *Review of Economic Studies*, vol.31, Oct. 1964; D. Dogas and A. G. Hines 'Trade Unions and Wage Inflation in the U.K.' *Applied Economics*, vol.7, Sept. 1975; D. L. Purdy and G. Zis, 'Trade Unions and Wage Inflation in the U.K.' *Applied Economics*, vol.8, Dec. 1976.

27 R. E. Caves, 'Productivity Differences among Industries' in Caves and Krause, *Britain's Economic Performance*.

28 Smith, 'Trade Union Growth' and studies quoted therein.

29 See J. Coakley and L. Harris, 'Industry, the City and the Foreign Exchanges: Theory and Evidence' *British Review of Economic Issues*, Spring, 1983.

30 See Coakley and Harris, *The City of Capital*; R. Minns, *Take Over the City: The Case for Public Ownership of Financial Institutions*, London, Pluto Press, 1982.

31 Coakley and Harris, *The City of Capital*, ch.6; *Committee to Review the Functioning of Financial Institutions Report* Cmnd 7937, London, HMSO, 1980 (Wilson Committee Report). Note that the reliance of UK banks on this 'security in liquidation' rather than the 'going concern' approach to lending policy has been less absolute than is sometimes implied.

32 V. I. Lenin, *Imperialism: the Highest Stage of Capitalism*, collected works, vol.22, Moscow, Progress Publishers, 1964.

33 See D. C. M. Platt, 'British Portfolio Investment Overseas Before 1870: Some Doubts' *Economic History Review,* 2nd Series, vol.XXXIII, 1980, p.16 and D. C. M. Platt, 'Some Drastic Revisions in the Sum and Direction of British Investment Overseas: 31 December 1913', University of London, Institute of Commonwealth Studies, The City and The Empire Seminar Series, May 1984 (unpublished).

34 Central Statistical Office, *UK Balance of Payments, 1983*, London, HMSO, 1983, table 8.1.

35 Coakley and Harris, *The City of Capital*, p.39.

36 J. Coakley, 'The Internationalisation of Bank Capital' *Capital and Class*, 23, 1984.

37 *Committee on the Working of the Monetary System: Report* Cmnd 827, London, HMSO, 1959 (Radcliffe Report).

38 Central Statistical Office, *UK Balance of Payments, 1983*, London, HMSO, 1983, tables 8.1 and 11.2.

39 G. Adam, 'Multinational Corporations and Worldwide Sourcing' in Hugo Radice (ed.),

International Firms and Modern Imperialism, Harmondsworth, Penguin, 1975.
40 R. F. Solomon and K. P. D. Ingham, 'Discriminating between MNC subsidiaries and indigenous companies' *Oxford Bulletin of Economics and Statistics,* vol.39, May 1977, quoted in Caves, 'Productivity Differences'.
41 J. H. Dunning, *Studies in International Investment*, London, Allen and Unwin, 1970, ch.6, quoted in Caves, 'Productivity Differences'.
42 J. H. Dunning and R. D. Pearce, *U.S. Industry in Britain*, 1977, quoted in Caves, 'Productivity Differences'.
43 D. Forsyth, 'Foreign Owned Firms and Labour Relations: A Regional Perspective' *British Journal of Industrial Relations*, vol. 11, March 1973, quoted in Caves, 'Productivity Differences'.
44 See Fine and Harris, *Peculiarities of the British Economy*.
45 *Trade and Industry*, 17 November 1978, quoted in A. Pollard, 'The Growing Concentration in Production?' in *Introduction to Economics* (D210, Unit 11a), Milton Keynes, Open University Press, 1984.
46 A. Pollard, 'The Structure of Production' in *Introduction to Economics* (D210, Unit 10a), Milton Keynes, Open University Press, 1984.
47 S. J. Prais, *The Evolution of Giant Firms in Britain*, Cambridge, Cambridge University Press, 1976, p.187, quoted in Pollard 'The Structure of Production'.
48 *British Business*, 19 January 1982, quoted in Pollard, 'The Structure of Production'.
49 See M. Ball, *Housing Policy and Economic Power*, London, Methuen, 1983.
50 *Committee of Inquiry on Small Firms: Report*, Cmnd 4811, London, HMSO, 1971 (Bolton Report).
51 R. Allard, 'The Position and Importance of small firms', *Economic Review, 1983*.
52 C. Freeman, 'Three studies on small firms' *Bolton Inquiry Research Report* No. 11, quoted in R. Allard, 'The Position and Importance of Small Firms'.
53 *Financial Times*, 5 April 1984, p.9.
54 L. Harris, 'Arms Spending and the British Economy' *World Marxist Review*, 1984.
55 K. O'Donnell and B. Fine, 'The Nationalized Industries' in D. Currie and R. Smith, *Socialist Economic Review*, London, Merlin Press, 1981; and Fine and Harris, *Peculiarities of the British Economy*. I am grateful to B. Fine for elaborating these arguments.

Chapter 2

1 R. Miliband, 'State Power and Class Interests' *New Left Review*, 138, 1983. See also B. Jessop, 'The Democratic State and the National Interest', in D. Coates and G. Johnston (eds), *Socialist Arguments*, Oxford, Martin Roberton, 1983.
2 A power bloc is an informal coalition of social groups which have been welded together, usually under the leadership of one group, in order to dominate the exercise of political power. The groups involved may be classes or fractions of classes.
3 J. Ross, *Thatcher and Friends*, London, Pluto Press, 1983.
4 T. Nairn, *The Break-up of Britain*, London, New Left Books, 1977.
5 J. Westergaard, 'Income, Wealth and the Welfare State', in Coates and Johnston, *Socialist Arguments*; J. Urry in this volume.
6 Minority control was defined as that situation where a dominant shareholder held between 10 per cent and 50 per cent of the shares. Limited minority control existed if a holding of slightly less than 10 per cent could be challenged by other large shareholders.
7 The links in the diagram take account only of lines directed from a person's base company, and not the 'induced' interlocks which these generate. Inclusion of induced interlocks would have produced a much denser network. Sir Eric Roll's directorship in Warburg, outside the top 250, has been counted as an interlock of its parent company Mercury

Securities, although Roll did not sit on the parent board.
8 N. Abercrombie and J. Urry, *Capital, Labour and the Middle Classes*, London, George Allen and Unwin, 1983.
9 R. Skidelsky, 'The Decline of Keynesian Politics', in C. Crouch (ed.), *State and Economy in Contemporary Capitalism*, London, Croom Helm, 1979.
10 B. Jessop, 'The Transformation of the State in Post-War Britain', in R. Scase (ed.), *The State in Western Europe*, London, Croom Helm, 1980.

Chapter 3

1 On the former, see R. Penn, *The Defensive Vanguard*, Cambridge, Cambridge University Press, 1984, and on the latter S. Walby, 'Women's Unemployment, Patriarchy and Capitalism' *Socialist Economic Review*, London, Merlin, 1983, pp.99–114.
2 Many of these are described in J. Urry and J. Wakeford (eds), *Power in Britain*, London, HEB, 1973; also in the chapter by John Scott (see above, pp.29–54).
3 See M. Wiener, *English Culture and the Decline of the Industrial Spirit*, Cambridge, Cambridge University Press, 1981, ch.7; and John Scott in this volume.
4 Ibid. p.126; and see P. Anderson, 'Origins of the Present Crisis' *New Left Review*, 23, 1964.
5 See J. Westergaard and H. Resler, *Class in a Capitalist Society*, Harmondsworth, Penguin, 1976, for example.
6 See the essays in H. Thomas (ed.), *The Establishment*, London, Anthony Blond, 1959, for example.
7 See pp. 36–44.
8 See J. Scott, *The Upper Classes*, London, Macmillan, 1982, p.21.
9 G. C. Harcourt and D. Hitchens, *Inheritance and Wealth Inequality in Britain*, London, George Allen and Unwin, 1979, p.136; and more generally see W. D. Rubinstein, *Men of Property*, London, Croom Helm, 1981.
10 A. B. Atkinson and A. J. Harrison, *The Distribution of Personal Wealth in Britain*, London, Cambridge University Press, 1978; p.159; and see Scott, *The Upper Classes*, table 6.2.
11 See A. B. Atkinson, *Unequal Shares*, Harmondsworth, Penguin, 1972.
12 Adapted from Atkinson and Harrison, *The Distribution of Personal Wealth*, p.159.
13 P. Townsend, *Poverty in the United Kingdom*, Harmondsworth, Penguin, 1979, table 9.3.
14 Westergaard and Resler, *Class in a Capitalist Society*, p.108.
15 See G. Routh, *Occupation and Pay in Great Britain, 1906–1979*, London, Macmillan, 1980, pp.54–5.
16 Ibid., p.57.
17 See Royal Commission on the Distribution of Income and Wealth, *Report no. 3, Higher Incomes from Employment*, London, HMSO, 1976, p.10; 'higher income' then meant earning over £10,000 p.a.
18 Ibid, p.116.
19 Routh, *Occupation and Pay in Great Britain*, p.58.
20 See M. Webb, 'The Labour Market', in I. Reid and E. Wormald (eds), *Sex Differences in Britain*, London, Grant McIntyre, 1982, pp.114–74, p.126.
21 A. B. Atkinson, *The Economics of Inequality*, Oxford, Oxford University Press, 1983 edition, p.63. See Routh, *Occupation and Pay in Great Britain*, ch.2, for an analysis of changes over this century for various occupational groupings.
22 See A. B. Atkinson, *The Economics of Inequality*, Oxford, Oxford University Press, 1975 edition, p.52.
23 See J. L. Nicholson, 'The Distribution of Personal Income in the UK', in Urry and

Wakeford, *Power in Britain*, pp.39–51, and Atkinson, *The Economics of Inequality*, 1983, p.63.

24 *Family Expenditure Survey*, Dept. of Employment, London, HMSO, 1981. See *Social Trends*, 1983, p.75.
25 Calculated from *Social Trends*, 1982, table 5.17.
26 See J. A. Kay and M. A. King, *The British Tax System*, Oxford, Oxford University Press, 1983, chs. 11 and 13.
27 Townsend, *Poverty in the United Kingdom*, p.302.
28 Ibid., p.898.
29 Ibid, chs. 7 and 26.
30 Royal Commission on the Distribution of Income and Wealth, *Report no. 7*, London, HMSO, 1979; Kay and King, *The British Tax System*, p.48. In the late 1970s they were equivalent to about 30 per cent of basic salary.
31 *Family Expenditure Survey*.
32 Routh, *Occupation and Pay in Great Britain*, ch.1.
33 See N. Abercrombie and J. Urry, *Capital, Labour and the Middle Classes*, London, George Allen and Unwin, 1983, chs. 3 and 7.
34 Routh, *Occupation and Pay in Great Britain*, p.124.
35 See Webb, 'The Labour Market', p.124.
36 *Labour Force Survey*, Dept. of Employment, London, HMSO, 1981.
37 Webb, 'The Labour Market', pp. 125–6.
38 See D. J. Smith, *Racial Disadvantages in Britain*, PEP Report, Harmondsworth, Penguin, 1977, p.83.
39 Ibid., pp.84–5
40 Ibid., p.85.
41 Ibid., chs. 9 and 10.
42 See A. Giddens, *The Class Structure of the Advanced Societies*, London, Hutchinson, 1973, p.107.
43 See D. Glass (ed.), *Social Mobility in Britain*, London, Routledge and Kegan Paul, 1954.
44 See Goldthorpe, *Social Mobility and Class Structure in Britain*, Oxford, Clarendon, 1980; A. H. Halsey, A. F. Heath, J. M. Ridge, *Origins and Destinations*, Oxford, Clarendon, 1980, and A. F. Heath, *Social Mobility*, London, Fontana, 1981, amongst many sources.
45 See R. Tawney, *Equality*, London, Unwin Books, 1931, p.142, and Halsey, Heath, Ridge, *Origins and Destinations*, p.205.
46 Ibid., p.204.
47 The gap increased from 2.4 years to 2.5 years; ibid., p.207.
48 Ibid., p.217.
49 Goldthorpe, *Social Mobility and Class Structure in Britain*, p.59; and see Routh, *Occupation and Pay in Great Britain*, ch.1.
50 See below, pp.76–98, as well as S. Macintyre, *Little Moscows*, London, Croom Helm; D. Massey, 'Industrial Restructuring as Class Restructuring' *Regional Studies*, 17, 1983, pp.73–90; and P. Cooke, 'Class Practices as Regional Markers: A Contribution to Labour Geography', in D. Gregory and J. Urry (eds), *Social Relations and Spatial Structures*, London, Macmillan, 1984.
51 See the famous M. Young and P. Willmott, *Family Life and Kinship in East London*, Harmondsworth, Penguin, 1962; although there are dangers of over-romanticizing this.
52 See *Census of Population*, 1961, 1981, *Employment Gazette* (various years).
53 H. Braverman, *Labour and Monopoly Capital*, New York, Monthly Review, 1974.
54 See R. Blackburn and M. Mann, *The Working Class in the Labour Market*, London, Macmillan, 1979.
55 On these issues see C. Littler, *The Development of the Labour Process in Capitalist Societies*, London, HEB, 1982, and S. Wood (ed.), *The Degradation of Work*, London, Hutchinson, 1982.

56 See B. Jones, 'Destruction or redistribution of engineering skills? The Case of Numerical Skills', in Wood, *The Degradation of Work*, pp.179–200.
57 This is well-shown in the film 'Nine to Five'.
58 See Abercrombie and Urry, *Capital, Labour and the Middle Classes*, chs. 3 and 7, for summary.
59 See *Race and Class*, 23, 1981/2, for a variety of analyses of race in Britain.
60 See C. Hakim, *Occupational Segregation*, Res. Paper no. 9, Dept. of Employment, London, HMSO, 1980.
61 See A. Stewart, B. Blackburn, K. Proudy, *Occupations and Social Stratification*, London, Macmillan, 1980, p.191, and A. Heath, 'Women Get On – Up to a Point' *New Society*, 12 February, 1981.
62 Note that I have not said anything here about housework and the inequalities generated within this sphere.
63 See P. Gilroy, 'You can't fool the youths . . . race and class formation in the 1980s' *Race and Class*, 23, 1981/2, pp.207–22.
64 See Abercrombie and Urry, *Capital, Labour and the Middle Classes*, ch.7.

Chapter 4

1 Acknowledgements to Nick Miles of the Open University for help with compilation of the data.

Chapter 5

1 For a critical discussion of such arguments see David Coates, 'The Question of Trade Union Power' in David Coates and Gordon Johnston, *Socialist Arguments*, Oxford, Martin Robertson, 1983.
2 Friedrich Engels, *The Condition of the Working Class in England in 1844*, London, George Allen and Unwin, 1968 (reprint of 1892 English edition), pp. 219, 224.
3 Karl Marx, *The First International and After* (ed. David Fernbach), Harmondsworth, Penguin, 1974, p.91.
4 Letter to Bernstein, 17 June 1879.
5 'England in 1845 and in 1885' *Commonweal*, 1 March 1885.
6 Letter to Liebknecht, 11 February 1878.
7 Central to Marx's contribution to the analysis of capitalism was his distinction between labour as a process and *labour power* as the commodity exchanged by the worker for wages. On the basis of this distinction it was possible to illuminate the exploitation at the heart of capitalism: the value of the typical worker's contribution to production was typically greater than the value of the commodity, labour power, purchased by the capitalist — who was able to pocket the surplus.
8 Karl Marx, *Capital*, Vol. 1, London, Lawrence and Wishart, 1959, p.331.
9 This notion was first used in the classic study by Carter Goodrich, *The Frontier of Control*, London, Pluto Press, 1975 (originally published in 1920).
10 For a discussion of official labour statistics see Richard Hyman and Bob Price, 'Labour Statistics', in John Irvine, Ian Miles and Jeff Evans, *Demystifying Social Statistics*, London, Pluto Press, 1979.
11 There is a discrepancy between the analysis of large unions in table 5.5 and the list given in table 5.7. It would appear that the Department of Employment figures for NUM and NUT include retired and student members respectively, bringing the totals to over 250,000; that the Royal College of Nursing (a non-TUC body claiming some 214,000 members) is

included in the total; and that neither TASS nor the Boilermakers are counted as separate organizations.

12 A far more detailed survey of the main unions, from a somewhat right-wing perspective, is provided by Robert Taylor, *The Fifth Estate*, London, Pan, 1980. Information on the TUC and every affiliated union is given at length in Jack Eaton and Colin Gill, *The Trade Union Directory* (2nd edition), London, Pluto Press, 1983.

13 For a discussion of the various dimensions of strike statistics see Richard Hyman, *Strikes*, London, Fontana, 1984; and for a historical analysis see James Cronin, *Industrial Conflict in Modern Britain*, London, Croom Helm, 1979.

14 For an interesting case study of such strategies see Theo Nichols and Huw Beynon, *Living With Capitalism*, London, Routledge and Kegan Paul, 1977.

15 By the late 1970s the TUC was able to nominate members to an array of positions (some at substantial salaries) on public bodies; many members of the General Council occupied multiple positions (see Ken Coates and Tony Topham, *Trade Unions in Britain*, Nottingham, Spokesman, 1980, ch.4). The Thatcher government has cut back on this 'quango' system and in particular on the number of trade-union appointments.

16 Perry Anderson, 'The Limits and Possibilities of Trade Union Action' in Robin Blackburn and Alexander Cockburn (eds), *The Incompatibles*, Harmondsworth, Penguin, 1967, pp.264–5.

17 Antonio Gramsci, *Selections from Political Writings 1910–1920* (ed. Quinton Hoare), London, Lawrence and Wishart. 1977, p.265.

18 I have made this point more fully in 'The Politics of Workplace Trade Unionism' *Capital and Class*, 8, Summer 1979.

19 The British situation with its tradition of lay involvement contrasts sharply with the context in which Michels developed his notion of an 'iron law of oligarchy' at the beginning of the century: a German labour movement top-heavy with full-time officials.

20 C. Wright Mills, *The New Men of Power*, New York, Harcourt Brace, 1948, p.9.

21 Gramsci, *Selections from Political Writings*.

22 The most detailed analysis of such tendencies has focused on sexism in trade unions; see for example Jenny Beale, *Getting It Together*, London, Pluto Press, 1983 and Anne Phillips, *Hidden Hands*, London, Pluto Press, 1983.

23 See for example Jill Rubery, 'Structured Labour Markets, Worker Organisation and Low Pay' *Cambridge Journal of Economics*, 2, 1, March 1978.

Chapter 6

1 *Shrew*, October 1969, quoted in B. Campbell and A. Coote, *Sweet Freedom*, London, Picador, 1982, p.23.

2 In what follows I shall be referring only to Britain. The structure of women's oppression takes a different form in other parts of the world.

3 E. Wilson, *Women and the Welfare State*, London, Tavistock, 1977.

4 S. Alexander and B. Taylor, 'In defence of patriarchy' *New Statesman*, 1 February 1980.

5 See for example J. Sayers, *Biological Politics*, London, Tavistock, 1982.

6 Sadie Robart, *Positive Action for Women, The Next Step*, London, NCCL, 1981.

7 Campbell and Coote, *Sweet Freedom*, p.124.

Chapter 7

1 Author, Booker Prize winner for *Midnight's Children*, London, Picador, 1982.

2 Substantial sections of this chapter were originally published as 'Racist Acts' by Kum Kum

Bhavnani in *Spare Rib*, nos. 115, 116 and 117, 1981.
3 We use 'black' to refer to people of both Afro-Caribbean and Indian sub-continental origin.
4 'Many Voices, one chant: Black Feminist perspectives' *Feminist Review*, no.17, 1984.
5 This qualification later became embodied in the legal concept of 'patriality' in 1971.
6 See the *Guardian* 21 March 1984.

Chapter 8

1 *Embrace the Earth: a Green view of Peace*, London, CND Publications, 1983, p.32.
2 Ibid., p.6.
3 David Bellamy, speaking at the Green Rally, organized by Friends of the Earth, Central Hall, Westminster, 27 April 1983, report by Judith Condon, *WEA News*, Autumn 1983.
4 *Embrace the Earth*, p.10.
5 Ibid., p.5.
6 Letter from Peter Cadogan to the author, 22 August 1983.
7 As cited in *The Directory of British Associations*, 1982.
8 Ecology Party, 1983 General Election Manifesto.
9 The details of the formation of the FOE is given in an article by Caroline Moorehead in *The Sunday Times*, 1 October 1980.
10 Ibid.
11 Aims as described in Peter Shipley (ed.), *Director of Pressure Groups and Representative Association*, London, Bowker, 1979.
12 This is the figure given for 1982 in *The Directory of British Associations*.
13 *Embrace the Earth*, p.35, citing Bob Overy.
14 Ibid., p.18.
15 Cadogan to author.
16 For a discussion of this earlier Movement, see Richard Taylor and Colin Pritchard, *The Protest Makers, The British Nuclear Disarmament Movement of 1958 to 1965, Twenty Years On*, Oxford, Pergamon Press, 1980; and Frank Parkin, *Middle Class Radicalism: the Social bases of the Campaign for Nuclear Disarmament*, Manchester, Manchester University Press, 1968.
17 For a discussion of one aspect of this, see Richard Taylor, 'The British Peace Movement and Socialist change', in R. Miliband and J. Saville (eds), *Socialist Register*, London, Merlin Press, 1983.
18 Brian Moynahan, 'Waif at the Heart of a Revolution', *Sunday Times Magazine*, 30 January 1983.
19 Aims as described in Shipley, *Directory of Pressure Groups*.
20 Ralph Schoenman, 'Civil Disobedience to Halt Polaris' *Peace News*, 17 February 1961.
21 Extracts from Neil Kinnock's replies to a questionnaire, in *New Ground*, journal of the Socialist Environment and Resources Association, Autumn 1983.
22 However, in the case of the Liberal Party, the conference policy rejecting Cruise missiles and advocating a broadly 'CND line' has been rejected by the parliamentary leadership, which in common with its SDP partners, is solidly pro-NATO, and follows to all intents and purposes a generally 'Healeyite' defence and foreign policy.
23 Direct Action strategies of the Peace Movement in the 1950s and 1960s were heavily influenced by Gandhian ideas and campaigns and by the US Civil Rights Movement. See Taylor and Pritchard, *The Protest Makers*.
24 See ibid.
25 To take just one example, from 1982, there were peace rallies of a quarter of a million people or more in each of seven Western European capitals.

26 See David Coates, *The Context of British Politics*, London, Hutchinson, 1984, ch.7, section 2.
27 Ralph Miliband's work on the nature of the capitalist state in Britain is of particular importance. See especially, *Capitalist Democracy in Britain*, Oxford, Oxford University Press, 1982, and *The State in Capitalist Society*, London, Weidenfeld and Nicholson, 1969.
28 Richard Taylor and Kevin Ward, 'Community Politics and direct action: the non-aligned Left', in D. Coates and G. Johnston (eds), *Socialist Strategies*, Oxford, Martin Robertson, 1983.
29 See Taylor and Pritchard, *The Protest Makers*.
30 The only major ideological perspective not to command significant support within the Greens is that of revolutionary mobilization.
31 For attempts at linking socialism, peace, and Green concerns see *Embrace the Earth* and the publications of the Socialist Environment and Resources Associaltion (SERA), 9 Poland Street, London, W1V 3DG.

Chapter 9

1 G. M. Young, *Victorian England: Portrait of an Age*, Oxford, Oxford University Press, 1936, 1953 edn, p.186.
2 Frederick Engels, 'History of Ireland', in *Marx and Engels on Ireland*, Moscow, Progress Publishers, 1971, p.171.
3 See Liam de Paor, *Divided Ulster*, Harmondsworth, Penguin, 1970, 1971 ed, pp.25–9.
4 See Andrew Boyd, *Holy War in Belfast*, London, Anvil Books, 1969, *passim*.
5 See Cecil Woodham-Smith, *The Great Hunger*, London, Hamish Hamilton, 1962, esp. pp. 54–5, 410.
6 J. C. Beckett, *The Making of Modern Ireland, 1603–1923*, London, Faber and Faber, 1966, 1969 edn, pp.61-2.
7 De Paor, *Divided Ulster*, p.57.
8 Ibid, p.75.
9 See de Paor, *Divided Ulster*, pp.105–6.
10 Sunday Times Insight Team, *Ulster*, Harmondsworth, Penguin, 1972, p.80.
11 J. Bowyer Bell, *The Secret Army, the IRA 1916–1979*, Dublin, Academy Press, 1979, p.376.
12 Sunday Times, *Ulster*, p.266.
13 See my article, 'Terrorism – Myths, Meaning and Morals' *Political Studies*, Vol. XXV, 1977.

Chapter 10

1 What follows relies heavily on the publications of, conversations with, and correspondence from, many activists in the various organizations discussed. A number of comrades in particular put time and effort into correcting earlier drafts of both this chapter and the Appendix; and I am very grateful to them. John Callaghan's *British Trotskyism* (Basil Blackwell, 1984) was an important source; as were the comments of Paul Hubert, John Charlton, Keith Venables and Andy Hollas. None of them, of course, bear any responsibility for any errors that remain.
2 All organizations so starred * are listed in the appendix, section 6.
3 This Labour Party figure, supplied by Party headquarters, is calculated on the basis of the number of membership cards requested by constituency parties, less those returned unused at the end of the year.

Chapter 11

1 See in particular Eric Hobsbawm, 'Labour's Lost Millions', *Marxism Today*, October 1983, and 'Labour: Rump or Rebirth', *Marxism Today*, March 1984.

2 See Robert Looker and David Coates, 'Basic Problems of Socialist Strategy', in David Coates and Gordon Johnston (eds), *Socialist Strategies*, Oxford, Martin Robertson, 1983, pp.272–7. More generally see Adam Przeworski, 'Social Democracy as a Historical Phenomenon', *New Left Review*, 122, 1980.

3 Looker and Coates, 'Socialist Strategy', p.278.

4 See Bo Sarlvik and Ivor Crewe, *Decade of Dealignment: The Conservative Victory of 1979 and Electoral Trends in the 1970s*, Cambridge, Cambridge University Press, 1983, for a view of the dealignment of voting with class. See also Andre Gorz, *Farewell to the Working Class*, London, Pluto Press, 1982, for a general statement of the 'death of class politics' view. There is more than an element of this perspective in Eric Hobsbawm, 'The Forward March of Labour Halted?', reproduced in Martin Jacques and Francis Mulhern (eds), *The Forward March of Labour Halted?*, London, Verso Editions, 1981.

5 For a discussion of the character of the 'new middle class' and its significance for socialist theory and practice see Alex Callinicos, 'the "New Middle Class" and Socialist Politics', *International Socialism*, 2,20, 1983. See also John Westergaard, 'Class of '84' *New Socialist*, 15, 1984, Richard Hyman and Robert Price (eds), *The New Working Class: White Collar Workers and their Organisations*, London, Macmillan, 1983, and D. Coates, *The Context of British Politics*, London, Hutchinson, 1984, ch.7.

6 Looker and Coates, 'Socialist Strategy'.

7 The phrase, of course, is taken from the title of Eric Hobsbawm's 1978 Marx Memorial Lecture. This, together with contributions to the debate it generated, are collected in Jacques and Mulhern (eds), *The Forward March of Labour Halted*.

8 Christopher Hampton (ed.), *A Radical Reader: The Struggle for change in England, 1381–1914*, Harmondsworth, Penguin, 1984, p.11.

9 Ibid.

10 John Saville: 'The Ideology of Labourism', in R. Benewick et al., *Knowledge and Belief in Politics*, London, George Allen and Unwin, 1973, p.215.

11 Eric Hobsbawm, *Labouring Men*, London, Weidenfeld, 1968, p.336.

12 Ralph Miliband, *Parliamentary Socialism*, London, George Allen and Unwin, 1961; David Coates, *The Labour Party and the Struggle for Socialism*, Cambridge, Cambridge University Press, 1975, and *Labour in Power? A Study of the Labour Government 1974–1979*, London, Longman, 1980.

13 Stuart Hall and Martin Jacques (eds), *The Politics of Thatcherism*, London, Lawrence and Wishart, 1983, p.11.

14 One of the more disturbing tendencies on the Left has been not only the reduction of political issues to personal ones, but also the resort to sexual stereotypes in the process. Hence the 'Ditch the Bitch' badges.

15 See the reference in footnote 1 above.

16 Stuart Hall, 'The Great Moving Right Show', in Hall and Jacques (eds), *The Politics of Thatcherism*, p.29.

17 Andrew Gamble, 'The Free Economy and the Strong State', in Ralph Miliband and John Saville (eds), *The Socialist Register 1979*, London, Merlin Press, 1979.

18 Coates and Johnston, *Socialist Strategies*. See in particular chapters 1, 2, 3 and 9 of that volume.

19 For a splendid recent discussion of the post-war world economy from a Marxist perspective see Nigel Harris, *Of Bread and Guns*, Harmondsworth, Penguin, 1983.

20 Looker and Coates, 'Socialist Strategy', pp.267–268. (For an alternative view, see chapter 1 of this volume.)

21 See Nigel Harris, *Competition and the Corporate Society: British Conservatives, the State and Industry 1945–1964*, London, Methuen, 1972, particularly part III.

22 Hall, 'The Great Moving Right Show', p.22.

23 Editorial in *Irish Times*, 4 April 1984.

24 Harris, *Of Bread and Guns*, particularly chapter 4.

25 An exception to this is provided by Dave Priscott, 'Popular Front Revisited', *Marxism Today*, October 1983.

26 For an excellent discussion of the ambiguities and tensions in Gramsci's thought and writings see Perry Anderson, 'The Antimonies of Antonio Gramsci' *New Left Review*, 100, 1976–77.

27 See Looker and Coates, 'Socialist Strategy', particularly pp.244–6 and pp.272–7.

28 See Nora Carlin and Ian Birchall, 'Kinnock's Favourite Marxist: Eric Hobsbawm and the Working Class' *International Socialism*, 2,21, 1983. For Eric Hobsbawm's happy acceptance of the 'Popular Front' tag see his 'Labour: Rump or Rebirth?', p.10.

29 For a fuller discussion see Fernando Claudin, *The Communist Movement from Comintern to Cominform*, Harmondsworth, Penguin, 1975, particularly chapter 4.

30 For a brief but useful discussion of both the historical background to, and contemporary relevance of, the strategy, see Pete Goodwin, 'The United Front' *International Socialism*' 1,104, 1978.

31 For useful discussions of the downturn and its impact on shop floor organization and militancy see Tony Cliff, 'The Balance of Class Forces in Britain Today' *International Socialism*, 2,6, 1979, and Dave Beecham, 'Updating the downturn: the class struggle under the Tories', *International Socialism*, 2,14, 1981.

Index